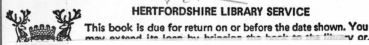

WILKIE COLLINS

THE NEW MAGDALEN

CHARING
THEATRE

Wilkie Collins

A BIOGRAPHY

Kenneth Robinson

DAVIS-POYNTER

LONDON

This edition published in 1974 by
Davis-Poynter Limited
20 Garrick Street London WC2E 9BJ
First published in 1951

ISBN 0 7067 0137 2

Printed in Great Britain by
Clarke, Doble & Brendon Ltd,
Plymouth

To Elizabeth

Contents

Acknowledgements

IN writing this book I have made use of published material from many sources, the more important of which are listed in the Appendix. I should like to acknowledge here my particular debt to Mr. C. K. Hyder, of Kansas University, for his two monographs on special aspects of Collins' life; and to the late Mr. S. M. Ellis whose study of the novelist in *Wilkie Collins, le Fanu and others* provided a valuable foundation on which to build.

My grateful thanks are also due to Mr. John Lehmann for allowing me access to unpublished letters and other material in his possession; to Mr. Frank H. Arnold, who not only entrusted me with the complete correspondence between his father (Frank Archer) and Collins, but went to great pains to send me other useful material; to Princeton University Library for permission to include letters from the Morris L. Parrish Collection; to Mr. Desmond Flower for allowing me to quote from his article in the *Book-Collectors' Quarterly* on 'Authors and Copyright' and to reproduce letters in his family's possession; to Messrs. Myers & Co., Ltd., of New Bond Street, for permission to copy unpublished letters; to Mr. Alan Tillotson and Mr. Evans for information concerning Collins' 'syndicated' stories; to Mr. Alexander Lagus for assistance with the illustrations; to Mr. Graham Pollard for a most valuable suggestion; and to the staffs of the British Museum Reading Room and the Borough Librarians of St. Pancras and St. Marylebone for their courteous co-operation.

The Executors of the late Alexander Pollock Watt, who was the first literary agent and Wilkie Collins' literary executor, have given me permission to publish Collins' letters in this biography; and the present partners in the firm of A. P. Watt & Son have allowed me to read a number of his other letters. Their help has been invaluable and I cannot thank them too warmly.

Foreword

WHEN this biography first appeared more than twenty years ago I explained in an introduction how it came to be written. It was while serving with the Royal Navy in India towards the end of World War II that I discovered *The Woman in White* and *The Moonstone*. These books led me to others by Wilkie Collins and stimulated a curiosity about the author which was not easy to satisfy. Relatively little seemed to have been written about him but the few facts known were sufficiently intriguing to encourage further research.

No full-length biography of Collins existed, though Miss Dorothy L. Sayers had vaguely hinted that she was collecting material for a book about Wilkie Collins. She died in 1957 with this intention still unfulfilled. It seemed to me that such an original writer and so unusual a man deserved a biography and with considerable temerity I decided to undertake the task myself.

The book was well received but went out of print within a few years. No other full-length biography has been published in Britain in the intervening period. Wilkie Collins covered his tracks well and gave little help to the would-be biographer. Since this book first appeared no new material of significance has come to light, apart from some information which reached me, from what I regard as a reliable source, about Wilkie's 'morganatic family'. It seems that they and their descendants did not disappear so completely as I had thought (p. 296).

Collins' two illegitimate daughters died in their eighties within months of each other in 1955. Their brother William died in 1913 at the age of 37 but his widow, daughter of a sea captain, was a dozen years ago still living in a town in the Home Counties. There are surviving children and three grandchildren, but they appear to have no wish publicly to acknowledge their distinguished if unconventional forebear.

KENNETH ROBINSON

I

William Collins R.A.

ON 18th September, 1788, William Collins, the father of Wilkie Collins, was born in Great Titchfield Street, London. His mother was a Scot, and his father, who bore the same name of William Collins, an Irishman from Wicklow. The elder William Collins earned a precarious living as an art-dealer, and specialised in the cleaning of old pictures. He was also a man of literary ambitions.

The boy grew up in this respectable middle-class environment surrounded by works of art, and delighted his father by starting to paint at an early age. The elder Collins did all he could to foster his son's obvious talent, instructing him in draughtsmanship and the use of paint, taking him on sketching expeditions to some nearby village such as Highgate or Willesden, and occasionally sending him to spend the day with his great friend, George Morland. Though deeply shocked by his dissipated habits, the boy was able to learn something of Morlands' masterly technique. As soon as he was eligible he became a student at the Royal Academy where, at the age of eighteen, he was also an exhibitor.

The elder William Collins was no man of business, and his family lived constantly on the edge of penury. The cleaning of pictures was an ill-paid occupation even if his services were in wide demand; as an art-dealer he was far too honest to be financially successful; and his literary work brought him, we are told, 'more popularity than profit.' He contributed to numerous periodicals, and published a handful of works including a *Poem on the Slave Trade*, a biography of Morland, and a sensational novel in three volumes entitled *Memoirs of a Picture*. This last book deserves a mention if only for the sake of a plot so complex as to invite comparison with the work of its author's grandson more than half a century later. *Memoirs of a Picture* tells the story of an Old Master which changes hands with the frequency of a coin of the realm, and is forever being stolen and copied by villainous collectors with such resounding names as Chevalier Vanderwigtie and Des-chong-fong. Perhaps the oddest feature of this curious literary hybrid is that the story occupies the first and third volumes, the second being devoted to a *Memoir of George Morland*. This section, in the words of Wilkie Collins, is 'filled with characteristic anecdotes, told with genuine Irish raciness of style.'

When the elder Collins died in 1812 he was heavily in debt. His son, now aged 23, was fortunate in being able to borrow from a patron enough money to meet the day-to-day household expenses. All the family's possessions had to be sold for the benefit of creditors, the furniture, the stock of pictures—including several by the younger William Collins which realised £57—even the dead man's spectacles and snuff-box. A friend who called at their house in Great Portland Street on the evening of the sale found the family eating their scanty meal off an old box, the nearest thing to a table they possessed.

For a time William Collins was too heartbroken to paint. His father had been to him master, critic, and friend; his encouragement had helped the young artist in all the difficulties and disappointments of his earliest attempts. The mood of despair only passed when he realised that the family now looked to the elder son for guidance and support. He went to work at his painting as he had never worked before. Of his two pictures exhibited during that year, one was sold for 150 guineas, his best price so far.

Henceforward, until his death, William Collins exhibited regularly at the Academy and was able to sell most of his work. He was elected an Associate of the Royal Academy in 1814, at the age of 26. A day or two later, the following resolve appeared in his diary:

November 12—To aim greatly at reformation in the leading features of my private character—the little weaknesses that almost escape detection, and which, notwithstanding their pettiness, seem to be the obstructing cause to all dignity of character in an artist, or a man.

And on the 17th of the same month:

From the great success I have met with, the eagerness I feel to deserve it and my struggles against sluggishness, I never was more confused in my intellects than now—dreadful want of confidence—my mind must be weeded—good habits may be gained by watchfulness—bad habits grow of themselves.†

Collins was ambitious, but seldom was ambition so tempered by humility and self-questioning.

The following year he moved from the small house in Great Portland Street to a 'larger and more eligible abode' at 11, New Cavendish Street, taking with him his mother and younger brother Francis. Within a few months the increased expenses had overtaken his income, and the diary sums up as follows:

One sixpence in my pocket, seven hundred pounds in debt, shabby clothes, a fine house, a large stock of my own handy-works, a certainty of about a couple of hundreds, and a determination unshaken of becoming a great painter.

He worked harder and still harder, only to see the gap between income and the necessary expenses of his household as wide as ever. At last, faced with the prospect of the immediate seizure of his goods for taxes, he sat down and wrote to Sir Thomas Heathcote, a generous patron, for an advance of money against a picture Heathcote had commissioned him to paint. The money was produced, accompanied by a note expressing surprise at 'the pecuniary distress of a person of such apparently prudent habits,' and the crisis averted. Economies were made which included the letting of half the New Cavendish Street house.

As Collins' fame increased so his circle of acquaintances widened. Among his intimates by this time were Sir David Wilkie, R.A., and Washington Allston, the American painter of historical subjects with whom Collins paid his first visit to Paris in 1817. Shortly afterwards he made the acquaintance of Constable. Despite his possessing, according to Collins, 'a capacity for dry, sarcastic humour and a character of marked eccentricity,' they became close friends until Constable's death in 1837. In a letter to Constable's biographer he mentions his friend's 'heartfelt love of his pursuit, independent of any worldly advantages to be obtained from it.'

† These and the following extracts from Collins' Journal are taken from *Memoirs of the Life of William Collins, Esq., R.A.*, by W. Wilkie Collins (*Longmans*, 1848).

If commissions were becoming more numerous, so were his
financial troubles. The diary of January 20th, 1818, opens
despairingly:

> Pecuniary difficulties, debilitating idleness, waging war upon me;
> dreading what, to my poor and finite capacity, appear insur-
> mountable embarrassments. Notwithstanding my conviction that
> my troubles are real, and their number great, yet I feel that
> my desultory habits are adding to the list . . . Fearing con-
> sequences, which God in His infinite mercy avert, I once more
> implore His assistance.

In addition, Collins sought assistance from Sir Thomas Heathcote
who once more obliged with a loan of a hundred pounds. This
loan, like the previous one, was scrupulously repaid and appears to
have been the last he was forced to seek.

The Academy of the same year (1818) set the seal on Collins'
fame. His main exhibit, *Scene on the Coast of Norfolk*, had just
been sold to the Earl of Liverpool, when he was informed that the
Prince Regent had been delighted with the seascape at the private
view and wished to possess it. Lord Liverpool graciously resigned
his purchase and commissioned Collins to paint another sea-piece
for the next year's exhibition. The Norfolk coast scene joined the
Royal Collection at Windsor Castle.

During the few remaining years of Lord Liverpool's life, Collins
was frequently his guest at Fife House and Walmer Castle. Here
he met a number of celebrities including Sir Robert Peel, who
became one of his most valued patrons. In the summer of 1818
he visited the Lake District where he was introduced to Words-
worth and Southey. At this point the Journal becomes tantalising
in its brevity.

> *September 2nd*—Showery all day. Lord Lowther and Mr. Words-
> worth at dinner. In the evening at Mr. Southey's—lightning in
> the evening.
> *October 3rd*—Walked to Ambleside with Wordsworth and his
> wife—sketched the mill there.
> *October 5th*—Rainy morning; Wordsworth read to me: walked
> out before dinner—took my farewell of the Lakes.

Whilst in the Lake District Collins had done a portrait of Sara
Coleridge. Writing from Highgate to Collins shortly after the

latter's return, Coleridge refers to 'your exquisite picture of Sara Coleridge, which had quite haunted my eye ever since.' He encloses two tickets for his first course of Lectures, and expresses the hope that there will be a tolerable number of auditors. Collins thanks him sincerely and asks for some prospectuses to distribute among his friends, for which kindness Coleridge's gratitude is almost pathetic: 'God knows I have so few friends that it would be unpardonable in me not to feel proportionately grateful towards those few who think the time not wasted in which they interest themselves in my behalf.' Many were the subsequent occasions on which Collins made the journey to Highgate to delight in Coleridge's 'extraordinary conversational powers.' A sincere friendship grew up between the two men which only ended with Coleridge's death some fifteen years later.

The Journal of this year shows how little Collins was affected by his mounting success, both professional and social.

March 20th—I believe that I must answer for every idle, vain, and unprofitable word that I utter; how absolutely necessary it is then, that I should use those means already in my power to attain the blessing of mental watchfulness. I know no cause so adequate to the entire frustration of the acquisition of this faculty, as indolence, which I believe to be of the will first, and then of the body; where, when it has once taken hold, it is cancerous. God, of His infinite mercy grant that I may escape its fatal grasp!

With all his humility Collins would not submit to dictation in matters affecting his professional pride or artistic conscience. One of his more exacting patrons, Sir John Leicester, had commissioned a landscape with figures to hang in his private gallery opposite a Richard Wilson, and having seen the work in progress thought fit to write to Collins suggesting that the subject chosen 'would not enable you to display your genius against so formidable a pendent as the Wilson.' After some indication how the picture should be treated in order to form a noteworthy companion to the Wilson and to 'partake of its magnificent character without servility or imitation,' Sir John blandly suggests that the half-completed picture should, when finished, be sent instead to the Academy Exhibition, Collins being compensated for work done on it to date, and that

B

he should begin another picture 'with fewer parts and more sim-
plicity.'

Collins' reply is politely firm :

Sir,—I know no event of my professional life attended with so
unpleasant a result as the one upon which you have written to
me this day.

With the utmost gentlemanlike regard for my feelings as a man,
and a solicitude for my reputation as an artist, you have thrown
me into a situation from which I must confess my utter inability
to extricate myself—each of your proposals being so entirely
impracticable. That a picture unfit to hang with a Wilson should
yet have nothing to fear upon a comparison with the works of
living artists at Somerset House (notwithstanding the very high
estimation I feel of Wilson's powers), is a reflection upon the
painters of this day to which I can never subscribe.

Respecting the other proposal—when I take the liberty to assure
you that my present picture engrossed my thoughts during the
whole of my tour in the north; . . . that I have already been
actually engaged upon it for nearly two months; and that I have
also put aside many considerable and lucrative commissions,
which it would be highly imprudent longer to neglect, solely for
the purpose of availing myself of an opportunity of painting
upon a larger scale, I trust you will see the futility of my attempting to complete another picture, either by February, or for some
time to come.

I remain, Sir,

Your most obedient servant,

William Collins.

After a further exchange of letters Collins won his point, and
the picture was hung in its intended position in Sir John Leicester's
Gallery.

Having failed the previous year by one vote, Collins was elected
a Royal Academician in 1820, at the age of 31. Some six years
earlier, he had met a young girl named Harriet Geddes to whom
he was immediately attracted. She was the daughter of an Associate
of the Royal Academy and younger sister of a Mrs. Carpenter who
was already known as a portrait-painter. Although he believed that
his affection was returned, Collins then considered his prospects
too uncertain to justify his asking Harriet to share them. During
the next seven years they met at intervals on social occasions and

it happened that both remained single. By 1821 he decided that his reputation was sufficiently secure, and with it his financial position, and asked Harriet to be his wife.

Though the couple became officially engaged there was an obstacle in the way of marriage. Mrs. Collins, whilst approving the match, urged delay until her son's position was still more firmly established, and not all his pleading could induce her to alter her view. Normally this would have been no obstruction to a determined couple of marriageable age, but there were, it seems, complications arising from a new Marriage Act recently passed into English law. Such was the vexatious position when Collins left London in August, 1822, for Edinburgh accompanied by Sir David Wilkie.

Their purpose was to provide a permanent record of the State Visit to Edinburgh of George IV, in a series of occasional paintings. The city put on its gayest dress to greet the Royal visitor. Its grey walls were decked with flags, cannon fired salutes of welcome, bonfires blazed in the streets. Every kind of entertainment was arranged. Collins and Wilkie were invited to Sir Walter Scott's house in Castle Street, where the food and wine were of equal excellence. The scene after dinner, according to Collins, would have defied 'the pen of a Rabelais or the pencil of a Hogarth.' The host, 'in the exuberance of his loyalty and hospitality,' gave a spirited rendering of his own song, 'Carle now the King's come,' loudly exhorting his guests to join in the chorus and then to dance round the table with him, despite his lameness, to its measure.

Within a fortnight the King had departed and the festivities were over. On August 16th Collins wrote to Harriet:

As I have received no letter from New Cavendish Street, where I hope to write today, I have it *not in my power decisively to say when or where the desired event may take place*. Would to heaven it were tomorrow, my affections and all my thoughts upon the subject of it are unchangeable. Our mutual love and confidence in each other have every night soothed my mind and every morning cheered my prospects. My dear love, how much of my happiness depends upon you . . . I have a space (being the whole of it) in my heart which, as 'tis yours, nought else can fill.

A few days later Sir David Wilkie returned to London but his companion, who had lighted upon a simple solution to his matrimonial problem, remained in Scotland. He wrote to Harriet asking her to join him in Edinburgh, where, after a brief residence, they could be married without regard to a law which was only effective south of the Border. The letter closed with the hope that they would 'return to London cemented by that tie which, please God, may brighten our future prospects.' To his mother he wrote of his intention to marry 'despite our unhappy difference upon the most vital of all subjects, connected as it is with happiness here, and the hope of it in a better world.' It was on the whole a mollifying letter and recognised that her opposition 'has arisen from an affection for me, which has never ceased to show itself upon all occasions; and this affection has been met, on too many occasions, by an apparently heartless neglect of your kindness.' It would be surprising if such a letter had not produced the forgiveness it sought.

Harriet duly arrived in Edinburgh and they were married in the English Episcopal Church in September, 1822. The ceremony was performed by the Rev. Dr. Alison, 'author of the celebrated work on *Taste*,' who declined to accept a fee, saying, 'You bear the name of a great poet, and you are yourself increasing the honours of that name by your progress in one of the intellectual Arts—I could receive no fees from *any* William Collins; and still less could I take them from you.'

Collins had not even confided his intentions to his friend Wilkie who wrote shortly afterwards:

Calling on Collins the other day, to my surprise he introduced me to his wife whom he brought from Edinburgh with him, and to be married to whom had been the reason of his delay in that place. When in Edinburgh he told me all about his engagement, but the marrying before returning home was an afterthought. They had been sighing for years, till they could sigh no longer; and he appointed her to come down in the James Watt steamer to Edinburgh. She seems a nice woman, not particularly handsome, but accomplished and intelligent, and I dare say much attached to him.

The elder Mrs. Collins had only to meet her new daughter-in-law to forget her opposition to the marriage and the married couple settled down happily at the house in New Cavendish Street. Harriet had an attractive personality and soon succeeded in winning her mother-in-law's affection. During the following summer Collins rented a small cottage at North End, Hampstead, at that time a village in rural surroundings, where he and his wife lived 'in perfect tranquillity and retirement.' The neighbourhood provided subjects for many of Collins' pleasantest works. He was happy to be removed from the interruptions of London life and derived all the more enjoyment from the occasional entertaining of his fellow-artists.

Towards the end of the year they returned to 11, New Cavendish Street, where, on January 8th, 1824, their first child was born, a son.† The boy was christened William Wilkie Collins, the second name being a tribute to his father's friendship with Sir David Wilkie, who was asked to be one of the sponsors. Wilkie was a bachelor and must have had little experience of infants, for it is recorded that when his godson was first presented for his inspection he exclaimed with astonishment, 'He *sees*!'

William Collins' fortunes continued to prosper, Commissions were coming in from such useful patrons as Sir Robert Peel, Lord Liverpool and the Duke of Bedford. His greatest honour so far was a commission from George IV who chose as a subject a Hastings Coast Scene; and to Hastings Collins duly removed his family for the summer of 1824. The picture was completed the following year and the artist was privileged to hear the King express his satisfaction with it in a personal interview at Windsor. We are told that 'the notorious ease and affability of the King's manners . . . was as apparent in his frank and kind reception of Mr. Collins as in all other instances.' Even when the artist ventured to correct His Majesty regarding the precise point on the Sussex coast which formed the subject of the picture, 'the propriety of the correction was acknowledged with the most perfect good-humour.'

The next summer was spent in the little village of Hendon, and the family did not return to London until December. A few months later, in the spring of 1826, Collins quitted the house in New Cavendish Street for good and went to live in Pond Street, Hampstead, where he remained apart from occasional visits abroad, for

† The *Dictionary of National Biography* incorrectly gives the birthplace as Tavistock Square.

the next four years. Few events interrupted the happy monotony
of their life in the country. From time to time William would leave
for a brief sketching tour but always his desire was to return home
to his family: 'I cannot tell you,' he writes to Harriet, 'when I am
alone how I long for home. Why should we be thus parted I say
continually, and my only consolation is that it is not for pleasure
alone, but for the "crumbs" I must take to my "nest." ' There are
the normal fond messages to his small son: 'Tell Willy I have this
day picked up two nice little scuttle-fish bones for him.'

During this period Sir David Wilkie was absent on an extensive
tour of the Continent and he too, at the end of a long letter
describing the Italian masterpieces he has seen, remembers his
godson: 'He is now old enough to learn that there is such a person
as his godfather—he will be able to speak to me when I return.'
A life-long bachelor, Wilkie never found it easy to talk to children,
though he developed a great affection for his young godson. Wilkie
Collins recalls sitting on his knee as a child and persuading him to
draw cats, dogs, horses and anything else he cared to name.

In January, 1828, Harriet Collins gave birth to their second son
whom, following the precedent, they named Charles Allston in
honour of his father's friend, Washington Allston. Allston became
a sponsor by proxy. Collins wrote to Wilkie: 'Your godson grows
a strapping fellow, and has a little blue-eyed, red-haired, bonny
bairn as a brother.' In the summer of the following year Collins
took his wife and children for a holiday to Boulogne. They rented
a house in the market-place and stayed about six weeks. For young
Willy, now in his sixth year, the first sight of a foreign country
was an exciting event. Twenty years later, he remembered, 'the
picturesque dresses, curious gestures and bustling employment' of
the peasants.

On returning home Collins moved into a larger house in Hampstead Square in order to accommodate his mother, now in poor
health and in need of constant attention. They remained only a
year before moving back into London where, in the summer of
1830, he rented a house in Bayswater. This possessed the double
advantage of 'a more commodious painting-room' and proximity
to Sir David Wilkie's Kensington residence. Despite these compen-
sations the Collins family left Hampstead with some regret. On
young Wilkie in particular the neighbourhood had left a lasting

impression. The quiet surroundings, the wild and solitary Heath, the view of London from the heights, invested Hampstead with an air of romance which not even the later development of the district quite dispelled. Time and again we find it used in his novels as the setting for some sensational event.

Wilkie Collins' childhood is scantily documented, and we know little of his progress between the ages of seven and twelve, while the family was living in Bayswater. There are letters describing a holiday at Ramsgate in September 1833 with his mother and Charley, and his uncle Francis, of whom he was particularly fond. Harriet writes: 'the boys are quite wild. Willy behaves nobly in the sea, he has had two 6 pennyworths'; and Collins asks if Willy has his book on ships. 'He might learn a good deal while at the sea about vessels.' There was the usual difficulties about lodgings, described in a cheerful, philosophical way by Harriet. Francis Collins fell seriously ill on his return to London and died in October. The elder Mrs. Collins' health gave way completely after the loss of her younger son and she too died three months later. William Collins was so stricken down by this double bereavement that he was forced to take a prolonged rest which he spent with his wife and children in Wales.

As his Journal shows, Collins' deeply religious nature coloured his entire life. One of the manifestations of his zeal was an inflexible Sabbatarianism. A story is told—not in the *Memoirs*—that he had a violent quarrel with his friend John Linnell because he found him nailing up his plums on a Sunday.

The children naturally came in for their full share of religious instruction. Fortunately, in the matter of their upbringing strictness was tempered by affectionate understanding. To Willy and Charley, aged 11 and 7, he writes:

Your mother's account, in her last letter, of you both, pleased me much. Go on praying to God, through Jesus Christ, to enable you, by His Holy Spirit, to be blessings to your parents; and then you must be happy. Both your letters were well written, and I was delighted to hear you were pleased with the holiday you had on Michaelmas-Day. I have made only a few sketches—one of them, however, will, I think, please you both. It is a drawing of a large gray horse, which was brought to me from the plough. The drawing occupied my time, I dare say, four hours. The horse is evidently of the Flanders breed, and I know Charley always likes to see horses of that class. I think I shall have it framed, and make a present of it to my own Charley. I have a sketch of a watermill, which I rode many miles yesterday to make and which, if Willy should take a fancy for, I shall have framed and give to him . . . A pretty *long* letter, methinks, for two such *short* fellows! However, I never regret any trouble I may have in doing anything for good boys.

That the boys were not invariably good is suggested by a letter to Harriet some days earlier :

Tell the dear children that the only way they can serve their parents, is to obey them in all things: let Charley find out the passages in the Scriptures where this duty is most strongly insisted on, and write them down for me.

The few letters from Harriet which have survived reveal a rather warmer, more humorous personality, and there is no doubt that she too adored her two boys. As so often happens, they received more indulgence at their mother's hands. It was, on the whole, a happy childhood for Willy and Charley, and the best was yet to come.

2

Early Years

SINCE Sir David Wilkie's return from the Continent in 1828 he had continually urged Collins to widen his acquaintance with the masterpieces of painting by taking a long holiday in Italy. Although eager to travel, Collins had always shown reluctance to leave England while his mother remained an invalid. This tie had now been broken and he at last allowed himself to be persuaded. Then followed the question of whether to take the boys or leave them behind to continue their education. Young Wilkie was at this time attending the Maida Hill Academy, where he won a First Prize—a copy of Southey's Essays—at the end of the Christmas term 1835. Most of Collins' friends held the opinion that it would be madness to interrupt the boys' schooling at such a critical stage. On the other hand, Sir David Wilkie and a Mrs. Somerville, for whose opinions Collins had the highest respect, took the opposite view, asserting that education embraced far more than mere schooling. To the boys' delight the minority view prevailed.

To transport a wife and two small boys to the Continent for a year, the period originally fixed, was in those days no minor task, and the arrangements occupied several months. At last preparations were completed, the routes mapped out and the luggage packed. On September 19th, 1836, armed with countless letters of introduction and Madame Stark's *Handbook to Italy*, the party set off for Paris via the Dover-Boulogne steamboat.

After a stay of ten days in Paris, during which visits were made to the Louvre and to various exhibitions, they left by diligence for Châlon-sur-Saône. Their experience of this mode of travel was unfortunate, and Collins became so disgusted with the surly conductor, who not only half-starved his passengers but transferred them from a carriage to a cart for part of the way, that he decided to post from Auxerre. At Châlon they took a river-steamer down the Saône to Lyons, and continued by road to Arles. The *Memoirs* recall 'the noble amphitheatre and the peculiar beauty of the female peasantry of Arles.' They covered the next stage by canal-boat across the Camargue, that strange wilderness which lies between the Mouths of the Rhône, and passed the night at Martigues, described as 'a most extraordinary place, built upon piles like a miniature Venice, inhabited by a race of people who seemed half-smugglers and half-fishermen, and furnished with one small inn.' Here they picked up the Marseilles diligence, but, disappointed with the dirtiness and general dullness of that city, they lost no time in pressing on to the 'pretty little coast town of Cannes,' staying there three days.

On arrival at Nice the travellers were met with disturbing stories of an outbreak of cholera in Italy and the establishment of severe quarantine regulations at the frontier. There was no choice but to remain in Nice for the present. Writing to Sir David Wilkie on November 4th, Collins announced his intention of leaving his wife and children in Nice, where the quarters were very comfortable, and of proceeding alone to Florence and Rome as soon as the cholera situation improved. In his reply Wilkie must have earned the boys' deepest gratitude by protesting against this plan. 'I shall answer for this,' he wrote, 'the young gentlemen have no dislike to travelling, with all its inconveniences, to any distance.' Wilkie's view again prevailed and the project was dropped. Six weeks after their arrival at Nice the situation had improved sufficient to justify taking the family across the frontier. Their first destination in Italy was Florence and, in the *Memoirs*, Wilkie Collins recalls the snow knee-deep in the streets, the immense icicles hanging from the housetops and the piercingly cold wind as they entered the city on Christmas Eve. Although not yet thirteen years old, he accompanied his father on numerous visits to churches and picture-galleries.

Finding no improvement in the weather, they moved south to Rome during the first days of 1837. Here Collins was offered lodgings in the house once occupied by Claude, but, finding the rooms filthy and the landlord of bad character, he declined the privilege in favour of a more comfortable apartment further down the street. They remained there two or three months during which, in addition to much sightseeing, Collins painted a number of pictures. His son retained a vivid recollection of two models employed during the stay in Rome.

He engaged one burly, handsome fellow to sit, who was ready to procure any dress and assume any appearance that was wanted, at a few hours' notice; and who was painted by him in the somewhat dissimilar characters of a cardinal in full dress, and a Roman gamekeeper—a monk in his everyday robe, and a country shepherd. Another of his models was a beautiful boy, with features dazzlingly perfect, who had sat to everyone for Cupids, angels, and whatever else was lovely and refined; and who was in 'private life' one of the most consummate rascals in Rome—a gambler, a thief, and a stiletto-wearer, at twelve years of age!

After witnessing the famous ceremonies of Holy Week, they left Rome for Naples, undeterred by reports of one or two cases of cholera. The two boys, no less than their parents, rejoiced in the city's gloriously romantic setting and the carefree gaiety of its people. They were happy weeks. Collins found subjects on every hand and sketched furiously, anxious not to miss anything, yet hardly knowing where to begin. After a few weeks, however, they began to notice strange-looking yellow sedan chairs, with closed windows, passing in front of their house. These, they were told, were carrying cholera patients to hospital. Collins decided not to risk being shut up in Naples in quarantine with pestilence raging in the streets, and hastily took his family across the Bay to Sorrento. The decision was a wise one, for within a week or so the epidemic was at its height in Naples, no fewer than four hundred people dying in a single day.

Wilkie Collins, in the *Memoirs*, tells the story of a trip they made by boat from Sorrento to Amalfi where the inhabitants had somewhat extreme ideas of quarantine. Permission to land having been refused, they ordered dinner to be served in the boat. The local innkeeper complied by sending his cooks down to the beach in procession, laden with the various dishes which were placed at the water's edge. Here they were collected by the boatmen and taken aboard. At the end of the meal the empty dishes and the money in payment had to be thrown into the shallow water to be disinfected by the sea before being touched by the cautious men of Amalfi.

More than thirty years later Wilkie Collins recalled, in a speech to the Lotos Club in New York, this stay at Sorrento. At the time, he said, his appetite for what was termed 'light literature' was insatiable, and he had soon read every such book within reach. Summoning his courage he approached a melancholy fellow-visitor, who turned out to be an American, for the loan of a book. The American reflected for some time and then produced the only books in his possession which came, in his opinion, within the prescribed category. They were *The Sorrows of Werther* and *A Sentimental Journey*. The loan was followed by an invitation to dinner, at which the thirteen-year-old Wilkie treated his host to a critical appreciation of the two works.

At the end of July, William Collins was struck down by a serious illness, the symptoms of which suggest rheumatic fever. He was confined to a sick-room for several weeks, suffering violent pain, before being removed in early October to the nearby island of Ischia. Ischia was celebrated for its natural sulphur-baths, which in this instance effected a remarkable cure. Within a month he was well enough to return to Naples where the cholera epidemic had by now subsided. Here the two boys became favourites of the small English colony, from whom they received presents of 'swords, colours, hoops and other heart-winning things.'

They returned to Rome in February and began the homeward journey by leisurely stages in the last days of April, 1838. Collins wanted to miss nothing and yet be home in time to see the Academy Exhibition. In Florence—very different from the snowbound city of a year earlier—they ran across a descendant of Michelangelo who showed them the original manuscript of the Sonnets. A detour had to be made to see the collection of Correggios in Parma, and towards the end of May they reached Venice. Wilkie Collins had something to say, in the *Memoirs*, of a remarkable figure whom they employed as a cook, but who acquired in addition the functions of guide and gondolier. Beppo, as he was called, had been a cook in the service of Lord Byron and spoke of his former master as most generous and indulgent, 'though he ate little but biscuits and fruit.' Beppo had certain fixed notions about English gentlemen, one of which was that they all had their names written

up over their house-doors. He accordingly set to and manufactured
a three-foot nameboard which he hung up in Collins' absence. The
painter's surprise was no less than his delight when he returned
home to read the inscription, in large white letters, 'WIMICHIM
COLLINS.' Thus it remained for the rest of his stay in Venice.
Leaving on June 26th, they spent a few days in the mountains
around Innsbruck and Salzburg before proceeding to Munich. The
ten days' stay in the Bavarian capital proved a disappointment
largely because Collins found himself out of sympathy with
contemporary German painting. The final part of the journey was
by way of Heidelberg and Mannheim, thence down the Rhine to
Cologne and Rotterdam. They arrived in London on August 15th,
1838, after an absence of almost two years.

The long residence in Italy, if an unorthodox part of Wilkie's
education, was probably the most important. Now the changing
scenes and strange customs of a foreign land were stored away in
his memory, there to mature and fertilize the imagination. Wilkie
Collins was a born story-teller and already, at fourteen years of
age, he had a wealth of first-hand experience on which to draw.

Back in England the family's first task was to find a home. While
abroad Collins had parted with the lease of the Bayswater house,
and he now had some difficulty in finding a suitable dwelling.
Eventually he decided upon a convenient house in Avenue Road,
Regent's Park, which was at that time 'in a quiet situation on the
outskirts of London.' A studio was quickly fitted up and he took
in hand the innumerable sketches he had brought back from Italy.
As long as the light lasted he painted and in the evenings Sir David
Wilkie would come round and talk until bedtime of Art and Italy.

Young Wilkie was sent to a private boarding-school run by a
Mr. Cole in Highbury, at a cost of £90 per year. He seems to have
been reasonably happy there, if we may judge from the half-dozen
or so schoolboy letters which have survived. There are one or two
interesting points about them. Two are in Italian, and correct
Italian at that, which suggests that he made good use of his two
years in Italy. All are neatly written, but certain of them are in
exquisite copperplate without a blot or a mistake. These no doubt
represented 'tasks,' closely scrutinised by Mr. Cole, and are addressed
to Mr. Collins; they comprise précis of various books of the *Aeneid*,
which 'celebrated poem' was one of Wilkie's form books for the

year 1839. The less formal letters, all written at the age of fifteen to his mother, are those of a thoroughly normal schoolboy:

I did not write until I had tasted the cake as I thought you would like to know that it was most *delectably luscious*. The whole parcel arrived quite safe, and I am very much pleased with the trowsers, I think they are the nicest pair I ever had . . . I suppose as you say nothing of yourself and Charles Allston that you are both quite bobbish.
The boys here do Themes three times a week and Mr. Cole has hinted at the probability of the senior boys of our class beginning after Midsummer holidays. Some of the boys in our class have begun to do the same. I suppose Charlie has had some sliding but has I hope had no misfortune with his breeks. On Sunday the frost was so severe that the ponds in the neighbourhood were covered with boys sliding. . . . I think I have now exhausted all my news and remain with love to all at home.

Sometimes he sounds oddly adult:

Poor Charlie's ear-ache was sad news indeed, I know that it is the hardest of all pains to bear, having felt it myself: between them both I really wonder how you keep as well as you do especially with Master Charles to nurse, whom we all know is not very easily pacified. I really hope I shall see poor papa 'himself again,' for our holidays would be most miserable if he was as unwell then as he was last Midsummer. Give him my best love and tell him that I hope he was be able to pass his opinion upon a whole host of *works of art, fecit his son*.

Many years later he used to amuse his friends with anecdotes of his schooldays. One of these, recounted to Mrs. Lucy Walford,† a once popular novelist, concerns a schoolmate who made a paying business of swallowing spiders. He charged a penny for admission to watch the performance, sometimes increasing the charge to two-pence or threepence if the spider were abnormally large. Having worked up the excitement like an experienced showman, the boy would take out of his pocket a pill-box from which he solemnly extracted the captive spider. This he placed on his lips and allowed to crawl slowly down his throat. 'It was really worth a penny,' said Wilkie. He then told Mrs. Walford that the boy had become

† *Memories of Victorian London*, L. B. Walford. (Arnold, 1912.)

one of the leading lawyers of the day and that he sometimes felt tempted to visit him with a pill-box and a spider and say, 'Swallow me this for six-and-eightpence.'

Another story concerned the senior boy of the school, who was placed in authority over the boys in Wilkie's dormitory. He was something of a bully and, in Wilkie's words, 'was as fond of hearing stories when he had retired for the night as the Oriental despot to whose literary tastes we are indebted for *The Arabian Nights*.' Wilkie's budding talent had been recognised and he was invariably the unhappy boy chosen to entertain the prefect. It was useless for him to beg leave to go to sleep. 'You will go to sleep, Collins, when you have told me a story.' The story had to be amusing, otherwise the wretched Wilkie felt the persuasion of a cat-o'-nine-tails. On the other hand, a good story would often receive its reward in the shape of a pastry. 'Thus,' he said, 'I learnt to be amusing on a short notice—and have derived benefit from those early lessons.'

He was often punished at school for petty misdemeanours. Many years later he recalled that the master used to turn him to good moral account, as a means of making his model scholars ashamed of their occasional lapses into misconduct. "If it had been Collins I should not have felt shocked and surprised. Nobody *expects* anything of *him*. But You!!!—etc., etc." The popularity usually accorded by his schoolmates to the victim of frequent punishment did not, however, extend to Wilkie. They could never forgive his proficiency at French and Italian, the result of his residence abroad. In vain, when denounced as a 'French frog' because only he could cope with Voltaire's *Le Henriade*, did he protest that his parents were English, his grandfather Irish and his grandmother Scottish.

During Wilkie's years at school his father's health began to deteriorate. In 1839 he developed acute inflammation of the eyes which his doctor attributed to the rheumatic complaint contracted at Sorrento. This disability did not prevent him from painting even though he was forced to give up reading and writing for a time. A year or so later he was taken ill with violent internal pains which were diagnosed as a form of heart disease. He was warned that he must avoid sudden emotion and violent exercise, either of which might bring fatal results. This information, his son tells us, occasioned him not the slightest depression and he continued to work with undiminished vigour. Far more distressing to him was the news of the death at sea, in June, 1841, of his very dear friend Sir David Wilkie, on his way home from the Holy Land.

Wilkie Collins apparently left school towards the end of 1840, shortly before his seventeenth birthday. It had long been his father's wish that he should take Holy Orders, but the young man showed little inclination toward such a career. In the circumstances Collins wisely refrained from exerting any pressure upon him, and the idea of the Church was regretfully dropped. Wilkie was then offered the choice of classics at Oxford, mathematics at Cambridge, or a commercial career. Left to decide for himself, he finally settled upon commerce, without much enthusiasm, as the least undesirable alternative. To this end his father sought the assistance of a Mr. Antrobus, who was both a patron and a personal friend, and some time in 1841, Wilkie Collins entered the firm of Antrobus & Co., tea importers of the Strand, as an apprentice.

In the summer of the following year he accompanied his father on a sea-trip to the North of Scotland and the Shetlands, which is described in some detail in the *Memoirs*. They stayed with a friend for a week in Thurso, where Wilkie 'rode 36 miles on horseback to John O'Groat's House,' as he informed his mother in a letter written 'without *any candle at midnight*'; and from Thurso they went on to the Shetlands where William Collins wished to make sketches for illustrating Scott's *The Pirate*.

While his father was at work on his drawings, Wilkie wandered over the island, the main features of which were 'Dutchmen, peat-bogs, ragged ponies, beggars and fine scenery.' He had several minor adventures. On one occasion he was riding a pony over a solitary moor when a heavy mist descended and the guide lost the way. Dangerous peat-bogs almost surrounded them, and it was mainly due to the sure instinct of the Shetland ponies, left to their own guidance, that the riders were brought to safety.† On another occasion, Wilkie and his father were looking over some Dutch fishing-boats in the harbour when they innocently stumbled upon a riotous Schnapps party. Under pressure from a couple of blind drunk Dutch sailors they joined in for an uncomfortable half-hour, and only with difficulty made their escape.

† A similar incident befalls one of the characters in Wilkie Collins' novel, *The Two Destinies*, written 30 years later.

The weather, for the most part, was unsuitable for sketching, but Collins was indefatigable in the pursuit of his art, and Wilkie gives us this picture of his father sketching under difficulties:

Mr. Collins, with one knee on the ground, steadying himself against the wind; his companion holding a tattered umbrella over him, to keep the rain off his sketch-book; the guide standing by staring at his occupation in astonishment; and the ponies browsing near their riders on the faded grass; with mane and tail ever and anon floating out like streamers on the gusty breezes that swept past them.

Writing home to his mother—they were now living in Oxford Terrace, Hyde Park—Wilkie expresses the hope that she has prepared Mr. Antrobus for his prolonged absence. Mr. Antrobus' generosity in the matter of his apprentice's holidays was to be subjected to repeated strain, as will be seen later.

All we know of Wilkie's reactions to the world of commerce is that they were unfavourable. There is an echo of this period of his life in his novel *No Name*. A job is found for the ne'er-do-well Frank Clare in a great mercantile firm in the City, importers of tea and silk. 'He would be received on a very different footing from the footing of an ordinary clerk; he would be "pushed on" at every available opportunity. If he possessed fair abilities and showed common diligence in exercising them, his fortune was made.' Frank Clare did not make his fortune in the City—nor did Wilkie Collins. Whether he even showed common diligence is doubtful, for he later told Edmund Yates that when he should have been concentrating on Bills of Lading, invoices and the state of the Chinese market, he spent his time composing 'tragedies, comedies, epic poems and the usual literary rubbish accumulated about themselves by young beginners.'

The important fact is that he began to write, and write incessantly. Now and again an article would be accepted by one or other of the periodicals of the day. Since with many of these anonymity was the rule, we cannot be sure of the first occasion of his achieving print, but the earliest signed story appeared in Douglas Jerrold's *Illuminated Magazine* for August, 1843, and was entitled 'The Last Stage Coachman.' The theme, the ousting of the stage-coach by the railway, is not particularly original though

Wilkie's love of the fantastic runs riot in his description of a special nemesis for railway pioneers, a vision of 'a fully-equipped stage-coach in the clouds, with a Railway Director strapped fast to each wheel and a stoker between the teeth of each of the four horses.'

Whilst in the tea business, Wilkie Collins wrote his first novel, of which all trace has disappeared. It was a wildly improbable story of savage life in Polynesia and was offered in vain to every publisher in London. The novelist's own account of his early failure appears in a letter written some twenty years later: †

> The scene of the story was laid in the island of Tahiti, before the period of its discovery by European navigation. My youthful imagination ran riot among the noble savages, in scenes which caused the respectable British publisher to declare that it was impossible to put his name on the title-page of such a novel. For the moment I was a little discouraged. But I got over it and began another novel.

This time he determined to use his knowledge of the Italian scene and embarked upon a long historical novel dealing with the Gothic invasion of Rome in the Fifth Century. Whenever he could escape during the day from the office in the Strand, he consulted his authorities in the British Museum, and in the evening wrote his story in the seclusion of his father's studio.

Among those who saw merit in these early scribblings was his father. In April, 1844, while staying with the President of Corpus Christi College, Oxford, he wrote and asked his wife to cut out Willy's stories from the various publications and 'send them by post directly.' They were no doubt submitted, with proper paternal pride, for his host's opinion. Collins's Journal for January 1st, 1844, opens with this entry: 'As I think it quite possible that my dear son, William Wilkie Collins, may be tempted, should it please God to spare his life beyond that of his father, to furnish the world with a memoir of my life, I purpose occasionally noting down some circumstances as leading points, which may be useful.' His failing health, however, prevented the fulfilment of this intention. He developed a constant cough which interfered with sleep and seriously weakened him. He struggled as long as possible 'not to sink into the mere invalid' but suffered so severe an attack

† Quoted in *Appleton's Journal* (New York), 3rd September, 1870.

after dining out one evening in July that all such invitations were thereafter refused. Such strength as remained to him was devoted to painting, at which he worked to exhaustion. A few months earlier the artist and his family had made yet another move, to a nearby house at 1, Devonport Street, Oxford Terrace, equipped with a fine studio.

In the meantime Wilkie Collins had emerged from adolescence, and a letter written to his mother in January, 1844, a few days after his twentieth birthday, reveals him in the character of a lively young man about town. 'I feel the spirit of *maturity* strong upon me, having been in a state of grace ever since the 8th of this month [his birthday] as regards my mental faculties; and in a state of deplorable feebleness as regards my bodily. The parties have knocked me up—I've made two speeches at supper and drunk so much of the juice of the grape that my belly is as wine. We got home after one of the festive scenes at 10 minutes past 4 a.m. Charlie was so horrified at hearing the cock crow that he showed a disposition to whimper and said that people out so late as we were not in a *fit state to die*.' Clearly he had broken free from the rigid paternal discipline of his earlier years, for the incidents described took place while his father was in fact at home.

A few months later William Collins and his wife stayed for a time in the New Forest and the Isle of Wight in an effort to restore his health. The boys were left to fend for themselves in Devonport Street, and Wilkie urged his mother not to return on their account, assuring her that they 'look into rooms in the dark, peep about at bars and fastenings, get up early in the morning, don't drink anything like a glass of wine in a day, and are on tremendously affable terms with the domestics.' In August, however, he reports that he has had to lecture Susan, the housemaid, upon 'inhumanity.' She had attempted 'to reintroduce by the kitten's *nose* that which the innocent animal had just previously expelled as worthless from an opposite and inferior portion of its body. Charlie tried rage with the cook, I tried philosophy with the housemaid. He failed. I succeeded. Purified is the nose of Snooks.'

The same letter to his mother refers to preparations for his forthcoming holiday in Paris, and contains a dissertation upon Carpet Bags:

I suppose I must take it though I hate Carpet Bags with a great and bitter hatred. They don't protect your linen from damp, your brushes from breaking and your waistcoats from crumpling as a portmanteau does. People sit upon a Carpet Bag because it is soft, trunks tumble upon it for the same reason. There is not an accident to which luggage is liable that a Carpet Bag does not fall a victim to. It never was meant for anything but a few shirts and stockings that may be knocked about anyhow. It is the most disagreeable machine to pack—the most troublesome to unpack—the most impracticable to carry that human science ever invented.

His companion on the Paris trip was to be his friend Charles Ward, a choice of which William Collins disapproved strongly, but in vain. 'I do not like his flippant companion,' he told Harriet, 'they seem to think of nothing but doing absurd things.' Charles Ward, who was a brother of the artist E. M. Ward, became one of Wilkie's most intimate friends over a period of twenty-five years. A number of letters to Ward have been preserved and show him as being completely in Wilkie's confidence, both in personal and business matters. Ward was employed at Coutts' Bank in the Strand where William Collins, and later Wilkie, had an account. In later years it was common for Charles Ward to be invited to lunch, or dinner, or a week-end with Wilkie, and enjoined to bring with him some sum of money against a cheque. Wilkie made extensive use, through Ward, of the facilities of Coutts' Bank, obtaining not only advice on his investments but anything from a courier to accompany him abroad to a parcel of books at trade price. Charles Ward, who was probably a few years older than his friend, married Wilkie's cousin and had a large family. He eventually attained a high position with Coutts & Co.

Armed with the Carpet Bag and in the company of Ward, Wilkie reached Paris on August 28th, 1844. He was at once enchanted with the city, and the enchantment never died. To his mother he wrote long, dutiful and often amusing accounts of what he reassuringly termed their 'non-adventures.' Within a few days of their arrival he is chiefly concerned to prolong the holiday as far as possible. 'Will you write to Mr. Antrobus to ascertain the utmost extension of leave of absence that he will allow me. Will he give me the first week in October? Or more? Or less? Or what? In the end Mr. Antrobus granted up to 3rd October, making five weeks in all. The weeks were spent in a whirl of sightseeing, some of it of the orthodox kind, theatres and the Opera, the churches, the gardens, Versailles and its pictures; some less so, as for instance 'a glorious subject for Charlie—a dead soldier laid out naked at the Morgue, like an unsaleable codfish all by himself upon the slab.' They propose to see Rachel at the Théâtre Français in *Les Horaces*, although he knows 'by bitter experience what a bore it will be—men in buff-coloured blankets with fuzzy heads growling about their beloved country through five long acts, with porticos *ad libitum* behind them for scenery—have taken care to secure comfortable seats with spring cushions, so as to sleep with dignity —shall lie furiously about it in England—say it was superb, etc., etc., to gain credit for a classical taste.' He returned to England an ardent Francophile and remained so for the rest of his life.

Although he kept up for his parents' benefit some pretence of taking his business career seriously—he described himself to his mother as being 'in a halo of commercial enterprise'—it is clear that much of his working day was devoted to literary composition of one kind or another. His general dislike of office routine was now reinforced by the limitations it placed upon the pleasures of travel, and he became more restless than ever. He could hardly wait until the following summer (1845) to visit Paris again, and on this occasion he travelled alone. Almost his first letter to his mother broached the annual subject. 'Pray find out, whenever you think it *politic to do so*, the *utmost extent* of leave that I can obtain from Mr. A.' Having left London on 7th September, he considered his liberty should be extended 'to the 15th or 20th of October— at least.'

Paris he found as delightful as before. 'The gutters hold their rights uninfringed, the churches rejoice in their accustomed emptiness, the sugar plums still glitter in gorgeous indelicacy of design, each shopkeeper leaves his business to his wife, and each grisette is redolent of sentiment and prodigal of smiles.' The only drawback is the presence of 'the beef-eating British,' among whom he has descried Harrison Ainsworth in Galignani's Library, 'sitting, as usual, in the positions of his different portraits.' French manners, especially those of the children, enchant him: 'An evening or two since, a creature (whether masculine, feminine or neuter, I know not) bowled his hoop against the toe of my boot and made me an apology (he seemed just able to walk and talk) so *elaborately civil* that I was perfectly astounded and took off my hat to him.'

Invited by some friends he had met in Paris to accompany them to Nice, Wilkie wrote to his mother, half-seriously, for an advance of £100 'upon the strength of my MS. and Chapman and Hall.' This was presumably the manuscript of the South Seas novel, and seems to have been regarded by his parents as inadequate security, for the project was quietly dropped. Indeed Mr. and Mrs. Collins were far from happy that their 21-year-old son should be wandering about Paris on his own, and their letters were full of warnings and parental advice. These Wilkie treated with some levity, replying on one occasion: 'Tell the Governor that I will eat plain food (when I get back to England) and read Duncan's *Logic* and Butler's *Analogy* (when I have no chance of getting anything else to peruse).' When William Collins reproves him for not reading his mother's letters carefully, Wilkie accuses him of 'a most unchurchmanlike disposition to scandalise other people.' This provoked a sharp reproof, to which Wilkie replied, 'My joke about Mr. Collins's scandalising propensities was an answer to one of yours; but it shall be my last witticism. People who live in the country and eat beefsteaks are not to be joked at with impunity.' As for the main purpose of this latest letter—'it contains no impiety and it attempts no jokes. It is devoted to a statement of my approaching INSOLVENCY.' The balance of his money will suffice for his miscellaneous expenses, but it will not pay his hotel-bill, nor his return fare. He has not of course ignored his mother's parting injunctions about living economically; the original sum has lasted for the trip, as she hoped, but will not unfortunately cover the return trip. To restore him to Devonport Street a further £10 will be needed. 'Should Mr. Collins vow that he will pay no attention to the above modest and, I may be permitted to say, luminous suggestion, do not be in the least alarmed or put out of the way. I can live here a long time upon my *credit*, and when that is exhausted I can go into a "spunging house"—the actual difference between imprisonment at Paris and imprisonment at the Strand being too inconsequential to be worth ascertaining to a nicety.'

After so dire a threat, Mrs. Collins must be cajoled.

I entirely disagree with you about the unworthiness of the world, for good people. The proof that you are wrong is in the existence of such individuals as Mrs. Collins in the habitable globe—(Don't forget the £10). Excellence such as yours, my dear Madam, cannot exist independent of usefulness, and would not be useful were people altogether unworthy of its softening and humanising influence. (The cheque must be crossed 'Messrs. Coutts & Co.') Therefore, I am inclined to conclude that, as long as you are in the world, the world must, logically and absolutely, be worthy of everybody and everything in it. (A letter must accompany the cheque directing Ward to forward it to Lafitte & Co., Paris.)

Is it surprising that Wilkie succeeded in wheedling the required sum out of his mother? His next letter thanks her for expressions of affection and for the despatch of the cheque. He will arrange to return to London on the evening of 14th October—Mr. Antrobus having again obliged—and to start work on the following day, thereby obtaining 'the utmost extension possible of my stay in Paris—a very pleasant and necessary achievement, considering that the Italian Opera has begun and that *Pâtés de Foie Gras* are daily expected at the principal restaurants.' Nor were these the only attractions. In his idle wanderings through the Paris streets, some morbid impulse had again drawn him into the chilly corridors of the Morgue. 'A body of a young girl had just been fished out of the river. As her bosom was black and blue I suppose she had been beaten into a state of insensibility and then flung into the Seine.' Fifteen years later he chose this grim setting for our final glimpse of Count Fosco in *The Woman in White*.

During these last two years William Collins's health had been steadily failing. In vain did Harriet take him into the fresh air and quiet of the countryside for long spells. About the time of his son's return from Paris in 1845, he began to cough blood and early the following year developed dropsy. Although he never entirely gave up hope he suspected, and his family knew, that he was a dying man. Still he continued to paint, working an hour or so a day in an effort to finish two Devonshire landscapes for the Academy, until the brush sometimes fell from his swollen hand from sheer weakness. Much of the time he was confined to bed. He did, however, collect his strength sufficiently to visit the Academy on varnishing day; many of his old friends clustered around him expressing the sincerest hopes for his recovery. Collins was deeply affected by their sympathy, and must have known that he was saying goodbye to most of them for the last time.

With a dying man's concern to set his family's affairs in order, he turned his attention to his two sons. Charley had already showed promise as a portrait-painter; on the eve of his eighteenth birthday his entry appears in his father's Journal: 'I most fully and sincerely believe that if this boy does justice to the genius with which he is endowed . . . he will, with his tact and taste, produce most satisfactory and popular works.' Of the elder son's literary abilities he was sufficiently convinced to approve his leaving the tea business, but pressed upon him the desirability of acquiring a regular profession as well. Accordingly, Wilkie Collins resigned from Antrobus & Co. and entered Lincoln's Inn in May, 1846, as a Law Student. He too had some idea of becoming a painter and for a time seemed undecided whether his future lay in the field of Art or of Literature. He did achieve, in 1848, the distinction of having a picture hung at the Royal Academy, but this success seems to have satisfied rather than stimulated his artistic aspirations, for there is no record of his ever painting another picture.

In a final effort to arrest the spread of her husband's disease, Harriet took him once more to the country, to a cottage she had leased at Iver in Buckinghamshire. This time the change did no more than perhaps delay the end. Collins was now in agonizing pain which he bore with great fortitude. Opiates had long since ceased to be effective. After three months he was taken back to London having said farewell to the English countryside he had loved so well and pictured so charmingly.

Soon after returning to Devonport Street, William Collins took to his bed for the last time. A few days before the end, according to Wilkie, 'happening to observe in the accidental arrangement of some writing and drawing materials placed in and about a small wooden tray at the foot of his bed, certain shades and outlines which resolved themselves to his fancy into the representation of an old ferry-boat lying at a deserted quay, he asked for some drawing materials, and being propped up with pillows, proceeded to make a small water-colour sketch.' Just before sinking into unconsciousness he pronounced 'an eloquent eulogium upon the Christian faith, impressing the advantages of its constant practice upon his family.' His intellect then clouded over and, after a period of delirium when he talked of his approaching recovery and of the many pictures he was going to paint, he died quietly and painlessly on the morning of 17th February, 1847.

In an obituary it was truly said of him: 'Only his intimate acquaintances could rightly estimate the high qualities of his mind and heart; generous and encouraging to young talent, he was always eager to accord praise; neither jealousy nor envy ever gave the remotest taint to his character.' These were among his virtues. He possessed other qualities of the kind less likely to find their way into an obituary. About his constant striving after moral excellence, sincere though it was, there was a touch of priggishness which showed occasionally in his dealings with those less deeply religious. From other sources there are stories which suggest that he paid more attention to social distinctions than was necessary, and endowed convention almost with the authority of law. To his family, however, he was all that was good and, though they had been long prepared for his death, they felt no less keenly the loss of a well-loved father and husband.

William Collins' influence on his children is more obvious in the case of Charley, who inherited many of his father's character-istics. With Wilkie the effect was different. We can trace his love of Art, his conscientious devotion to work, perhaps his capacity for handling his affairs, to his father's influence, but the pattern of his life is essentially a recoil from the somewhat austere atmosphere of his early home, and a reaction against the ascetic in the person of his father. On the positive side, the dominant influence in the forming of Wilkie's character was almost certainly that of his mother.

3

Literary Beginnings

WILKIE COLLINS laid aside the manuscript of the historical novel upon which he had been working for some time, in order to carry out his father's wish that he should write his biography. He set to work collecting letters and reminiscences of friends to supplement the Journal, even going so far as to trace almost every picture his father had painted, a task which involved visits to Public Galleries and private collections all over Britain.

Towards the end of July, 1847, he interrupted his labours to take a short holiday in Normandy with Charles Ward. Normandy proved somewhat disappointing and after about ten days they found themselves, despite Mrs. Collins' warnings, once more in Paris. Reassuring his mother, Wilkie wrote: 'We find provincial cities insupportably oppressive to our mercurial characters.' Paris, as always, landed him in financial straits. At first it was merely a matter of whether his mother had a spare five-pound note which she could send him, even though he had money enough for a short stay. No cash arrived, and Charles Ward left for home a day or two later. Ever optimistic, Wilkie remained, expecting a cheque from one post to the next, until after a week he was compelled to write in desperation to Charles Ward at Coutts' Bank:

Up to this moment I have received no communication—monetary or epistolary—from England, and I now write to you, with eight francs in my pocket, and in debt for two pair of boots, to ascertain whether I am to expect any remittances at all before I become bankrupt—an event which I have my suspicions will take place tomorrow.
On the day you left me I made a calculation of my resources—including the five pounds I expected from England—and found

to my horror and astonishment that if I paid for my boots, my bill here and my journey back, like an honest man I could not stay more than two days longer at Paris, at the furthest. I made up my mind therefore to start for London today rather than spend a single farthing more money, but on Saturday no money arrived—on Sunday no money arrived—on Monday no money arrived—and today—this present Tuesday—par le sang bleu! I have changed my last 'Nap' and have not a banker at Paris to go to for any more!

I suppose Mrs. Collins is determined to punish me for going to Paris at all, by keeping me there as long as she pleases in a state of *pauperism*. This may seem at the first glance a monstrous good joke, but it will be found on closer inspection to be rather an expensive one. Every day I stay here enlarges my bill in the Hotel and increases my current expenses, which, carefully as I watch them, grow upon me as fast as moss on an old house or pimples on a drunkard's face.

I breakfast for a franc and a half, I dine for three francs and a half. I have never entered a hackney coach since I have been at Paris, I have missed the Theatre *one whole* night, I occupy myself all day in painting and taking salubrious walks, I have had three glorious bowel complaints since I saw you which have done my stomach a world of good and made my complexion as pure as milk of roses. Can anything be more economical, more salubrious, more virtuous than such a mode of life as this?

Have the goodness to show (or send) this letter to Mrs. Collins, directing her attention particularly to the above paragraph and also to the statement of my assets and liabilities exposed beneath.

LIABILITIES (supposing that W.W.C. departs from Paris ASSETS
in a solvent state on Saturday next. N.B. This is only Frs. 8
allowing proper time for securing my place in the
Diligence and getting the money from London)

Probable amount of Lodging, Washing, Candles,
Servants, or in two words: 'Hotel Bill.'   Frs. 40
Journey back (cheapest way)   Frs. 65
Bill for boots   Frs. 68

(This bill for boots includes two new pair at 50 frs. (charged £3 in London) and new fronting an old pair the leathers and soles of which have burst, at 18 frs.—charged £1 in London.)

Board and pocket money for five days at 10 frs.
a day (i.e. 15 frs. *less* than I spent at Paris per
diem on my last visit)   Frs. 50

                         TOTAL   223
                                    8

                  Liabilities   215 Frs.
                          or £8-12-6

This will doubtless appear very horrifying to Mrs. Collins, but
it is not entirely my fault . . . If you have already forwarded
five pounds to Lafitte's, forward another five *immediately* on the
receipt of this, without waiting to get it from Mrs. Collins. I
will settle with you on my return. If you have not remitted me
a rap (Mrs. Collins being unpropitious) ask her boldly for £10
at one fell swoop and send the money with all possible despatch
to Lafitte's. If Mrs. Collins refuses to touch the estimate let me
know by return of post. It will then be time to pawn my watch
and coat at the Mont de Piété and try my fortune with the
proceeds at a table of Rouge et Noir (Horror! Horror!!) . . . I
have been very ill-used by the Devonport Street Dynasty, to
which however in a fine spirit of Christian piety I extend my
forgiveness and desire my love.

Within a year of his return home the biography was finished
and arrangements were made for publication. In November, 1848,
Memoirs of the Life of William Collins R.A. was published in two
volumes by Longmans, Brown, Green and Longmans. One of the
first subscribers was Charles Dickens.

A few days before publication Wilkie wrote to R. H. Dana, the
American author, to thank him for information about Washington
Allston, who had been the friend of both Dana and William
Collins. The letter continues:

Many causes connected with delay in engraving the illustrations
to the book and with changing the arrangement of parts of the
MSS., have contributed to put off the publication of my work—
it will, however, be 'out' at last in about a week or ten days
hence. It occupies two volumes, is dedicated by permission to
Sir Robert Peel, and will be published by Messrs. Longmans.
What chances of success can be predicted for a book devoted
to so peaceful a subject as the Art, amid the vital and varied

interests of home politics and foreign revolutions now attracting everybody's attention in England, it is impossible to say. I resign myself philosophically to await the event of my experiment—hoping little and foreboding less.

It is not surprising that the *Memoirs* show signs of immaturity: the writing is careful but the style too often ponderous. Page after page is devoted to painstaking descriptions of Collins' paintings down to the smallest detail. If these remind one sometimes of an art-dealer's catalogue, they were also a form of apprenticeship and developed in Wilkie Collins a sense of landscape which enabled him, in later books, to set his scene with marked effect.

The sky is tinged by a mild, dawning light, which arises over a bank of misty vapour, and touches the wild, sharp edges of a large cloud, stretching across the heavens towards the light. Above this, still lingers the deep, purple, transparent atmosphere of the departing light, studded in one or two places with the glimmer of a fading star. Beneath, the fresh, buoyant sea dances onward to the foreground, garnished here and there fantastically with the rising light. In front, a single fishing-boat—whose large sail, flapping lazily against the mast, rises grandly against the lighter part of the sky—is stranded in shallow water. Around, and on it, stand the burly fishermen, hauling in their nets over the wet sand. In the distance is seen a town, faintly discernible on the cliffs that rise on the right hand of the picture; while, on the horizon, appears the sail of another boat approaching the beach. The tone of colour in this elaborate work is dark, yet transparent—representing a sort of brightening obscurity, and suggests at every point the mysterious morning stillness which reigns over the scene.

A living portrait of William Collins emerges from this biography. If a blemish is concealed here and there, this was only to be expected. On its first page the author admits that he is 'perplexed at being called upon to delineate a character which it has hitherto been his only ambition to respect' but he sets about his task modestly and with complete sincerity and achieves no small success.

To the biographer of Wilkie Collins the *Memoirs* hold a special disappointment in the deliberate self-effacement of their author, who so seldom intrudes upon his father's story. His own opinions are but rarely expressed. When we do come across them they reveal a shrewd and alert mind, as for example in his judgment upon the uninformed art-critic, hardly less apposite today than when it was written.

There is probably no department of intellectual Art which is so incautiously approached by those who have never studied it, as painting. . . . People who, in music, will silently submit to the infliction of a modern symphony, because they suppose that their professional friends, who assure them that it is 'full of tune,' must know better than they do; or, who toil boldly through a volume of metaphysical poetry because a learned acquaintance has described it as 'earnest' or 'hopeful' or 'subjective' or 'æsthetic,' are in many cases, the very people who in matters of Art, scorn all guidance and decide, *ex cathedra* upon everything pictorial over the last sip of a cup of coffee, or during a passing salutation in the crowd of an Exhibition-Room.

Nor is the book entirely lacking in wit: 'He scouts logic and probabilities with all the serenity of a juryman waiting for his dinner, or a politician with a reputation for consistency.'

On the whole the *Memoirs* are a remarkable achievement for the first book of a young man of twenty-four. Mr. Walter de la Mare, in his interesting essay, *The Early Novels of Wilkie Collins*, sums up the biography as 'the quiet and veracious record of the life of a man who manifestly deserved every ounce of loving admiration his son accorded him—of a father whose companionship must have been a priceless blessing to such a son.'

Some six weeks after publication Wilkie wrote again to Dana, this time at some length:

> 38 Blandford Square,
> London.
> January 12th, 1849.

My dear Sir,—On Saturday the 30th December last, I gave Messrs. Longmans directions to send a copy of my *Memoirs* of my late father's life to their Boston Correspondents—Little and Brown, addressed to you. They assured me that the parcel should be despatched at the first opportunity—I hope you will receive it with as little delay as possible.

The book has hitherto succeeded very satisfactorily. It has been received with much greater indulgence, and reviewed at much greater length, by the Press, here, than I had ventured to anticipate. More than half the edition of 750 copies is already sold; and this success thus far, trifling as is its importance in itself, is a matter of some gratification to me—not merely as showing that I have not entirely failed in my undertaking—but also as relieving me from some pecuniary responsibility; for the *Memoirs* are my own speculation, and by the sale of the larger half of the edition, the somewhat heavy expenses connected with their publication are already more than paid.† I sincerely hope that you may be led to form a favourable opinion of the work, on perusal.

You ask what is the opinion among artists here of Ruskin's *Modern Painters*. Although I do not follow my father's profession (being a student of Lincoln's Inn; and only painting at leisure moments, in humble *amateur-fashion*, for my own amusement) I live very much in the society of artists, and can therefore tell you something of the impression made by Ruskin's work. The violent paradoxes in the first volume had the effect which violent paradoxes, when cleverly argued, usually produce; they amused some, displeased others, and startled everybody. It was pretty generally admitted that the Author was a vigorous and dashing writer, who had studied Art with genuine enthusiasm, but with doubtful judgment. On the other hand, however, the greater part of his readers (with whom I came in contact) while doing justice to his capacities, thought them woefully misdirected; and considered him as a man, who having determined to say something new on every subject that he touched, resolutely overlooked or dogmatically contradicted any received and tested principle of intellectual or critical truth that came in his way; and fancied that he had achieved originality when in many cases he merely succeeded in producing what was eccentric or absurd. His book had its small circle of resolute admirers—but it made a sensation, and only a sensation, among the larger class of readers—artists and amateurs.

His *second Volume*, published some time after his first, and containing an expression of regret for the arrogance of manner in his preceding publication, has, however, raised him immensely

† Messrs. Longmans' records indicate that Collins arranged for the printing and binding, and that they distributed the book for him on commission terms, retaining 10% on bookshop sales. The published price was 21/-. The author himself disposed of 200 copies, the publishers some 300 at the trade price of 15/-, and the rest of the edition was remaindered in 1852 at 2/6. The author's final profit on the transaction may have been about £100. The book has never been reprinted.

in the estimation of cultivated and thinking readers. I have merely looked into it myself, but I have heard it spoken of by artists who have read it carefully as a work of very unusual power, exhibiting a deep sympathy with the highest purpose of Art—poetical observation of Nature—and profound critical appreciation of many of the works of the 'Old Masters.' Some paradoxical opinions it might contain, in common with the preceding volume; but they were urged in a different spirit, and were amply compensated by the general intention of the book, and the real good to be gained from it—philosophically as well as pictorially—by attentive readers. Such is the general opinion of this second Volume, so far as it has reached me.

All *literary* London is now astir, however, about a work of a very different order—Macaulay's *History of England*. It is regarded everywhere, as a really great achievement, and as tending to found a new school of Historical writing. The first edition of three thousand copies was out of print in a fortnight. This is indeed a great age for great authors. Dickens told a friend of mine, that he had made *four thousand guineas* by his last year's Christmas book—(*The Battle of Life*)—a five shilling publication (!) which everybody abused, and which, nevertheless, everybody read. Eighteen thousand copies of his present Christmas book (*The Haunted Man*) were 'subscribed for' by the book, sellers, before publication . . .

It has been one of the greatest sources of gratification to me, since the publication of my work, that the *Memoirs* have gained the favourable opinion of Sir Robert Peel; whose long and kind friendship for my father, and whose well-known judgment in matters of Literature and Art, concurred to give the highest importance to any criticism of his on my undertaking. I had the pleasure of visiting him, by invitation, at his country seat, to receive his personal congratulations . . .

Mrs. Collins had moved with her two sons to 38 Blandford Square, a rather smaller house than the one in Devonport Street, some six months after her husband's death. William Collins had learned to be prudent in matters of money, though he seems not to have been parsimonious; he had received considerable sums by the sale of his pictures and his mode of living had never been luxurious. It is not surprising, therefore, that he left to his widow an income which enabled the family to live in some degree of comfort.

Although, as he takes care to mention to Dana, Wilkie remained a student of Lincoln's Inn, his exertions seem to have been mainly directed towards eating the requisite number of dinners; he later admitted to having read seriously for the Bar for perhaps six weeks. The study of law he found as irksome as the importing of tea; its pursuit would have interfered with his writing and writing had already become a ruling passion. Even as late as August, 1850, he had some idea of eventually practising at the Bar ('I resign myself to the Queen's Bench,' he wrote in a letter to his mother) but discovering that he could earn a living in more pleasant ways he seems to have changed his mind soon afterwards. It was not difficult, however, for a gentleman in the mid-nineteenth century to become a barrister and, in November, 1851, Wilkie was duly called. It is probable that he did not entirely abandon his legal associates, since no characters are more closely observed or sharply delineated than the lawyers who figure in his novels. They are certainly drawn, not without a wry affection, from the life. He once described himself as 'a barrister of some fifteen years' standing, without even having had a brief, or ever having even so much as donned a wig and gown.'

It was, however, from the painting fraternity that most of Wilkie's friends were drawn at this time and indeed he was able to enjoy the friendship of artists all his life. First among them was E. M. Ward, the painter and brother of Charles Ward, who became, like his brother, Wilkie's life-long friend. Nine years older than Wilkie, Ward was originally his father's friend, having first met William Collins in Rome. Some years before his death Collins had written: 'Yesterday, Jones offered to take my evening duty at the Library, so I came home to Willie, who would have been dull enough by himself—as it was he was amused; for I had asked Mr. Ward to spend the evening with us.' Among E. M. Ward's friends, who became Wilkie's too, were John Leech, Maclise, painter of several portraits of Dickens, and Augustus Egg, R.A. Then there were the friends and fellow-students of Wilkie's younger brother Charles, who included Millais, Frith, Holman Hunt and the Rossettis. Wilkie Collins was well qualified to express, as in his letter to Dana, what artistic London was thinking.

E. M. Ward was deeply in love with a sixteen-year-old girl, daughter of a painter also named Ward, although no relation. They were determined to get married and, aware of both parents'

D

disapproval on account of Henrietta's extreme youth, they decided upon a secret wedding. The plan was confided to Wilkie, to whose sense of adventure it made an immediate, if vicarious, appeal. He became a fellow-conspirator and willingly undertook all arrangements. The wedding took place at All Souls, Langham Place, on May 4th, 1848, with Wilkie as best man, and was followed by a dinner in celebration. The dinner over, husband and wife departed to their respective homes. The final step was not taken until three months later, when they ran away to spend a delayed honeymoon in a country cottage found for them by Wilkie.

For his share in organising the runaway marriage, Wilkie Collins was invited to be godfather to the Wards' first child, Alice, who was born the following year and christened at St. Pancras Church. Mrs. Ward relates that, after the ceremony, he joined in the celebrations to such effect that he was observed to gaze at the sleeping infant and say, 'The baby sheems to be moving in a very odd way and is making funny faces. Why! 'Pon my soul, the baby's drunk! The baby's drunk!'

The Wards, who lived in Harewood Square, Marylebone, were close neighbours of the Collins family. Wilkie and E. M. Ward shared a love of amateur theatricals, and used to stage ambitious productions in what Wilkie called the 'Theatre Royal Back Drawing Room' at Blandford Square. Among the performances given were Sheridan's *The Rivals* and Goldsmith's *The Good-Natured Man*. These shows remained among Wilkie's most affectionate memories; writing to Ward in 1862 he said: 'I thought certain old memories of ours would be roused by that Chapter [in *No Name*] about the private theatricals. I read *The Good-Natured Man* and *The Rivals* again while I was writing it, and saw you once more in 'Croaker' as plainly as I see this paper. I have been engaged in far more elaborate private theatrical work since that time—but the real enjoyment was at the Theatre Royal, Blandford Square.'

The first recorded instance of Wilkie's appearance on a public stage is on February 26th, 1850, when he played the part of Soubise in *A Court Duel*, adapted from the French by himself. The performance took place at the Soho Theatre (late Miss Kelly's), 73, Dean Street, Soho, and was in aid of The Female Emigration Fund. It was followed by a short play by an anonymous author called *Raising the Wind!!*; from the two exclamation marks and the fact that Wilkie played a character named Jeremy Diddler one may make a reasonable guess at the nature of its plot.

Encouraged by the favourable reception of the *Memoirs* Wilkie Collins took up again the manuscripts of his historical novel. Much of the earlier draft was revised and re-written and, about the middle of 1848, the work was finished. It was offered without success to Henry Colburn and to George Smith, of Smith, Elder. It was Ruskin who brought the manuscript to Smith but the latter did not consider a first novel with a classical subject a tempting proposition. On 8th September Wilkie wrote to his mother: 'Two volumes of my book are in Bentley's hands. I wrote a civil letter offering them on trial, received a civil answer accepting them on trial; and expect, in process of time, a second civil answer refusing them on trial.' His fears were unfounded, for Richard Bentley accepted the book and it was published in February, 1850, under the title of *Antonina, or the Fall of Rome*.

In this novel Wilkie had taken Bulwer Lytton, for whom he shared at that time the public's extravagant admiration, as his model, and *Antonina* is to a large extent imitative. Abounding in scenes of violence, it describes the sacking of Rome early in the Fifth Century by the Visigoths. The subject was an ambitious one for a writer of his inexperience to tackle, and his courage at least can be commended. The book is, unfortunately, long and dull, the style flamboyant and the dialogue mainly disclamatory. *Antonina* bears little resemblance to anything else he wrote and is today almost unreadable.

The work nevertheless gained for its author a certain reputation. Some ten years later, Wilkie wrote that the reviewers acclaimed it 'with such a chorus of praise as has never been sung over me since.' There were dissentient voices, however, and discussing *Antonina* with his friend Frank Archer towards the end of his life, Wilkie said, 'There was a man who came down on me heavily, and prophesied that I should never make a novelist. Many years afterwards I met him and we had a hearty laugh over his prediction. Though I must honestly say that the story was anything but a good one.' He must have appreciated that the historical novel was not to be his medium, for he made no effort to repeat the experiment.

He was amused to find himself a minor celebrity following the success of *Antonina*. In a letter to E. M. Ward he wrote:

> An awful crowd at the Mayor's last Thursday, stewards with names of distinguished individuals on private printed lists— charged to make civil speeches to all authors and artists, made hideous mistakes instead: Cardwell taken for Bulwer, your humble servant taken for a P-R.B., and asked whether the author of *Antonina* was there that night. Gallons of cider-cup in a vessel like a gold slop-pail, out of which the company drank like horses out of a trough. Seedy next morning and miserably unfit to be in the house of a virtuous man whose servant had never heard of Brandy and Soda-water in the whole course of his life. I met Bulwer at a party on Monday night. He is looking bright and plump. Now is the time to take his portrait.

During the summer months following the publication of *Antonina* Wilkie determined to take a holiday—but it must be one that he could turn to literary account. The year 1850 roughly marks the end of the first frenzied period of railway-construction in England; by then the net had spread over most of the country despite every protest from the partisans of the stage-coach. One of the few counties still to escape the penetration of the locomotive was Cornwall: on the maps of 1850 the thin black line stops short at Plymouth. To the average Londoner, Cornwall, with its remote fishing-villages and its superb coastline was an unknown land. According to Wilkie Collins, books of travel crowded the shelves of the circulating libraries relating to every country of the Globe 'except perhaps Cornwall and Kamchatka.' Of the two he thought he preferred Cornwall, and, accompanied by a young artist friend, H. C. Brandling, he set out in July for Plymouth and the end of the railway.

The tour lasted several weeks during which they visited many places that have since become well known to Cornish holiday-makers, among them Looe, Kynance Cove, St. Michael's Mount, Land's End and Tintagel. It was a happy tour and Wilkie and Brandling got along excellently together. They found the Cornish hospitable and courteous, although then, as now, anyone coming from east of the Tamar was regarded as a foreigner. They were mistaken for travelling pedlars and for 'Mappers,' come to survey the land in preparation for the railroad. Everywhere their misfortune in having to carry their baggage on their back elicited sympathy. At Fowey 'the mere sight of two strangers walking along with such appendages as knapsacks strapped on their shoulders seemed of itself to provoke the most unbounded wonder. We were stared at with almost incredible pertinacity and good humour. People hard at work left off to look at us; whole groups congregated at cottage-doors, walked into the middle of the road when they saw us approach. Little children ran indoors to bring out large children.' At Liskeard, on the other hand, their landlady liked them for being 'nice strong young Englishmen who walked about independently and didn't mind the weight of their knapsacks,' and because they were not 'effeminate dandies.' So much Wilkie proudly records in a letter to his mother.

Among their adventures was the descent of a copper mine at Botallack, for which Wilkie was provided with a miner's suit several sizes too large—he was only five feet six inches in height. After a climb down many hundreds of feet of vertical ladders, complicated for Wilkie by his voluminous garb, they are conducted along a gallery leading out under the sea. They stop and listen:

A distant, unearthly noise becomes faintly audible—a long, low, mysterious moaning, that never changes, that is *felt* on the ear as well as *heard* by it—a sound that might proceed from some incalculable distance—from some far invisible height—a sound unlike anything that is heard on the upper ground, in the free air of heaven—a sound so sublimely mournful and still, so ghostly and impressive when listened to in the subterranean recesses of the Earth, that we continue instinctively to hold our peace, as if enchanted by it, and think not of communicating to each other the strange awe and astonishment which it has inspired in us both from the very first.

At last the Miner speaks again, and tells us that what we hear is the sound of the surf lashing the rocks a hundred and twenty feet above us, and of the waves that are breaking on the beach beyond. The tide is now at the flow, and the sea is in no extraordinary state of agitation : so the sound is low and distant . . . But, when storms are at their height, when the ocean hurls mountain after mountain of water on the cliffs, then the noise is terrific; the roaring heard down here in the mine is so inexpressibly fierce and awful, that the boldest men at work are afraid to continue their labour.

Wilkie collects facts as a squirrel gathers nuts. He tells us that the miner's normal wage is between forty and fifty shillings a month; that five per cent of the population of the Penzance area emigrated to Australia and New Zealand in 1849, chiefly as a result of the potato-blight; that a dozen pilchards sell for a penny; that good cottages are to be had in Cornwall for between fifty shillings and four pounds a year; that no one dies of starvation in Cornwall—a fact apparently worthy of remark.

He is interested too in folklore and superstition, relating with gusto the story of how the people of Looe once rid themselves of a plague of rats by cooking and eating them, liberally flavoured with onion; and of Old Daniel Gumb whose addiction to mathematics led him ultimately to seek solace in a hermit's life, his dwelling a small cave on the walls of which he scratched out his Euclidean problems. He retails the local superstition that no wound will fester as long as the instrument which has caused it is kept bright and clean. In one village they visited the inhabitants took comfort from the belief that no one baptised with water from a certain well would be hanged—surely a classic example of the anti-social superstition.

The wind-swept cliffs and desolate heaths of Cornwall stirred his imagination; the sea, which he loved, was never far away:

> Far out on the ocean the waters flash into a streak of fire; the sails of ships passing there, glitter bright; yet a moment more, and the sunlight in triumphant brilliancy bursts out over the whole view. The sea changes soon from dull grey to bright blue, embroidered thickly with golden specks, as it rolls and rushes and dances in the wind.

Cornwall was to furnish the setting for many a chapter to come. Wilkie's account of the holiday is as unpretentious as its title, *Rambles Beyond Railways; or Notes in Cornwall taken A-foot*. It appeared early in 1851 with Brandling's illustrations, Bentley again being the publisher. In its small way the *Rambles* proved most successful, and ran into several editions. Shortly after publication, Wilkie wrote to George Bentley, with whom he was on cordial terms, seeking advice as to how best to deal with a certain menace named Britton :

This is the third occasion on which the Venerable B. has lain in ambush for my books and bounced out upon me with a letter of broad hints. On the first occasion, I gave him a copy of the *Life of Collins* and received in return a treatise on *Junius*. I couldn't read it, but suppose I ought to consider myself a gainer by my swop . . . On the second occasion I determined to protect *your* rights of property and evade paying tribute with *Antonina* by writing a polite, grateful and complimentary letter. This answered my purpose for *Antonina*, but, as you will see by the enclosed letter, has not protected *Rambles Beyond Railways*. What am I to do? Am I to return a *gift* of illustrations by a *loan* of *Rambles*? Or am I, now and henceforth, to consider the Venerable B. as a sort of second British Museum, regularly entitled to a copy of every book I write? If you decide to send the book, I will toss up with you for the proprietorship of the promised illustrations.†

Soon after his return from Cornwall, Wilkie Collins sat to Millais, then about 21 years of age, for the attractive little portrait which hangs in the National Portrait Gallery. It is one of the very few likenesses which show him as clean-shaven, exhibiting features which, a few years later, were to be swallowed up for ever in a jungle of beard. The eyes peer through gold-rimmed spectacles—he was so near-sighted that he could hardly see without them; the bulbous forehead adds a hint of intellectuality to a face which is pale and sensitive. The sitter's elbows rest on the arms of his chair; his small hands touch only at the tips of heavily-ringed fingers. It is a characteristically precise pose suggesting a mood of studious reflection.

† Quoted in 'The Camel's Back, Michael Sadleir. *Nineteenth Century Essays.* (*Oxford University Press*, 1948.)

4

The Dickens Circle

IN view of the many friends and acquaintances they possessed
in common, it is remarkable that Wilkie Collins and Dickens
did not meet before 1851. Wilkie's friend, Augustus Egg, who
assisted not only at the Blandford Square theatricals but also at
the grander entertainments organised by Charles Dickens at his
house in Devonshire Terrace, received the following letter from
Dickens, written on 8th March, 1851:

My dear Egg,—I think *you* told *me* that Mr. Wilkie Collins would
be glad to play any part in Bulwer's comedy; and I think *I* told
you that I considered him a very desirable recruit. There is a
Valet, called (as I remember) Smart—a small part, but, what there
is of it, decidedly good; he opens the play—which I should be
delighted to assign to him, and in which he would have an
opportunity of dressing your humble servant, frothing some
chocolate with an obsolete milling-machine that must be revived
for the purpose, arranging the room, and dispatching other similar 'business,' dear to actors. Will you undertake to ask him if
I shall cast him in this part? If yes, I will call him to the reading
on Wednesday; have the pleasure of leaving my card for him
(say where) and beg him to favour us with his company at
dinner on Wednesday evening. I knew his father well, and should
be very glad to know him.

Wilkie lost no time in accepting the invitation and the two
writers met a few days later at Ivy Cottage, Egg's house in Bayswater. Thus began a friendship which was only to end with Dickens'
death nearly twenty years later.

Dickens was in his fortieth year; *David Copperfield* had been
recently published and for two years the novelist had been editing
his own periodical *Household Words*. His industry was tremendous.

Besides writing his novels, engaging in amateur theatricals on the grand scale, editing and contributing to his magazine, communicating with a host of friends in a flood of brilliant letters, bringing up a large family and undertaking periodical Reading Tours in the provinces, he still contrived to live a crowded social life and even to find, on those seemingly rare occasions when his energies flagged, some quiet relaxation such as a country walk.

Dickens was a many-sided personality, and each of his biographers from Forster down to the present day, has, from much the same raw material, fashioned a different figure. In one respect, however, there is substantial agreement. Most of the biographers express surprise that their subject should have become intimate with one whom they regard as so unworthy of his friendship, so obviously his intellectual inferior as Wilkie Collins. Collins is usually dismissed as a mere second-rater, a seeker after pleasure, possessed of none of Dickens' warmth of character or broad humanity.

Dickens, like other great men with a genius for friendship, was surrounded by a crowd of admirers, each of whom strove towards a greater intimacy than the next and among whom, partly for that reason, disharmony was not rare. Two contemporaries who wrote extensively about their idol after his death were Percy Fitzgerald and, of course, Forster. Neither was at any pains to disguise his hostility towards Wilkie Collins, the one by calculated omission, the other by direct statement. The less important of the two, Fitzgerald, was a prolific novelist and journalist of the mid-Victorian era, most of whose work has been long forgotten. He sought to establish, in his last book,† a claim to have been Dickens' closest friend, the one in whose company alone the Great Man relaxed and spoke his inmost thoughts. Hardly a shred of evidence is adduced in support of this fantasy, which does not bear investigation. Fitzgerald only knew Dickens for the last seven years of his life and nowhere is there any suggestion from a third party that he stood in any different relationship to him from the other 'Dickens' young men' who contributed to All the Year Round.

Fitzgerald's efforts to foist his claim upon the public, at a time when nearly all Dickens' contemporaries were safely buried,

† Memoirs of Charles Dickens, Percy Fitzgerald (Arrowsmith, 1914).

involved him in a systematic belittling of those close to Dickens during his later years, and in particular of Wilkie Collins. 'I always think,' Fitzgerald wrote, 'that Dickens' noble, unselfish, generous nature expended itself rather vainly on such a character, certainly not endowed with anything likely to respond to such affection.' Then follows the surprising admission: 'Not that I knew him sufficiently to judge him, but he had not the warm and rather romantic tone of feeling that "Boz" looked for.'

Forster's case was different. He had, of course, been Dickens' closest friend for fifteen years when Wilkie Collins came upon the scene. He had acquired that distinction by virtue of his intelligence and acumen, his forthrightness and his sincere admiration of one who frankly liked to be admired; he had managed to retain his position despite his proprietary attitude towards Dickens and his rather childish jealousy which was the occasion of many an embarrassing scene. Dickens frequently sought Forster's advice in literary as well as business matters, and through his assistance was much relieved of the irksome details of the writer's profession. Dickens trusted his judgment, and valued his friendship highly. At the same time, there were aspects of Forster's character that Dickens found, as he grew more restless in middle age, harder to tolerate. He lacked both humour and tact; he was inclined to be dogmatic and to stand upon his dignity to the point of pomposity. His Scottish dourness became more and more of a damper on Dickens' periodic exuberance of spirits.

At this period of Dickens' life, he was under considerable mental strain. Apart from the bewildering variety of his activities, his domestic affairs were not running smoothly. Although appearances were still maintained, he and Catherine were gradually drifting apart. In such circumstances Dickens needed someone in whose company he could forget his eminence, his domestic worries, even his public, and who would yet lend a sympathetic ear when the mood was upon him to talk of his troubles. Forster's was not the temperament to cope with this new situation.

From the moment he met Wilkie Collins, Dickens seems to have taken him to his heart. Here was a man, clever, amusing, young— Wilkie was then 27—who enjoyed good food and wine, and yet who already displayed in his calling those qualities of industry and application to which he attached such great importance. In short, here was at least a promising recruit to the little band of 'Mr. Dickens' young men,' and perhaps even the kind of companion of whom he stood in need.

Forster's possessive instinct was aroused at the outset. With his notorious lack of tact, he was heard to comment unfavourably upon Dickens' new acquaintance. When, in the face of his disapproval, the acquaintance ripened into lasting friendship, Forster made the grudging admission some years later that 'Collins was a decidedly clever fellow,' which was reported by Dickens forthwith to his sister-in-law, Georgina Hogarth, with unconcealed satisfaction. Notwithstanding the sincere efforts made over many years by Wilkie, whose nature was without a spark of jealousy, the two men never became friends. Forster never forgave him for having appropriated his position. Forster remained Dickens' friend until the end, but he ceased to enjoy the privileged relationship to which he felt entitled. For details of the last two decades of Dickens' life his biographer had to rely more on the testimony of others than on the first-hand knowledge and voluminous personal correspondence which had supplied the material for the earlier years. For this Forster held Collins largely responsible and retaliated, in his biography of Dickens, with a display of pettiness which only mars what is unquestionably a great book. The references to Collins in Forster's *Life* are deliberately reduced to a minimum, and do scant justice to the part he played in the last twenty years of Dickens' life. It is difficult to attribute such omission to any other motive than jealousy.

Later biographers of Dickens seem to have taken their cue from Forster and are content to deplore instead of trying to explain the undoubted influence of Collins on the other novelist. Insofar as this influence extended to Dickens' writing, it may have been detrimental—although this is a matter of opinion, but there is little doubt that in Collins' company he spent some of the happiest periods of his life. A study of the published letters from Dickens to his friend hardly supports the suggestion, made by Dame Una Pope-Hennessy in her *Charles Dickens*, that Collins was merely 'the indispensable companion of his more frivolous hours.'

The performance of Bulwer-Lytton's comedy, *Not So Bad as we Seem*, duly took place on May 16th, 1851, at Devonshire House,

in the presence of the Queen and Prince Consort. The Duke of
Devonshire not only lent his house for the occasion but temporarily
converted the great drawing-room into a theatre and the library
into a green-room. He entertained the company to supper after
the performance and Dickens' earliest surviving letter to Wilkie
concerns the latter's request that a certain friend might be included
in this invitation. Dickens makes rather heavy weather of it but
concludes by giving way: 'I do not like to refuse compliance with
any wish of my faithful and attached valet, whom I greatly esteem.'

This production of Lytton's play was the first public venture of
the Guild of Literature and Art, an organisation sponsored by
Dickens and Bulwer-Lytton for the purpose of providing a fund
for indigent authors and artists in sickness and old age; or, to
quote the playbill, 'To encourage Life Assurance and other Provi-
dent Habits among Authors and Artists; to render such assistance
to both as shall never compromise their independence; and to
found a few Institutions where honourable rest from arduous
labour shall still be associated with the discharge of congenial
duties.' All seats for the Devonshire House production were sold
at £5 apiece, and with further performances at the Hanover Square
Rooms and in the provinces, an initial total of £4,000 was raised
for the Fund.

The provincial tour, which took place during 1852, was highly
successful and reached its climax in the concluding performances
at Liverpool and Manchester where an audience of nearly 3,000
stood up and cheered. Besides Dickens, the company included
Mark Lemon, famous editor of *Punch*, Douglas Jerrold, Tenniel
and Augustus Egg. Early in the tour Jerold deserted them without
warning, and Wilkie Collins took over his roles for the remaining
performances. In a letter to Bulwer-Lytton, Dickens said that Wilkie
'fell upon his new part with great alacrity and heartiness,' and
wrote to his wife, 'Collins was *admirable*—got up excellently,
played thoroughly well, and missed nothing.' Wilkie assured his
mother that he was not in the least nervous before these large
audiences.

In addition to Lytton's comedy the Guild company produced on
tour Charles Mathews' *Used Up* and a farce by Dickens and Mark
Lemon entitled *Mr. Nightingale's Diary* in which Wilkie Collins
played Lithers, landlord of the 'Water Lily.' In some quarters the

programmes were regarded as too frivolous. Writing from the Royal Hotel, Derby, Wilkie told his mother: 'Here the parsons have been preaching against us. One reverend gentleman, we hear, solemnly adjured his flock, all through last Sunday evening's sermon, not to compromise their salvation by entering our Theatre. Considering that we do not act on Sunday evening, and that congregations are to let on weekdays, these parsonic prohibitions seem slightly unreasonable.'

Forster's account of the provincial tour contains the one generous reference to Collins in the whole of the *Life*: 'Mr. Wilkie Collins became for all the rest of the life of Dickens one of his dearest and most valued friends.' Shortly after the conclusion of the tour we find Wilkie and Egg staying with Dickens at 10, Camden Crescent, Dover, 'within a minute's walk of baths and bathing-machines.' In letters home Wilkie described the pleasant life they led. Breakfast was at 10 minutes past 8 sharp, after which Dickens would disappear into his study until 2 o'clock, when he would be 'available for every pleasant social purpose that can be imagined for the rest of the day,' such as a long country walk, or a swim in the sea. Dinner was at half-past five, often followed by card games played for modest stakes, and bedtime between ten and eleven. One evening Dickens read the opening chapters of *Bleak House*, 'making his audience laugh and cry with equal fervour and equal sincerity.' When Wilkie suffered an acute attack of earache and faceache he was cosseted by Mrs. Dickens, and cured in no time. Invited to stay an extra week, he accepted with alacrity.

Wilkie was now living with his mother and brother at 17, Hanover Terrace, a pleasant Regency house facing the Park, the family having moved from the less elegant neighbourhood of Blandford Square in August, 1850. Mrs. Collins entertained a good deal at Hanover Terrace and her small dinner-parties acquired quite a reputation among her son's friends. She was in many ways a remarkable woman. Millais found her a charming hostess and would make an elaborate pretence of being in love with her, a game in which Mrs. Collins, who possessed a keen sense of humour, joined with spirit. Holman Hunt recalls, in his autobiography, her telling him that many years earlier Coleridge had singled her out at an evening party and had discoursed to her for nearly half an hour 'in the highest strains of poetical philosophy.' She had not understood one word and only remembered a stream of eloquence pouring from the lips of a man who had fixed her with large and brilliant blue eyes.

She held decided views on domesticity and considered that Mrs. E. M. Ward should have abandoned Art when she married, telling her that if she devoted her energies to the home, to tending and cooking for her husband and to making the children's clothes, there would be no time left for painting. She had her eccentricities; according to Mrs. Ward's son Leslie, who later became 'Spy' the cartoonist, 'she wore her kid boots carefully down on one side and then reversed them and wore them down on the other.' He also records her horror of Highlanders, whose kilts she regarded as scandalous. Dickens' daughter Kate, who became Mrs. Collins' daughter-in-law, summed her up as 'a woman of great wit and humour—but a Devil!' If she appeared thus to those outside her immediate family, she was an affectionate and indulgent mother, and both sons were very attached to her.

Holman Hunt was a frequent guest at 17, Hanover Terrace. He describes Wilkie at this time as 'slight of build, about five feet six inches in height, with an impressive head, the cranium being noticeably more prominent on the right side than the left, which inequality did not amount to a disfigurement; perhaps indeed it gave a stronger impression of intellectual power.' He adds that Wilkie was 'redundant in pleasant temperament.'

A year or so earlier, towards the end of 1849, Millais, Holman Hunt and the Rossettis had founded the Pre-Raphaelite Brotherhood. Despite the propaganda put out by *The Germ*, the official voice of the Movement, the public was confused as to the aims and methods of the Pre-Raphaelites. Wilkie Collins, although not a member of the Brotherhood, was one of its earliest supporters and was once pressed to write an article, designed for the widest circulation, explaining the Movement and trying to correct the public's misapprehensions. The Collins' house in Hanover Terrace was a favourite venue of the P-R.B.s, who were accustomed to call at tea-time and consume vast quantities of bread and butter washed down with beer or sherry-cobbler.

Wilkie's brother, Charles, though not a 'founder-member,' soon became an enthusiastic adherent of the Pre-Raphaelites. Unfortunately their self-imposed style did not entirely suit his talent, a fact which probably contributed to his abandonment of painting in favour of literature some years later. Charles Collins was a highly-strung man, much given to sudden enthusiasms and extreme attitudes. Shortly after joining the Pre-Raphaelite Brotherhood he adopted a most severe form of religious conduct. He began to observe Church fasts and other ordinances with a rigid self-discipline. Wilkie, always the more worldly of the two, became concerned less for his brother's spiritual well-being than for his physical health, which had never been robust and was unlikely to benefit from such abstinence. He wisely persuaded Hunt and his friends not to worry Charles by commenting on his eccentricities, as Millais persisted in doing, but rather to leave him alone to his religious devices, until he tired of them. Within a few months, to his brother's relief, Charles became once again his normal self.

Wilkie Collins' entry into the Dickens' circle brought him many new friends. Among them was W. H. Wills, Dickens' sub-editor—or assistant-editor as he would be called today—on the staff of *Household Words*, who was married to a daughter of Robert Chambers, the Edinburgh publisher. Another daughter, Nina Chambers, whom Wilkie had met at the Will's house, married shortly afterwards Frederick Lehmann, a Leith merchant and the son of a German portrait painter. His friendship with the Lehmanns was an enduring one and later extended to their three children. In the early years of this century, R. C. Lehmann, Frederick's son, wrote: 'Wilkie Collins was the kindest and best friend that boy or man ever had. To us he was not merely the grown-up and respected friend of our parents, but our own true companion and close associate.'†

The influence of Dickens on Wilkie Collins' writing soon showed itself. Prompted no doubt by the enormous sales of Dickens' Christmas Books, perhaps encouraged by 'Boz' himself, Wilkie produced in January, 1852, a Christmas story of his own. *Mr. Wray's Cash Box* is a trivial little sketch, remarkable only for its successful imitation of the Dickens' model.

Wilkie's first contribution to *Household Words*, a story in the Grand Guignol manner called 'A Terribly Strange Bed,' appeared

† *Memories of Half a Century*. R. C. Lehmann. (*Smith, Elder, 1908.*)

on April 24th, 1852. This sensational tale of a four-poster-bed designed to smother its occupant, has appeared in several anthologies of the macabre, and is said to have been based on fact. It points the way in which, after one or two false starts, Wilkie Collins' talents were to develop most effectively.

For some months he had been at work on a long novel which was to unfold a melodramatic story against a background of everyday middle-class life. It marked a departure from the conventional mid-Victorian novel in which high society provided the only possible setting for the passions and pangs of love. So much we learn from the Preface to *Basil*, as the novel was ultimately named:

> Directing my characters and my story towards the light of Reality wherever I could find it, I have not hesitated to violate some of the conventionalities of sentimental fiction . . . In certain parts of this book where I have attempted to excite the suspense or pity of the reader, I have admitted as perfectly fit accessories to the scene the most ordinary street-sounds that could be heard, and the most ordinary street-events that could occur, believing that by adding to the truth, they were adding to tragedy.

Few Wilkie Collins novels are without a Preface. Rejecting Dickens' argument that a work of fiction should be left to tell its own story, he remained addicted to preface-writing to the end. However deplorable they may be on artistic grounds, these Prefaces are of interest in revealing something of the writer. They underline his intentions, even where these are perfectly clear from the pages that follow; they tell us a little of his working methods; they are sometimes addressed to his critics, not always in terms calculated to evoke a favourable review; from time to time they attack the prudes, or the snobs; but above all they seek to establish a closer relationship between author and reader. The reader is often warned, sometimes encouraged, occasionally flattered, but all the time Wilkie is assuring him of the author's friendly interest in him, an interest which he modestly hopes will be reciprocated.

Although we cannot be certain, it is probable that Wilkie had recently undergone a violent emotional experience and wrote *Basil* as a form of catharsis. Indeed he goes so far as to state: 'I have founded the main event out of which this story springs, on a fact within my own knowledge. In afterwards shaping the course of the narrative thus suggested, I have guided it where I knew by my own experience or by experience related to me by others, that it would touch on something real and true in its progress.' The course of the narrative suggests that the experience was not a happy one for Wilkie, though it may well have been valuable to him as a novelist.

Basil is the story of a young man's infatuation with a worthless girl of inferior social position, his strange form of marriage to her, and her seduction by another man before the marriage is consummated; the latter part of the novel deals with the seducer's hunting down of Basil, who has disfigured him for life. Basil himself is a colourless figure, vacillating and foolish. Although he bears some superficial resemblance to the author—he is for instance engaged upon an historical novel—Wilkie does not seem to have put much of himself into the character. More interesting are the two fathers, the one inordinately proud of his ancient family, the other a successful linen-draper, mean and hypocritical, by far the greater snob. The gulf that separates their two classes is an essential part of the plot, and the author's acceptance of current social conventions land him into situations which today approach the ludicrous. Basil's father—who in some respects calls to mind William Collins—has just learned of his son's marriage in a trades-man's family:

'I did not come prepared to hear that unutterable disgrace had been cast on me and mine, by my own child. I have no words or rebuke or of condemnation for this: the reproach and the punishment have fallen already where the guilt was—and not there only. My son's infamy defiles his brother's birthright, and puts his father to shame. Even his sister's name—' He stopped, shuddering. When he proceeded his voice faltered and his head drooped low. 'I say it again. You are below all reproach and all condemnation.'

The most successful character is the seducer, Mannion. As the *déclassé* confidential clerk who carries out his duties to perfection, he is admirably drawn, and it is only when the mask is lifted that one recognises some features of the stock villain of melodrama. Even so Wilkie is careful to furnish him with a credible excuse for

E

his villainy and to obtain for him a measure of the reader's sympathy.

The scene in which Basil virtually witnesses in an adjoining room, Mannion's seduction of his wife is described with uncommon realism: 'I listened; and through the thin partition, I heard voices—*her* voice and *his* voice. *I heard and I knew*—knew my degradation in all its infamy, knew my wrongs in all their nameless horror.' The reviewer of *Antonina* who had written: 'We must warn Mr. Collins against the vices of the French school—against the needless accumulation of revolting details—against catering for a prurient taste,' doubtless felt that his advice had been deliberately rejected. Perhaps he might have been included among 'those persons who deny that it is the novelist's vocation to do more than merely amuse them; who shrink from all honest and serious reference, in books, to subjects which they think of in private and talk of in public everywhere; who see covert implications where nothing is implied, and improper allusions where nothing improper is alluded to; whose innocence is in the word, and not in the thought; whose morality stops at the tongue, and never gets on to the heart.' To them, concludes Collins in his Preface, 'I do not address myself in this book, and shall never think of addressing myself to them in any other.'

Basil: A Story of Modern Life was published by Bentley in three volumes in November, 1852. The work met with a mixed reception, and not surprisingly, was attacked in some quarters as being immoral. The reviewer of *The Athenaeum* took the opportunity to pontificate: 'Mr Collins should know that the proper office of Art is to elevate and purify in pleasing.' After charging the author with adopting the 'æsthetics of the Old Bailey,' he sums up: '*Basil* is a tale of criminality, almost revolting from its domestic horror. The vicious atmosphere . . . weighs on us like a nightmare.' Wilkie's somewhat naïve attempt in his Preface to disarm criticism of this type, failed completely. On the other hand, there was much praise for the telling of the story, and it was generally agreed that the author had succeeded in what he had, so misguidedly, set out to do.

In many respects *Basil* marks a great advance, particularly in the creation of atmosphere and the description of scene. The drawing-room at North Villa affects the reader as it affected Basil, waiting for an interview with his future father-in-law:

> Never was a richly furnished room more thoroughly comfortless than this—the eye ached at looking around it. There was no repose anywhere, The print of the Queen, hanging lonely on the wall, in its heavy gilt frame, with a large crown at the top, glared at you: the books, the wax flowers in glass-cases, the chairs in flaring chintz-covers, the china plates on the door, the blue and pink glass vases and cups ranged on the chimney-piece, the over-ornamented chiffoniers with Tonbridge toys and long-necked smelling bottles on their upper shelves—all glared on you. There was no look of shadow, shelter, secrecy, or retirement in any one nook or corner of those four gaudy walls. All surrounding objects seemed startlingly near to the eye; much nearer than they really were. The room would have given a nervous man a headache, before he had been in it a quarter of an hour.

A copy of *Basil* had, of course, been sent to Dickens, probably with some misgivings on the part of the author, since Dickens took, on the whole, a narrow view of the bounds of literary propriety. A week or two elapsed before Wilkie received the following letter:

Tavistock House,
Monday, 20th December, 1852.

My dear Collins,—If I did not know that you are likely to have a forebearing remembrance of my occupation, I should be full of remorse for not having sooner thanked you for Basil.
Not to play the sage or the critic (neither of which parts, I hope, is at all in my line), but to say what is the friendly truth, I may assure you that I have read the book with very great interest, and with a very thorough conviction that you have a call to this same art of fiction. I think the probabilities here and there require a little more respect than you are disposed to show them, and I have no doubt that the prefatory letter would have been better away, on the ground that a book (of all things) should speak for and explain itself. But the story contains admirable writing, and many clear evidences of a very delicate discrimination of character. It is delightful to find throughout that you have taken great pains with it besides, and have 'gone at it' with a perfect knowledge of the jolter-headedness of the

conceited idiots who suppose that volumes are to be tossed off
like pancakes, and that any writing can be done without the
utmost application, the greatest patience, and the steadiest
energy of which the writer is capable.

For all these reasons I have made Basil's acquaintance with great
gratification, and entertain a high respect for him. I hope that I
shall become intimate with many worthy descendants of his,
who are yet in the limbo of creatures waiting to be born.

Wilkie could hardly have hoped for more generous encouragement from one whom he regarded as the greatest literary figure
of his time.

5

Grand Tour

I is unfortunate that hardly a single letter from Wilkie to
Dickens survives. In September, 1860 Dickens, incensed by what
he considered 'the misuse of the private letters of public men,'
burned in the field at Gad's Hill every letter he possessed which
did not deal exclusively with business, and was determined to
destroy all such letters in the future as soon as they were answered.
Although he is reported as exclaiming, 'Would to God every letter
I have ever written was on that pile!' it is an ironical reflection
that, while so much biographical detail concerning others went
up in smoke on that September afternoon at Gad's Hill, more than
six thousand of his own letters have since been published. Those
written to Wilkie Collins, interesting as they are, afforded only
an occasional reflection of Wilkie's personality, seen as it were in
a mirror.

Collins' next contribution to *Household Words* was a story of the
Breton fishing community called 'Gabriel's Marriage' which appeared
on April 16th and 23rd, 1853. Some weeks earlier Dickens had
turned down a better story, 'Mad Monkton'—later published in the
collection entitled *The Queen of Hearts*—for the reason that it
dealt with hereditary insanity, a subject which might occasion
distress 'among those numerous families in which there is such a
taint.' Writing to Wills, Dickens is at pains to emphasise that his
objection lies only in Wilkie's choice of subject, and continues: 'I
think there are many things, both in the inventive and descriptive
way, that he could do for us if he would like to work in our direction. And I particularly wish him to understand this, and to have
every possible assurance conveyed to him that I think so, and that
I should particularly like to have his aid.' The rejected short-story

was shelved by Wilkie for a year or so, eventually appearing in *Fraser's Magazine* for November and December, 1855.†

For some months Dickens had been discussing with Wilkie and Augustus Egg the possibility of a tour of Italy. The original plan would have entailed an absence of three months or more, but Dickens came to the conclusion that the editorial chair of *Household Words* could not remain empty for so long. In a letter to Wilkie dated January, 1853, which incidentally offers 'a bellyful of Gin Punch on Sunday next at 5 at the "Family Arms," Tavistock,' Dickens writes: 'I have been thinking of the Italian project, and reducing the time to two months—from the 20th October to the 20th December—see the way to a trip that shall really not exclude any foremost place, and be reasonable, too. Details when we meet.'

For the summer of 1853, Dickens had taken the Château des Moulineaux, on the outskirts of Boulogne, for himself and his family—and of course, for his friends. In June, Wilkie was summoned for a long visit.

> We are established in a doll's country house of many rooms in a delightful garden. If you have anything to do, this is the place to do it in. And if you have nothing to do, this is also the place to do it in to perfection. You shall have a Pavilion room in the garden, with a delicious view, where you may write no end of Basils. You shall get up your Italian as I raise the fallen fortunes of mine. You shall live, with a delicate English graft upon the best French manner, and learn to get up early in the morning again. In short, you shall be thoroughly prepared, during the whole summer season, for those great travels which are due to come off anon.

Unfortunately Wilkie, who, far from having nothing to do, was working seven days a week on a new novel, fell ill and was unable to make the journey for some weeks. As soon as his health began to improve Dickens again insisted on his coming to Boulogne to recuperate and guaranteed 'the pure air, regular hours and perfect repose' of the Château des Moulineaux to do as much for Wilkie as they had for his own complaint. 'And what was the matter with me? Sir—I found this reads like Dr. Johnson directly—Sir, it was

† It was included by Dorothy L. Sayers in the First Series of *Great Short Stories of Mystery, Detection and Horror*.

an old afflicted KIDNEY, once the torment of my childhood, in which I took cold.'

Not until the end of July was Wilkie well enough to travel to Boulogne. Besides such entertainments as town fêtes and country fêtes, picnics (often in the rain) and excursions to Amiens or Beauvais, there was, for Wilkie, the opportunity for work in the most delightful surroundings. Dickens was a superb host, though he was apt to be tyrannical in the matter of punctuality. He made it a rigid rule of the Château des Moulineaux that breakfast was served at nine o'clock and that those who were not down in time went without. It is recorded that Wilkie, never an enthusiast for early rising, was discovered more than once at the Casino around eleven o'clock breakfasting in solitary state on *pâté de foie gras*.

From time to time Dickens would make a flying visit to London to attend to the affairs of *Household Words*, Wilkie accompanying him early in September in order to discuss with Bentley the publication of his next novel. On the return journey the crossing was very rough and Wilkie described the ladies with their white basins as resembling 'an immense picnic-party with everybody intent upon a pigeon pie of her own.' Guests came and went, and towards the end of the holiday there was an enormous dinner ('the best that Boulogne could supply') to celebrate the completion of *Bleak House*. For this event they were joined by Forster and Mark Lemon, and the publishers and illustrator of the book. The bill of fare Wilkie carefully preserved as 'a memorable document.'

The final plans for the Italian tour were made in London and on October 10th, after a week-end at Boulogne, Dickens, Egg and Wilkie set off for Paris accompanied by Edward, Dickens' newly-acquired personal servant. We have, from Wilkie's letters home and from Dickens' letters, mostly to his wife, a fairly detailed account of the tour. Dickens projects himself as the 'father' of the party, the experienced foreign traveller, tolerantly leading two enthusiastic but occasionally embarrassing tourists. He is, however, at some pains to stress, after a description of some irritating incident or other, that they remained on excellent terms throughout.

After a day or so in Paris, 'very full and extraordinarily gay,' they travelled by rail to Strasbourg and Basle. Already Dickens inclined to the belief that Wilkie was the better traveller of the two: 'He takes things easily and is not put out by small matters —two capital requisites.' From Basle they posted to Lausanne where they arrived on the evening of the 15th. By this time Egg was engaged in a desperate struggle with the Italian language and found it impossible to remember what he learned. As for the other member of the party, 'Collins eats and drinks everything. Gets on very well everywhere, and is always in good spirits.' In Lausanne they hired an excellent carriage, four horses and a postilion, made an excursion to Chillon, and set off the following morning for Chamonix, 'with a Strasbourg sausage, a bottle of wine, brandy, kirsch-wasser and plenty of bread to keep off hunger on the road.' It was a tiring journey over appalling roads, but nobody seemed to mind. 'We travel in a state of mad good spirits,' Wilkie told his mother, 'and never flag in our jollity all through the day. I am Keeper of the Privy Purse, for roadside expenses of an irregular nature, and am in this capacity the purveyor of all the picnic eatables and drinkables consumed on the way between breakfast and dinner. Egg is constantly exercised in Italian dialogue by Dickens. The courier turns out to be a perfect treasure.' The night's rest at Chamonix revived them sufficiently to make an ascent the next morning of the Mer de Glâce, where the holiday nearly ended in disaster. Dickens' account of the incident is quoted in Forster's *Life*:

> We were a train of four mules and two guides, going along an immense height like a chimney-piece, with sheer precipice below, when there came rolling from above, with fearful velocity, a block of stone about the size of one of the fountains in Trafalgar Square, which Egg, the last of the party, had preceded by not a yard, when it swept over the ledge, breaking away a tree, and rolled and rumbled down into the valley. It had been loosened by the heavy rains, or by some woodcutters afterwards reported to be above.

Wilkie, understandably, omits all reference to this adventure in writing to his mother.

At Chamonix the junior travellers begin to show their inexperience. 'Egg sometimes wants trifles of accommodation which could hardly be got in Paris, and Collins sometimes wants to give people too little for their trouble.' But a word from the seasoned tourist 'puts it all right in a moment.'

It was Dickens himself who ordered three hot baths and provoked the scene described in a letter to his wife.

Women ran backwards and forwards across the bridge, men bore in great quantities of wood, a horrible furnace was lighted, and a smoke was raised which filled the whole valley. This began at half-past three, and we congratulated each other on the distinction we should probably acquire by being the cause of the conflagation of the whole village. We sat by the fire until half-past five (dinner time) and still no baths. Ever since, the smoke has poured forth in enormous volume, and the furnace has blazed, and the women have gone and come over the bridge, and piles of wood have been carried in, but we observe a general avoidance of us by the establishment which still looks like failure.

For this failure, dinner, consisting of soup, beefsteak admirably cooked, boiled fowl and rice, roast leg of chamois, roast leg of mutton, and a pudding served in a blaze of rum, must have afforded some compensation.

After dinner, 'Collins (with his short legs stretched out as far as they will go) is reading, and Egg writing in a marvellous diary . . . concerning the materials of which he remembers nothing, but is perpetually asking Collins as I write, about the names of the places where we have been, signs of hotels we have put up at, and so forth—which Collins with his face all awry, blowing old snuff down one nostril and taking new snuff up the other, delivers oracularly.'

Travelling twelve to fifteen hours a day over the Swiss mountain roads, they continued their journey in the direction of Milan. Wilkie, dazzled as he was by the majesty of the landscape, was still able to observe the large number of cretins in the Swiss villages, and the prevalence of goitre among the peasants. These maladies he attributed to 'exhalations from the marshy ground' around the valley streams which, shut in by the unbroken chains of mountain, poisoned the air of the villages. Crossing the Italian frontier by Lake Maggiore, they took the ferry across the river at the foot of the lake. On board was an old blind fiddler who sang Italian folk-songs to the passengers in a harsh but strangely moving voice. Describing the scene in a letter, Wilkie wrote: 'I don't know whether it was the music, which reminded me of old times in Italy, or the scenery, or the gliding motion of the boat over the clear water and through the lovely river-landscape, or the state of incessant excitement that I had been in for the last three or four days, that affected me—or whether it was all these things together —but I never felt nearer astonishing everybody by bursting out crying!'

They covered the final stage of the journey to Milan in a fusty carriage dating, according to Wilkie, from the period of Louis XIV. The innkeeper warned them of robber-bands on the route, who would certainly steal their luggage from the roof unless they took special precautions. These measures consisted of tying to each trunk a string, the end of which was led into the carriage through the window and held firmly by the owner travelling within. 'It was,' wrote Wilkie to Charles Ward, 'like sitting in a shower bath and waiting to pull the string—or rather, like fishing in the sea, when one waits to feel a bite, by a tug at the line round one's finger. You would have imagined we were taking all the treasures of Golconda to Milan.' By this time they had travelled in a weird variety of vehicles—'like swings, like boats, like Noah's Arks, like barges and enormous bedsteads.'

They arrived at Milan on the night of October 24th tired, dusty and a trifle out of humour. A performance of the latest Verdi opera at La Scala Wilkie found 'utterly miserable and incapable.' In his tour of the art galleries his enthusiasm was reserved for Raphael's 'Betrothal of the Virgin'; da Vinci's 'Last Supper' he described as 'the utter ruin of something which was once a picture,' so disastrously had the restorers—or 'picture-patchers'—done their work. To complete his disenchantment his favourite snuff-box was stolen by a pickpocket. From Dickens comes a hint of irritation in a letter to Georgina Hogarth: 'I have long entertained that other men in general (and Collins in particular) spit and snort rather more than I have ever found it necessary to do, particularly in the early part of the day.'

From Milan, they made a wearily slow journey by carriage to Genoa, where they embarked on the P. & O. steamship *Valetta* for Naples. The voyage, short as it was, proved something of a nightmare. The steamer was already more than filled with passengers from Marseilles and all was in confusion. They found that there were no berths or accommodation of any kind available despite the heavy first-class fares they had paid; even their meals had to be taken on deck. At Leghorn there was some delay and the ship had to lie off all night. Dickens describes the scene on board: 'Ladies and gentlemen lying indiscriminately on the open deck, arranged like spoons on a sideboard. No mattresses, no blankets, nothing . . . We three lay together on the bare planks covered with our coats. We were gradually dozing off, when a perfectly tropical rain fell, and in a moment drowned the whole ship. The rest of the night we passed upon the stairs, with an immense jumble of men and women. When anybody came up for any purpose we all fell down, and when anybody came down we all fell up again.' The next morning Dickens managed to get a state-room for himself and used his influence with the Captain to have the store room opened up for Collins and Egg; here they slept amid cheeses, fruit, spices and moist sugar with the steward, a cat and a stowaway for company.

The voyage lasted four days; on arrival at Naples they took rooms in the Hotel des Etrangers, facing the sea. During their week's stay, the three tourists explored Pompeii, ascended Vesuvius —and, incidentally, suffered agonies from fleas and mosquitoes. Wilkie paid some social calls, renewing acquaintances of his former visit. He described, in a letter to his brother Charley, his call upon Iggulden, the Naples banker and an old friend of the family:

He was extremely depressed and gloomy, and surrounded by wretched pictures, on which he had been lending money, I suspect. He grievously desired to know whether I was still going on 'writing books,' and whether I ever meant to 'practise my profession.' He asked after you and my mother with great interest, and then introduced me to a tall young gentleman with a ghastly face, immense whiskers, and an expression of the profoundest melancholy, who was casting account and reckoning up dollars in the outer office. Do you remember little Lorenzo, who was the lively young 'Pickle' of the family in our time? Well! this was Lorenzo!!! He asked me whether I had not broken my arm when I was last in Naples. I told him *you* had. He rejoined gloomily: 'Galway dead'—and then waited for me to say something. I said, 'God bless me! Is he indeed?'—And so we parted. I must not forget to say that Charles Iggulden— the pattern *goodboy* who used to be quoted as an example to me—has married a pretty girl *without* his parents' consent—is out of the banking business in consequence—and has gone to Australia to make his fortune as well as he can. I was rather glad to hear this as I don't like 'well-conducted' young men! I know it is wrong, but I always feel relieved and happy when I hear that they have got into a scrape.

They had intended to visit Sicily but, being already behind schedule, went direct to Rome, where they stayed at an excellent hotel overlooking the Piazza del Popolo; a large dining-room, a handsome front drawing-room and three front bedrooms cost them four shillings a day each. Both Naples and Rome were, of course, familiar to Wilkie, their sights and sounds evoking memories of the happy months he had spent there as a boy. Coming back was like reliving a dream. Rome, in particular, had provided his young imagination with the germ of those ideas which, years later, had matured to produce his first novel. 'Nothing has astonished me,' he wrote to Charley, 'more than my own vivid remembrance of every street and building in this wonderful and mournful place . . . Not the least changeless object in Rome was our old house in the Via Felice. The Virgin is still in her niche—the cabbage stalks and rubbish are strewn about underneath—the very door looks as if it had never been painted since we left it.' In the old surroundings Wilkie began to boast mildly, as travellers do, about his earlier visit. It is hardly likely that he expected to be taken literally, and one may consider Dickens' comments, in a letter to Catherine, unduly tart:

> But the best of it is, that he tells us about the enormous quantities of Monte Pulciano and what not, that he used to drink when he was last there, and what distinguished people said to him in the way of taking his opinion, and what advice he gave them—being then exactly thirteen years of age.

He adds, however,

> All these absurdities are innocent enough. I tell them in default of having anything else to tell. We are all the best of friends and have never the least difference.

It was now the middle of November and there were several Italian cities on Dickens' list still to be visited. Leaving Rome for Florence, they spent the first night at Bolsena, on the shore of a dismal lake, in malaria-ridden country. The inn was wretched and dirty, offering little to eat and nothing but sour country-wine to drink. 'However,' said Dickens, 'we made a great fire, and strengthened the country wine with some brandy (we always carry brandy) and mulled it with cloves (we always carry cloves) and went to bed, and got up before 5 and breakfasted on our own tea (we always carry tea), and came away in the dark.' The next night was spent at Siena and the travellers reached Florence the following evening.

Wilkie had taken the opportunity to start growing a moustache. Once again Dickens is disapproving:

> You remember how the corners of his mouth go down, and how he looks through his spectacles and manages his legs. I don't know how it is, but the moustache is a horrible aggravation of all this. He smooths it down over his mouth ... Likewise he tells Egg he must 'cut it for it gets into his mouth'—and he and Egg compliment each other on that appendage.

The journey to Florence seems to have put Dickens out of humour for, having told his wife that he will not enter a picture-gallery with his companions, nor will he join in their discussions on Art, he continues:

> To hear Collins learnedly holding forth to Egg . . . about reds, and greens, and things 'coming well' with other things, and lines being wrong, and lines being right, is far beyond the bounds of all caricature. I shall never forget it. On music, too, he is very learned, and sometimes almost drives me into frenzy by humming and whistling whole overtures—without one movement correctly remembered from the beginning to the end. I was obliged to ask him, the day before yesterday, to leave off whistling the Overture to *William Tell*. 'For by heaven,' said I, 'there's something the matter with your ear—I think it must be the cotton—which plays the Devil with the commonest tune.' He occasionally expounds a code of morals, taken from modern French novels, which I instantly and with becoming gravity smash.

Fortunately, there is no suggestion that the good-tempered Wilkie took offence at this headmasterly behaviour on the part of his friend.

There was only time to remain one day in Florence, after which the party pressed on to Venice. The travelling arrangements and general organisation appear to have been Dickens' responsibility. 'We observe the Managerial punctuality in all our arrangements,' he remarks in a letter. He also notices 'that the expenses make the Neophytes wink a little, and that the shirts do a good deal of duty.'

In the matter of dress it is clear that Egg and Wilkie were no match for the elegant Dickens. Here is his account of a visit to the opera in Venice:

> It is the usage that when you go to the play the chief of your two gondolieri lights you up to your box with an enormous lantern. Last night . . . this ceremony was observed with great state, through brilliantly lighted passages, where the lantern, big as it was, became a mere twinkle. Imagine the procession—led by Collins with incipient moustache, spectacles, slender legs, and extremely dirty dress gloves—Egg second, in a white hat, and a straggly mean little black beard—Inimitable bringing up the rear, in full dress and big sleeved greatcoat, rather considerably ashamed.

The performance of the opera—Verdi's 'Nabucco'—was good, the ballet capital, and the best box in the house cost them approximately seven-and-sixpence. They wound up the evening at Florian's in the Piazza San Marco drinking punch. In a letter to his mother Wilkie wrote: 'We lead the most luxurious, dandy-dilettante sort of life here. Our gondola (with two rowers in modern footmen's liveries!) waits on us wherever we go. We live among pictures and palaces all day, and among Operas, Ballets and Cafés more than half the night.'

For the two poorer members of the party, funds were beginning to run low and they made one or two pathetic attempts at economy. 'This morning at breakfast,' wrote Dickens,

> 'they settled that there was no need for them to have the Servitore di Piazza today . . . Downstairs we all go. In the hall is the Servitore. To whom Collins—in Italian, expounds that they don't want him. Thereupon he respectfully explains that he was told to come, has lost his day, and has been waiting an hour. Upon that, they are of course obliged to take him; and the only result of the great effort is (as it always is) that it has been a profoundly mean, and utterly fruitless attempt at evasion. We

brought some good tea with us from Genoa, and if you could
have seen them, when it was first going to be used, devising how
a teapot and boiling water were to be got from the hotel for
nothing, you would never have forgotten it. Of course I clinched
the matter very speedily by ordering tea for one (tenpence in
price) which we didn't use. Egg is always reasonable on all such
points if he is spoken to, seriously. But there is a ridiculous contrast sometimes between their determination to have good things
and their tremendous readiness to complain—and their slight
reluctance in paying afterwards.'

By implication, Wilkie was less reasonable when spoken to
seriously, and who can blame him? Obviously there were occasions
when Dickens was not the most sympathetic of travelling companions.

The journey home from Venice lasted only ten days. After a
brief glance at Parma and Verona the travellers reached Turin
whence they took the mail-coach over the Mont Cenis to Lyons.
They went by river-steamer up the Saône to Châlon where they
caught the Paris train and eventually arrived back in London on
December 10th, having been away two months.

The expenses of the trip seem remarkably high, and Wilkie and
Egg may not have found the holiday quite as 'reasonable' as Dickens
had promised. Wilkie received the reckoning within a few days of
their return:

The total expenses (deducting of course all charges incurred for
Edward and Charley) have been in French money 9510 francs.
That is, in English money, £380-8s.-4d.—or, say in round
numbers, £380-10s.-0d.

One-third share of this sum is	£126	16	8
You have actually contributed	90	0	0
Leaving a balance for you to pay of	36	16	8
To which is to be added, money lent	6	15	0
Making a total for you to pay of	£43	11	8

Back in Hanover Terrace, Wilkie got down to work again on
the new novel, which was concerned to some extent with Art and
Artists. This may explain his current preoccupation with the details

and techniques of painting; the 'reds and greens' which had irritated Dickens on the Italian tour. It is plain that these minor skirmishes which figured so often in Dickens' letters home were of no real significance, for the three remained as good friends as ever. Egg, incidentally, had acquired the nickname of 'The Colonel'—sometimes 'Kernel'—and thus he was known to Dickens and Wilkie evermore.

Wilkie, now 30 years old, spent most of July and August, 1854, with the Dickens family at the Villa du Camp de Droite at Boulogne, a house rather larger than the Moulineaux, which they had taken for the summer. In inviting him to the villa, Dickens expressed the hope that he would finish the third volume of his new book there, but the book was already finished and in the printer's hands; not until after it was published in June, 1854, did Wilkie cross the Channel.

Hide and Seek, as the new novel was called, could hardly have appeared at a less propitious moment. The Crimean War had flared up and was absorbing the attention of all England; people were reading newspapers rather than novels. The first printing of *Hide and Seek* just met the public demand and no further copies were printed for several years. Wilkie did, however, receive two tributes from fellow novelists which must have offset the comparative apathy of the public. Macaulay, whom he had not met, wrote a letter full of lavish praise; Dickens, generous as always in his enthusiasm for Wilkie's work, made no reservations this time. Writing to Georgina Hogarth he said: 'I think it far away the cleverest work I have ever seen written by a new hand. It is in some respects masterly . . . In short, I call it a very remarkable book, and have been very much surprised by its great merit.' And in reply to a criticism by Georgina, he concluded: 'Nor do I really recognise much imitation of myself.' The echoes are there, certainly, even if Dickens failed to notice them, but this is the last of Collins' novels to show to any marked extent the Dickens manner. Soon the influence was to be seen working in the opposite direction.

Hide and Seek, or the Mystery of Mary Grice is an altogether more lighthearted affair than the sombre *Basil*, from which it marks an abrupt departure. As a story it carries less conviction. Of the strange bunch of characters one is pleased to have made the acquaintance of Zach Thorpe, an engaging young extrovert in revolt against his puritan upbringing, and of Valentine Blyth who paints potboilers to support his paralysed wife, Lavvie. Less credible is the mysterious Mat, who has been scalped by Indians and wears a skull-cap to conceal the fact. The author's obsession with physical infirmity leads him to make the other leading character, Madonna, a deaf-mute, his object being to illustrate 'the patience and cheerfulness with which the heavier bodily afflictions are borne, for the most part, by those afflicted,' a favourite Wilkie Collins theme. He claimed to be the first novelist to draw such a character but his failure to make her live suggests all too clearly why his predecessors left this particular ground unexplored.

It is a tribute to his narrative skill that one follows with interest, if without excitement, the search for the solution to Madonna's identity; the *dénouement*, however, depends upon an incredible series of coincidences. Contemporary readers of the novel found its ending objectionable for a different reason. By revealing a close blood-relationship between two characters who had, in all ignorance, been in love with each other, the author was held to have committed a grievous offence against moral standards.

Wilkie Collins' powers of evoking atmosphere were developing; here is Baregrove Square on a wet Sunday :

The garden in the middle of the Square—with its close-cut turf, its vacant beds, its brand-new rustic seats, its withered young trees that had not yet grown as high as the railings around them —seemed to be absolutely rotting away in yellow mist and softly-steady rain, and was deserted even by the cats. All blinds were drawn down for the most part over all windows; what light came from the sky came like light seen through dusty glass; the grim brown hue of the brick houses looked more dirtily mournful than ever; the smoke from the chimney-pots was lost mysteriously in deepening superincumbent fog; the muddy gutters gurgled, the heavy raindrops dripped into empty areas audibly.

Here and there he allowed himself a tilt at one of the conventions.

The smug human vultures who prey commercially on the civilised dead, arranged themselves, with black wands, in solemn Undertakers' order of procession on either side of the funeral vehicles. Those clumsy pomps of feathers and velvet, of strutting horses

F

and marching mutes, which are still permitted among us to
desecrate with grotesquely-shocking fiction the solemn fact of
death, fluttered out in their blackest state grandeur and showed
their most woeful state paces, as the procession started mag-
nificently with its meagre offering of one dead body more to the
bare and awful grave.

With *Hide and Seek* off his hands, Wilkie felt entitled to enjoy
two months of 'Elysian laziness' with Dickens at the Villa du Camp
de Droite. The house stood upon a hill overlooking Boulogne; as he
approached Wilkie saw fluttering from its flagstaff the Tricolor and
the Union Jack side by side in honour of the recently-concluded
Alliance between the two countries. All around were French
soldiers, ten thousand of them, waiting to take part in manœuvres
before the Emperor. They were remarkable, he told his mother, for
'good breeding and quiet behaviour,' a marked contrast to the
British Grenadiers. The diversions of Dickens' house-party during
the next week or two took on something of the prevailing military
atmosphere. They attended a Military Mass performed in the open
by a 'meek-looking old curé who came shambling in through all
the magnificent military preparations, with his rusty black cassock
trailing in the dust, and his green umbrella under his arm.' Wilkie
strolled into the market-place to find 'a whole regiment in it, with
a real live *vivandière* serving out drams to the men in the most
operatic manner possible.' The arrival of the Emperor was celebrated by illuminations all over the town, to which Dickens made
a typical contribution. He ordered a candle to be fixed in each of
the 114 window-panes of the villa, and so arranged his household
that at the ringing of a bell every candle was lit in less than a
minute. The evening concluded with a brilliant display of fireworks.

6

Amateur Theatricals

Towards Christmas of 1854, amateur theatricals were in the air again at Tavistock House. This time the entertainment was to be a pantomime, in order that the Dickens children should have an opportunity of acting. The play selected was Planché's *The Fairy Extravaganza of Fortunio and his Seven Gifted Sons*, the only grown-up parts being played by Mark Lemon, Wilkie and Dickens. Wilkie, as Gobbler, had only a dozen words to say but the part offered 'great Pantomime opportunities—which require a first-rate old stager to devour Property Loaves'; his instructions from the producer were to make up 'dreadfully greedy.' He appeared in the playbill as Wilkini Collini.

Dickens was becoming increasingly restless, and in February, 1855, took Wilkie with him for a fortnight's holiday in Paris. The cold was intense on both sides of the Channel, but, wrote Wilkie, 'compared with French frost our national frost seems to be always wrapped up in more or less soft fog. We should have felt this difference unpleasantly enough on the railway from Boulogne to Paris—but for the excellent metal cases of boiling water placed in each carriage, and renewed several times in the course of the journey. These kept our feet and legs warm and made the air like the air of a room.' He was most impressed with the accommodation secured by Dickens at the Hotel Meurice. 'We are settled here in a delightful apartment, looking out on the Tuileries, gorgeously-furnished drawing-room, bedrooms with Turkey carpets, reception-room, hall, cupboards, passages—all to ourselves.' Wilkie was not in the best of health, and Dickens wrote to Georgina: 'Collins continues in a queer state, but is perfectly cheerful under the stoppage of his wine and other afflictions.' They dined in 'all manner of places' and usually visited two or three theatres each day. Wilkie just managed to last out the fortnight but retired to bed immediately on his return to London, where we find him dispensing hot gin-and-water to visitors at his bedside, and turning over in his mind an idea for a play.

Ever since the Blandford Square days the theatre had held a special fascination for him. The time had now come to try his hand as a playwright. Some months earlier he had written to Charles Ward: 'I have plenty of hard work in prospect—some of it, too, work of a new kind, and of much uncertainty as to results. I mean the dramatic experiments which I have been thinking up, and which you must keep a profound secret from everybody in case I fail with them. This will be an anxious winter for me. If I were not constitutionally reckless about my future prospects, I should feel rather nervous just now.' During the intervening period the secret had been well kept, and even Dickens knew nothing of the play until it was finished. He wrote to Wilkie on May 11th:

> I will read the play referring to the lighthouse with great pleasure if you will send it to me—of course I will at any time, with cordial readiness and unaffected interest, do any such thing.

And a week later, to Clarkson Stanfield, the artist:

> I have a little lark in contemplation, if you will help it to fly. Collins has done a melodrama (a regular old-style melodrama), in which there is a very good notion. I am going to act in it, as an experiment, in the Children's Theatre here [Tavistock House]. I, Mark, Collins, Egg, and my daughter Mary, the whole *dram. pers.* . . . Now there is only one scene in the piece, and that, my tarry lad, is the inside of a lighthouse. Will you come and paint it?

Stanfield accepted the commission and also painted an Act-drop depicting the Eddystone Lighthouse, the original sketch for which fetched the remarkable sum of 1,000 guineas at the Gad's Hill sale after Dickens' death.

The Lighthouse called for a more elaborate production than anything previously done at Tavistock House and Dickens lavished every care upon it. No time was lost, however; rehearsals started within a fortnight of his reading the play for the first time, and the opening performance took place on June 16th. The play at least provided some strong melodramatic situations, and a fine acting opportunity for Dickens in the part of Aaron Gurnock, the old lighthouse-keeper who believes himself to be an accessory to murder. Carlyle, who was one of the enthusiastic first-night audience, gave high praise both to the play and to Dickens' performance. *The Lighthouse* became the talk of the town and Dickens remarked that, at a dinner-party at Lord John Russell's, it was the chief topic of conversation. The demand for seats greatly exceeded the capacity of the tiny auditorium and Dickens was persuaded by a friend, Colonel Waugh, to give a series of performances in his private theatre at Campden House, Church Street, Kensington.

Already one actor-manager, Benjamin Webster, was nibbling, through the agency of Mark Lemon, to whom Wilkie wrote on June 28th:

I am anxious to know what Mr. Webster's intentions are on the subject of *The Lighthouse*. If you will kindly communicate to him the terms on which I am willing to dispose of the play for a limited period, I think we shall come to a definite understanding immediately.

The terms, then, that I propose (if *The Lighthouse* is acted in public) are: Five pounds a night to be paid to me during the first twenty nights of the run of the piece—the Play to be, so far as the dramatic right over it is concerned, Mr. Webster's property for twelve months from the first night of its production on the stage at his Theatre. After that period, all rights over it are to revert to me.

There are one or two minor arrangements which it will be time enough to talk over when I know how Mr. Webster is disposed to receive this proposal.

In spite of the far from onerous terms, set down with typical preciseness by Wilkie, Mr. Webster declined the proposal. According to Dickens, he developed cold feet at the prospect of playing Aaron and, presumably, of having his performance compared with that of the famous amateur. Negotiations with Wigan, manager of the Olympic Theatre, broke down because he too was unable to cast the play—a situation which provoked Wilkie to write: 'The principal part really requires a first-rate serious actor—and where is he to be found Anno Domini 1855?' Dickens, though he considered Wigan's refusal a lucky escape, was most anxious to secure for Wilkie a professional production and arranged for a dozen leading critics to attend one of the Campden House performances. Despite favourable notices, the managers remained aloof and it was not until two years later that *The Lighthouse* first appeared on a public stage. The theatre was the Olympic and the 'great little' Robson was imported into the company to play Aaron Gurnock. On this occasion, Wilkie wrote to his mother, on August 10th, 1857: 'Everybody breathless. Calls for me at the end of the first Act. A perfect hurricane of applause at the end of the play—which I had to acknowledge from a private box. Dickens, Thackeray, Mark Lemon publicly appearing in my box. In short an immense success.' These were optimistic words, for not even Robson's remarkable performance did in fact secure for *The Lighthouse* more than a moderate success.

Dickens, who threw himself into acting with the same whole-hearted vigour that characterised all his activities, needed a rest at the end of the *Lighthouse* season. He took the family to Folke-stone where Wilkie joined him at 3, Albion Villas, towards the end of July. Here they discussed future plans for *Household Words*, including the Christmas Number for 1855, *The Holly Tree Inn*, to which Wilkie contributed two stories, 'The Ostler' and 'The Dream Woman.' Wilkie's other two contributions to *Household Words* during 1855 were 'The Yellow Mask,' another essay in the macabre, and 'Sister Rose,' a story of the French Revolution. They were longer than his earlier stories, and each appeared in four parts. He was remunerated at the rate of about £10 for each weekly part.

From Folkestone, Wilkie went off to join Edward Pigott on a sailing expedition to the Scilly Islands. Pigott was a great friend of his for many years, and passionately keen on yachting. He owned and edited the *Leader*, a paper which he had founded in 1850, and to which Wilkie was an occasional contributor. Some years later Pigott was appointed Examiner of Plays in the office of the Lord Chamberlain, a task he performed with notable success. He has been described by an acquaintance as 'courteous and kind, well-read, especially in French literature, and agreeably witty.'

The Scillies trip provided the material for Wilkie's first non-fiction article in *Household Words*, 'The Cruise of the Tomtit,' in which the protagonists are lightly disguised as Jollins and Migott. They hired a 36-foot cutter of 13 tons and sailed her from the Bristol Channel. Several friends had declined to join the crew,

taking a different view of the hazards involved, and in the end—
and perhaps wisely—they engaged three brothers well-versed in ship
handling. Apart from bad weather at the start which forced them to
run for shelter, it was an uneventful and pleasant voyage. Wilkie
proudly records that they made the return trip in only 43 hours.

He was back at work in Hanover Terrace by the end of September preparing a book of short stories which Smith, Elder had
undertaken to publish. He selected for inclusion five of his
Household Words stories and wrote a sixth especially for the
occasion. This last story, 'The Lady of Glenwith Grange,' is one
of his most successful—a strangely moving tale, told with a rare
economy of words. He also devised an ingenious connecting thread
which gives to *After Dark*, as the collection of stories was named,
a certain measure of coherence.

This same year, 1855, was a notable one in the life of his friend
John Everett Millais. The Ruskins' strange and unhappy marriage
had recently been annulled after a painful lawsuit, and Effie Ruskin,
whom Millais had painted in 'The Order of Release,' was free at
last. After an interval no longer than propriety demanded, Millais
asked her to marry him, and a month or so later she consented.
To celebrate the event Wilkie gave a last bachelor dinner for
Millais on the eve of his departure for Scotland, where the marriage
was to take place.

One of the guests on this occasion was the already well-known
author of the *Book of Nonsense*, Edward Lear, who also became
a lifelong friend of Wilkie Collins. It is however a friendship of
which hardly a trace remains. Over thirty years later Lear wrote,
in one of his depressed moods: 'I am about to make a new
arrangement, i.e. to correspond only with those I have been in the
habit of writing to since 1850. They include Lushington, Tennyson,
Wilkie Collins. . . .'; and yet in the two volumes of Lear's published
letters not one to Wilkie appears. The single other reference is in
a letter dated January 7th, 1884: 'Received long and very nice
letter from Wilkie Collins.' It is also known that he was one of
the few friends to whom Lear sent, in 1886, a manuscript copy of
his last nonsense-poem, 'Uncle Arly.' A piquant aspect of the
friendship of the two writers was their close personal resemblance.
Lear remarked once that he was frequently being mistaken for
Wilkie Collins.

It is about this time that we see signs of a deterioration in
Wilkie's health. Hitherto he had led a normal, moderately active
life and despite occasional ailments there was nothing to indicate,
in the first thirty-two years of his life, that his health was below
average. In 1856, however, he had three distinct periods of sickness,
the nature of which is not specified, although Dickens in one
instance refers vaguely to 'a chill.' In the light of Wilkie's subsequent medical history it is at least probable that these troubles
were largely rheumatic, and the forerunner of the gout to which
he later fell a chronic victim. His proneness to rheumatic complaints was almost certainly inherited either from his father or,
as he himself believed, from his paternal grandfather.

The first of the attacks in January, 1856, delayed his visit to
Paris to see the Dickens family who were spending the winter
there. In inviting him Dickens had held out the prospect of
'theatrical' and other lounging evenings, and also of articles in
Household Words, adding, 'it will not be the first time that we
shall have got on well in Paris, and I hope it will not be by many
a time the last.' Not until the end of February was Wilkie able
to leave for Paris where Dickens had found for him an apartment
at 63, Champs Elysées, which he described as 'the snuggest little
oddity I ever saw—the lookout from it the most wonderful in
the world.' Wilkie was enchanted with the place as soon as he
set eyes upon it, and wrote to E. M. Ward: 'I have got a most
perfect little bachelor apartment; a "Pavilion" like a house in a
Pantomime, and the most willing, pleasant *concièrge* and wife in
the world to wait on me.'

Wilkie, who was quite accustomed to receiving communications
such as:

My Dear Collins:

Day	....	Thursday
Hour	....	Quarter past 11 a.m.
Place	....	Dover Terminus, London Bridge
Destination	...	Tunbridge Wells
Description of Railway Qualification		
		Return Ticket
Entd.		(signed) Charles Dickens

Form of trip appointment, in
compliance with Act of Parlia-
ment, Victoria, cap. 7, sec. 304.

was probably not surprised when a messenger arrived at the Pavilion, bearing the following document from No. 49, a few doors away:

The Humble Petition
of
Charles Dickens
A Distressed Foreigner

SHEWETH,—That your Petitioner has not been able to write one word today, or to fashion forth the dimmest shade of the faintest ghost of an idea.
That your Petitioner is therefore desirous of being taken out, and is not at all particular where.
That your Petitioner, being imbecile, says no more. But will ever etc. (whatever that may be).

It is not recorded where Wilkie took his distressed friend; one result of the expedition was that Wilkie developed a chill, accompanied by 'rheumatic pains and aguish shiverings,' which kept him indoors for a fortnight.

The invalid, confined to his sick-room, is apt to develop a morbid preoccupation with ill-health in all its manifestations. In the changing scenes of Parisian life which Wilkie watched from his window, only those incidents which could be in some way related to his own sick condition held any real interest for him. Of the hundreds of passing vehicles, two in particular impressed themselves on his memory.

A sober brown omnibus, belonging to a Sanitary Asylum, and a queer little truck which carries baths and hot water to private houses, from a bathing establishment near me. The omnibus, as it passed my window at a solemn jog-trot, is full of patients getting their airing. I can see them dimly, and I fall into curious fancies about their various cases, and wonder what proportion of the afflicted passengers are near the time of emancipation from their sanitary prison on wheels. As for the little truck, with its empty zinc bath and barrel of warm water, I am probably wrong in sympathetically associating it as frequently as I do with cases of illness. It is doubtless often sent for by healthy people, too luxurious in their habits to walk abroad for a bath. But there must be a proportion of cases of illness to which the truck ministers; and when I see it going faster than usual, I assume that it must be wanted by some person in a fit; grow suddenly agitated by the idea; and watch the empty bath and hot water barrel with breathless interest, until they rumble away together out of sight.

Similarly, of the people he comes to know by sight, one figure he cannot forget.

She is a nursemaid, neither young nor pretty. Very clean and neat in her dress, with an awful bloodless paleness in her face and a hopeless consumptive languor in her movements. She has only one child to take care of—a robust little girl of cruelly active habits. There is a stone bench opposite my window; and on this the wan and weakly nursemaid often sits, not bumping down on it with the heavy thump of honest exhaustion, but sinking on it listlessly, as if in changing from walking to sitting she were only passing from one form of weariness to another. The robust child remains mercifully near the feeble guardian for a few minutes—then becomes, on a sudden, pitilessly active again, laughs and dances from a distance, when the nurse makes weary signs to her, and runs away altogether, when she is faintly entreated to be quiet for a few minutes longer. The nurse looks after her in despair for a moment, draws her neat black shawl, with a shiver, over her sharp shoulders, rises resignedly, and disappears from my eyes in pursuit of the pitiless child. I see this mournful little drama acted many times over, always in the same way, and wonder sadly how long the wan nursemaid will hold out.

In his careful observation of this moving little scene we can see that Wilkie Collins of later years, a semi-invalid himself, morbidly fascinated by human infirmity and always interpreting it with sympathy and understanding.

By March 19th he was able to announce to Charles Ward that, 'after relieving my mind by swearing,' he had emerged victorious from the struggle. In the same letter he mentions that Paris has been illuminated in celebration of the birth of the 'Imperial Infant, who was created Prince of Peace and King of Algeria as soon as he could squall and dirty his napkins.' Wilkie was soon caught up again in the stream of entertainment provided by his unflagging companion. Dickens arranged a continuous round of theatres, art galleries, and social occasions of every kind. At various functions they met leading figures in French literature and drama, many of whom were known to Dickens already. Wilkie too made a number of friends. Among them was Emile Forgues, editor of the *Revue des Deux Mondes*, who had recently brought Wilkie's work to the notice of the French public through an article in his paper, and who later translated many of his books; Scribe, who on the evidence of a single story (Mad Monkton) prophesied his success as a novelist; and Regnier, of the *Comédie Française*, who subsequently collaborated with him in a dramatisation of *Armadale*.

Paris afforded an opportunity for Dickens and Collins to indulge their passion for the theatre. Their most memorable experience was Frédéric Lemaitre's performance in the hoary old melodrama, *Thirty Years of a Gambler's Life*, at the Ambigu. As the last curtain fell they were so overcome with emotion that neither moved or spoke for several minutes. Dickens wrote half a dozen ecstatic pages to Forster which, according to Wilkie, were 'not one whit exaggerated.' The Ambigu's next production, *Paradise Lost*, was of a very different type. Before the opening night the wildest rumours were current in Paris concerning the measure of nudity to be displayed by Adam and Eve, and tickets were rapidly sold out. Wilkie and Dickens attended the first night only to discover that the play was a ludicrous compound of Milton's epic and Byron's *Cain* and that, contrary to expectation, Eve was dressed 'very modestly.'

Ristori, the Italian actress over whom Paris was going mad, was dismissed by both of them as an imposter. Writing to E. M. Ward, Wilkie reports:

Perfect conventionality of the most hopelessly stage kind—walk, attitudes, expression, elocution, all nothing but commonplace in a violent state of exaggeration. We saw her in a play of Alfieri's exhibiting the unnatural bestiality of a daughter in love with her own father in long classical speeches. Virtuous females of all nations, sitting in balloons of crinoline petticoat, observed the progress of this pleasant and modest story with perfect composure.

On the more frivolous side they were delighted with a farce, *Les Cheveux de ma Femme*. A man surreptitiously secures a lock of his wife's hair and takes it to a clairvoyante who possesses an infallible gift for telling character from such evidence. She announces that the owner of the hair has been engaging in the most frightful dissipations, and the husband returns home distraught and mad with jealousy; only to discover what his wife had successfully concealed hitherto—that she wears a wig.

A trivial incident which occurred during this visit had a far-reaching effect on Wilkie Collins' subsequent career. He told the story many years afterwards to a friend: 'I was in Paris, wandering about the street with Charles Dickens, amusing ourselves by looking into the shops. We came to an old book-stall—half-shop and half-store—and I found some dilapidated volumes and records of French crime—a sort of French Newgate Calendar. I said to Dickens: "Here is a prize!" So it turned out to be. In them I found some of my best plots.' These volumes, Maurice Méjan's *Recueil des Causes Célèbres*, remained in Wilkie's library until his death. But for them *The Woman in White* would probably never have been written.

Wilkie returned to London in April, a sick man again. The house in Hanover Terrace had been let for a short term to the Wards and the family were staying in the country. He went to an hotel for a night and set off the next morning to look for a Furnished Apartment. At almost the first notice he saw advertising Rooms to Let, which was in the window of a house in Howland Street, off Tottenham Court Road, he stopped his cab and went in to inspect them. They were uninviting, and the street was gloomy, but he felt too depressed and ill to continue the quest, and paid his deposit. In Howland Street he suffered from the most devastating of afflictions, an obtrusive and maternal landlady. Mrs. Glutch—the name Wilkie gives her in writing of these experiences—is likened to a healthy bluebottle waiting on a sick fly, 'a woman suffused in a gentle melancholy proceeding from perpetual sympathy for my suffering condition.' He is however far too weak to think of escaping.

Dickens writes from Paris: 'The Pavilion looks very desolate and nobody has taken it as yet . . . I found the evening sufficiently dull, and indeed we all miss you very much.' And again a week later:

I have been quite taken aback by your account of your alarming seizure; and have only become reassured again, firstly by the good fortune of your having left here and got so near your Doctor; secondly by your hopefulness of now making head in the right direction. On the 3rd or 4th I purpose being in town, and I need not say that I shall forthwith come to look after my old Patient.

Several pages of this long letter are devoted to anecdotes calculated to cheer the convalescent. Dickens has seen the Comédie Française version of *As You Like It*—

Which is a kind of Theatrical Representation that I think might be got up, with great completeness, by the Patients in the asylum for Idiots. Dreariness is no word for it, vacancy is no word for it, gammon is no word for it, there *is* no word for it. Nobody has anything to do but sit upon as many grey stones as he can.

Chauncey Hare Townshend has called with his dog Bully, whose antics are described in a paragraph primly expurgated by Georgina Hogarth in her edition of the *Letters*.

The Bully disconcerted me a good deal. He dined here on Sunday with his master, and got a young family of puppies out of each of the doors, fell into indecent transports with the claw of the round table, and was madly in love with Townshend's boots, all of which Townshend seems to have no idea of, but merely says —'Bul-la!' when he is on his hind legs like the sign of a public house. If he dines here again, I mean to have a trifle of camphor ready for him, and to try whether it has the effect upon him that is said to have upon the Monks.

There have been hints that 'Paris pleasures' for Dickens and Wilkie were not all of an intellectual or gastronomic nature, and the final paragraph might be construed as lending substance to these suggestions.

On Saturday night I paid three francs at the door of that place where we saw the wrestling, and went in, at 11 o'clock to a Ball. Much the same as our own National Argyle Rooms. Some pretty faces, but all of two classes—wicked and coldly calculating, or haggard and wretched in their worn beauty. Among the latter was a woman of thirty or so, in an Indian shawl, who never stirred from a seat in a corner all the time I was there. Handsome, regardless, brooding, and yet with some noble

qualities in her forehead. I mean to walk about tonight and look
for her. I didn't speak to her there, but I have a fancy that I
should like to know more about her.

By the beginning of May when Dickens visited him at Howland
Street, Wilkie was very much better and shortly afterwards was
able to turn his back on the tiresome Mrs. Glutch for good. The
three miserable weeks in lodgings formed the subject of an article
for *Household Words*, which he subsequently included in *My
Miscellanies*.

The article is chiefly remarkable for an expression of his views
on domestic service, a matter in which he was quite at variance
with his time. In the Victorian novel, as in the Victorian household,
servants were only permitted to obtrude their personalities so long
as these were of regulation pattern. Usually they were excluded
from any real participation in the plot. In Trollope's novels the
domestics are seldom more than mere accessories to the story;
even Dickens is embarrassed in his handling of the master-servant
relationship on more than one occasion. Wilkie Collins, however,
depicts the domestic servant of his novels without a trace of
condescension as real people with real emotions, not as stock
figures but as characters in the round. In this article he is writing
of one of several maids who came and went during his short time
in Howland Street:

She looks very much surprised, poor creature, when I first let
her see that I have other words to utter in addressing her besides
the word of command; and seems to think me the most eccentric
of mankind, when she finds that I have a decent anxiety to spare
her all useless trouble in waiting on me. Young as she is, she has
drudged so long over the dreariest ways of this world, without
one leisure moment to look up from the everlasting dirt on the
road at the green landscape around, and the pure sky above, that
she has become hardened to the saddest, surely, of human lots
before she is yet a woman grown. Life means dirty work, small
wages, hard words, no holidays, no social station, no future,
according to her experience of it. No human being ever was
created for this. No state of society which composedly accepts
this, is the cases of thousands, as one of the necessary conditions
of its selfish comfort, can pass itself off as civilized, except under
the most audacious of all false pretences.

Such an attitude was bound to incur the obloquy of the employing class, and as late as the nineties it was possible for Percy Fitzgerald to write:

Another feature of Wilkie Collins's work was his odd interest in the secrets of servant-life, which he seemed to think were of extraordinary value. The housekeeper's views, the still-room maid's opinions and observations, were retailed with much minuteness, and made to influence the story. Such things are below the dignity of official narrative: for it is notorious that the opinions and judgments of servants are not only valueless, but are often actual distortions of the truth.†

It is to Collins' lasting credit that he was not prepared to treat the domestic servant as an inferior species. One hardly imagines that he would have been dismayed by Fitzgerald's sneers.

More stories from Wilkie's pen appeared in *Household Words* during 1856. 'A Rogue's Life,' for which he received £50, came out in five successive numbers during March, and 'The Diary of Anne Rodway' in two parts in July. Concerning the latter, Dickens writes:

I cannot tell you what a high opinion I have of 'Anne Rodway,' I read the first part at the office with strong admiration, and read the second on the railway coming back here . . . My behaviour before my fellow-passengers was weak in the extreme, for I cried as much as you could possibly desire. Apart from the genuine force and beauty of the little narrative, and the admirable personation of the girl's identity and point of view, it is done with an amount of honest pains and devotion to the work which few men can have better reason to appreciate than I, and which no man can have a more profound respect for. I think it is excellent, feel a personal pride and pleasure in it which is a delightful sensation, and know no one else who could have done it.

In their discussion of future plans the thoughts of both writers were turning once more towards the Drama. The success of *The Lighthouse* had meant as much to the principal actor as to its author. The acclamation of a whole world of readers, accorded him in a measure hardly known by a writer before or since in his

† *Memoirs of an Author.* Percy H. Fitzgerald. (Bentley, 1894).

lifetime, was not enough for Dickens; he was beginning to find it too distant, too impersonal. What he needed more and more was the applause he could see and hear, the excitement of the theatre. The same streak of exhibitionism which was to drive him to undertake the reading-tours that sapped his strength and ultimately killed him, now prompted him to seek still greater renown as an actor.

The writing of a new play would have to devolve upon Wilkie, since Dickens was up to his eyes in *Little Dorrit* and the day-to-day affairs of the magazine. They sketched out the plot together in Paris during March. The subject, Arctic Exploration, was very much in the public mind—and in Dickens'—because of the recent Admiralty publication of a Report on Sir John Franklin's tragic expedition. The two leading characters, Naval officers forming part of a similar expedition, were to be played by Wilkie and Dickens. Both men began to let their beards grow in order that, by the time the performance took place nine months later, they should really resemble Arctic explorers. Wilkie retained his beard until the end of his life.

After his illness he seems to have laid the draft aside for a time, but Dickens, who had set his heart on the project, keeps on prodding in letters with such phrases as 'All to come—in the fulness of the Arctic Seasons.' In April he tells Wills, 'Collins and I have a mighty original notion (mine in the beginning) for a play,' and offers Mrs. Wills the part of a Scotch housekeeper.

In June, Wilkie and Pigott chartered the *Coquette*, a 'delightful vessel' attached to the Royal Yacht Squadron, and sailed with one or two professional hands from Gravesend to the Bristol Channel, by way of Cowes, Cherbourg and Torquay. Their intention had been to sail to Dublin, but the winds were unfavourable. They crossed the Channel instead, calling at Cherbourg—'a dull, neglected place, full of the most intricately composite Continental stenches' —in order to take on board a stock of champagne and sauterne. On his return in early July, Wilkie received a letter from Dickens pressing him to join the party at the Villa des Moulineaux which had been rented again for the Summer:

On the 15th we shall, of course, delightedly expect you, and you will find your room in apple-pie order. I am charmed to hear you have discovered so good a notion for the play. Immense excitement is always in action here on the subject, and I don't think Mary and Katey will feel quite safe until you are shut up in the Pavilion on pen and ink.

His stay was cut short by a diphtheria epidemic in Boulogne which drove the whole party back to England early in September. He had, however, made good progress with the play, and on September 10th, Dickens wrote: '*An Admirable idea*. It seems to me to supply and include everything the play wanted.' Some suggestions follow, and the letter ends: 'Turn it how you will, the strength of the situation is *prodigious*; and if we don't bring the house down with it, I'm a—Tory.'

Another matter which Dickens had been turning over in his mind was Wilkie's position in relation to *Household Words*. He had become one of its most frequent contributors of stories, and had also written some non-fiction articles. Would it not be preferable to have him on the staff of the magazine, at a regular salary? Dickens was satisfied that *Household Words* would benefit from such an addition to its strength, and he knew that occasional payments to Collins were running at a high rate. Striking a careful balance between a desire to treat his friend fairly and a disinclination to swell the salary list more than he need, Dickens wrote to his sub-editor on September 16th:

My dear Wills—I have been thinking a good deal about Collins, and it strikes me that the best thing we can just now do for *H.W.*, is to add him on to Morley, and offer him Five Guineas a week. He is very suggestive, and exceedingly quick to take my notions. Being industrious and reliable besides, I don't think we should be at an additional expense of £20 in the year by the transaction.

I observe that to a man in his position who is fighting to get on, the getting his name before the public is important. Some little compensation for its not being constantly announced is needed, and that I fancy might be afforded by *a certain engagement*. If you are of my mind, I wish you would go up to him this morning, and tell him this is what we have to propose to him today, and that I wish him, if he can, to consider beforehand. You could explain the nature of such an engagement to him, in half a dozen words, far more easily than we could all

G

open it together. And he would then come prepared. Of course
he should have permission to collect his writings, and would be
handsomely and generously considered in all respects. I think
it would do him, in the long run, a world of good; and I am
certain that by meeting together—dining three instead of two—
and sometimes calling in Morley to boot—we should knock out
much new fire.

What it is desirable to put before him, is the regular association
with the work, and the means he already has of considering
whether it would be pleasant and useful to him to work with
me, and whether any mere trading engagement would be likely
to render him as good service.

If Wills expected Wilkie Collins to jump at this offer he was
quickly disillusioned. As Dickens had foreseen, Wilkie was fully
aware that unsigned stories and papers in *Household Words* did
little to enhance his growing reputation as a writer of fiction. He
seems to have had the temerity to suggest that he might suffer
by the readers' confusing his work with that of Dickens. No less
acute than Dickens in pecuniary matters, Wilkie also appreciated
that Five Guineas a week was not much of an increase over his
current remuneration, and that the acceptance of a salary must
in some degree limit his freedom. On the whole Wilkie was
disinclined to accept the offer as it stood. If, however, Dickens
and Wills could make certain concessions, he would be very willing
to reconsider the proposal. Would they, perhaps, agree to his
contributions being signed? Or, failing that, to undertake the
serialisation of a full-length novel—over his name of course? Wills
was doubtful, but promised to communicate with his chief.

Back came Dickens' reply by the next post:

Don't conclude anything *un*favourable with Collins, without
previous reference of the subject, and the matter of your consultation, to me. And again put before him clearly, when he
comes to you, that I do not interpose myself in this stage of the
business, solely because I think it right that he should consider
and decide without any personal influence on my part.

I think him wrong in his objection, and have not the slightest
doubt that such a confusion of authorship (which I don't believe
to obtain in half-a-dozen minds out of half-a-dozen hundred)
would be a far greater service than dis-service to him. This I

clearly see. But, as far as a long story is concerned, I see not the least objection to our advertising, at once, before it begins, that it is by him. I *do* see an objection to departing from our custom of not putting names to the papers in *H.W.* itself; but to our advertising the authorship of a long story, as a Rider to all our advertisements, I see none whatever.

Now as to a long story itself, I doubt its value to us, and I feel perfectly convinced that it is not one quarter so useful to us as detached papers, or short stories in four parts. But I am quite content to try the experiment. The story should not, however, go beyond six months, and the engagement should be for twelve.

On these terms agreement was reached and Wilkie joined the staff of *Household Words* about October 1st, 1856. More than one publisher was later to lament that Wilkie Collins drove a hard bargain, but he seldom had better cause to be satisfied with his negotiating ability than on this occasion, when his personal relationship with Dickens placed him at something of a disadvantage. Dickens obtained his services cheaply, but Wilkie made a great stride forward in achieving such a wide circulation for the serial version of his next novel.

Dickens, it must be admitted, interpreted the arrangement generously. Wilkie suggested that serial publication should only begin after he had written half, or at least a third of the story, and had submitted it for the Editor's approval. Dickens, however, brushed aside the suggestion and assured Wilkie of his confidence in the novel. *The Dead Secret* was, in consequence, written 'hot,' or virtually instalment by instalment, and began to appear in January, 1857, barely three months after Wilkie was taken on to the staff of the paper.

Wilkie Collins lost no time in getting down to work for the magazine. In addition to pushing ahead with the novel, and completing *The Frozen Deep*, both of which were pressing commitments, he found time to collaborate with Dickens on the coming Christmas Number to be entitled *The Wreck of the Golden Mary*. To this, Wilkie contributed two chapters, 'John Steadiman's Account' and 'The Deliverance.'

By the middle of October the first two acts of *The Frozen Deep* are finished; suggestions for dialogue and details of the action continue to pervade Dickens' letters. A little later he is learning his part and writes in a postscript, 'Took twenty miles today, and got up all Richard's words, to the great terror of Finchley, Neasdon, Willesden, and the adjacent country.' In November the play is finished; rehearsals begin; Stanfield gets to work on the scenery; Francesco Berger is consulted about the incidental music; the play-bills are sent to the printer. Next, and most important, there are the invitations to be despatched. Even after a careful pruning of the list, Dickens finds that four hundred guests represent the irreducible minimum. At a pinch the 'Smallest Theatre in the World' will accommodate an audience of a hundred, so there must be four performances. The Duke of Devonshire must be allowed to choose this evening, and there are other important guests to be invited on the same evening to meet him at supper. On December 16th, Dickens was able to write to Wilkie, 'All progressing satis-factorily. Telbin painting on the Stage. Carpenters knocking down the Drawing-room.'

The first performance was given on January 6th, 1857. Forster declaimed a Prologue in verse on a darkened stage, to the strains of 'soft music' throughout, beginning:

> One savage footprint on the lonely shore,
> Where one man listn'd to the surge's roar,
> Not all the winds that stir the mighty sea
> Can ever ruffle in the memory.
> If such its interest and thrall, O then
> Pause on the footprints of heroic men,
> Making a garden of the desert wide
> Where Parry conquer'd death and Franklin died.

At the closing words, 'Vanish ye mists!' the lights were turned up to reveal the living-room of a house in Devon. Clara Burnham is affianced to Frank Aldersley, played by Wilkie Collins, and is loved by but has rejected Richard Wardour, played by Dickens. Both men, unknown to one another at the time, have left England some months earlier as members of an Arctic expedition. Clara is distracted by premonitions of disaster and visions of blood on the icy wastes. The second act is set in an Arctic encampment; supplies are nearly exhausted and a small party is selected by lot to search for relief. It includes both Wardour and Aldersley. Just before the fall of the curtain, Wardour discovers that Aldersley is the man

who has robbed him of Clara's love and whom he has sworn to
kill. The last act takes place on the shores of Newfoundland,
whither Clara and the wives of other officers in the Expedition
have been transported to greet the survivors Wardour and Aldersley
are not among them. Clara is convinced that the worst has
happened and that her lover has met death at his rival's hand,
when a haggard, half-demented figure appears, whom she recognises
with difficulty as Wardour. He leaves the stage, to return a few
moments later carrying in his arms the insensible Aldersley whom
he has snatched from the jaws of death at the cost of his own life.
Clara understands his sacrifice as Wardour expires at her feet and
the curtain falls.

Such is the brief outline of what is emphatically not a good play.
By the standards of Victorian melodrama it is perhaps no worse
than the average, and has the advantage of an original background.
That it created something of a sensation among the audiences at
Tavistock House and elsewhere must be attributed chiefly to
Dickens' performance as Wardour. By all accounts this eclipsed
anything he had ever done on the stage; he played, according to
Wilkie, 'with a truth, vigour, and pathos never to be forgotten by
those who were fortunate enough to witness it.' Dickens himself
records that 'For about ten minutes after his death, on each occasion of that event occurring, Richard Wardour was in a floored
condition. And one night . . . he very nearly did what he never
did—went and fainted off, dead, again. But he always plucked up,
on the turn of ten minutes, and became facetious.' He adds that
Wilkie, when the time came for him to be carried on to the stage
in the last act, 'always shook like a mound of jelly, and muttered,
"This is an awful thing." '

The theatre at Tavistock House was dismantled, but the last had
not been heard of *The Frozen Deep*. This cruel melodrama had one
effect out of all proportion to its small intrinsic merit. The
character of Richard Wardour made a deep impression on Dickens'
dramatic sense and the notion of a man achieving regeneration
through self-sacrifice began to germinate in his mind. From this
small seed sprang the ideas which ultimately found expression in
A Tale of Two Cities. Richard Wardour was transformed into
Sydney Carton. In his preface to the novel, Dickens wrote: 'When
I was acting, with my children and friends, in Mr. Wilkie Collins's

drama of *The Frozen Deep*, I first conceived the main idea of this story.' For its French Revolution background Dickens drew upon other sources, including Carlyle and perhaps Bulwer-Lytton, but here again the influence of Wilkie Collins can be seen. There are striking similarities of detail between Dickens' novel and Wilkie's story of the French Revolution, 'Sister Rose,' which appeared in 1855. It is also clear from their correspondence that Wilkie was more than once consulted during the writing of *A Tale of Two Cities*, and that his suggestions were always carefully considered. All this indicates, not of course that the novel is derivative in any but a minor way, but that Wilkie Collins was beginning to exercise a certain influence upon his friend's work. One sees this influence at work in the increasing attention that Dickens pays to the plot in his last four or five novels, which display a tautness of construction not to be found in the earlier books, The process culminated in *Edwin Drood*, the only Dickens' novel where plot is supreme, and an undisguised invasion of the territory Wilkie had by then made his own.

7

'Household Words'

DURING the months following the performance of *The
Frozen Deep*, while Wilkie was at work on the *The Dead
Secret*, Dickens was straining to finish *Little Dorrit* on
schedule. Restless and dispirited, he sought Wilkie's company more
and more. The letters of this period make frequent reference to
dinners together at the *Household Words* office, jaunts into the
country and, later, visits to Dickens' new home near Rochester,
Gad's Hill Place, of which he took possession in May. He writes to
Wilkie in March, 1857:

> *I cannot tell you* what pleasure I had in the receipt of your letter
> yesterday evening, or how much good it did me in the depression
> consequent upon an exciting and exhausting day's work. I
> immediately arose (like the desponding Princes in the *Arabian
> Nights*, when the old woman—Procuress evidently, and probably
> of French extraction—comes to whisper about the Princesses
> they love) and washed my face and went out; and my face has
> been shining ever since.
> Ellis [proprietor of a Brighton hotel] responds to my letter that
> rooms shall be ready! There is a train at 12 which appears to me
> to be the train for the distinguished visitors. If you will call for
> me a cab at about 20 minutes past 11, my hand will be on the
> latch of the door.
> I have got a book to take with me of which I have not read
> a line, but which I have been saving up to get a pull at it
> in the nature of a draught—*The Dead Secret*—by a Fellow
> Student.

In May *Little Dorrit* was finished and Wilkie is informed that 'any
mad proposal you please will find a wildly insane response in
Yours ever, C.D.' And a week or so later Dickens writes:

Tomorrow I am bound to Forster; on Sunday to solemn Chief Justice's in remote fastnesses beyond Norwood; on Monday to Geographical Societies dining to cheer on Lady Franklin's Expedition; on Tuesday to Proctor's; on Wednesday, sir—on Wednesday—if the mind can devise anything sufficiently in the style of sybarite Rome in the days of its culminating voluptuousness, I am your man . . . If you can think of any tremendous way of passing the night, in the meantime, do. I don't care what it is. I give (for that night only) restraint to the Winds!

Wilkie Collins was no longer, if indeed he had ever been, merely the companion of Dickens' 'Inimitable' moods.

In *The Dead Secret*, published in two volumes in June, 1857, by Bradbury & Evans, part-owners of *Household Words*, Wilkie Collins is still feeling his way. Although it did much at the time to enhance his reputation, it can hardly be said to mark any great advance on *Hide and Seek*. For a Collins novel it is strangely deficient in plot; the 'secret' does not remain for long a secret from the reader, and there is scarcely enough intrinsic interest in the rest of the story to carry it through. In his portrait of the lady's maid, Sarah Leeson, the principal character of the book, he tells us that he wished to trace 'the influence of a heavy responsibility on a naturally timid woman whose mind was neither strong enough to bear it, nor bold enough to drop it altogether.' Unfortunately Sarah never quite comes to life and her dilemma seems altogether too contrived. Leonard Frankland, the hero, is blind—one of the long succession of Collins' characters suffering from some major disability. Uncle Joseph, with his musical-box and his passion for Mozart, is an entertaining figure, and we see all too little of the Reverend Dr. Chennery, one of Wilkie's most delightful clerics. The misanthropic Andrew Treverton and his attendant, Shrowl, are drawn several sizes larger than life in the early Dickens' manner. Competent, if unoriginal, *The Dead Secret* can best be described as a tentative move in the direction of the sensation novel, that department of fiction of which Wilkie Collins was soon to become the best known exponent. Dickens found the book of absorbing interest. It is doubtful if even he could have been prepared for the astonishing work which was to follow it.

The same month there appeared an article on Wilkie Collins in

The Train, a short-lived periodical founded by that enthusiastic young journalist Edmund Yates. The magazine featured a series of articles on literary figures of the day, written by Yates himself and entitled 'Men of Mark.' Number Two, which appeared in June, 1857, was devoted to Wilkie Collins; on the strength of half-a-dozen books, all more or less immature, he is startlingly accounted 'fourth among his contemporaries, after Dickens, Thackeray and Charlotte Brontë.' That such an estimate, extravagant as it was, could have been seriously advanced is at least an indication of Wilkie Collins' growing popularity with the novel-reading public. Yates adds that he considers him the most conscientious novelist of the day and a story-teller without equal. Alluding to *The Lighthouse* and *The Frozen Deep*, he says that they were performed with great success 'before the most refined and critical audiences in the land.'

In June, Douglas Jerrold, friend of both Dickens and Collins, died suddenly and Dickens decided on an impulse that they must do something to assist Jerrold's widow. He had been longing for an excuse to revive *The Frozen Deep*, ever since the last performance, and here it was. There had been hints of Royal interest in the play and at one time Dickens had passed on to Wilkie a rumour that the Queen intended to command a performance at Windsor Castle. Nothing had come of it, but, having decided on a further series of performances in aid of Jerrold's family, Dickens made discreet soundings at Court. The result was favourable and he was able to announce a short season, with the same cast as before, at the Gallery of Illustration, Regent Street, of which the first night would be a Command Performance.

The Queen, the Prince Consort, the King of the Belgians and their party numbering about fifty formed, on July 7th, 'a most excellent audience,' and at the public performances which followed the earlier success was repeated. Among the handful of 'outsiders' invited by Dickens to the first night was Hans Andersen, who was wonderfully impressed with the whole affair.

Andersen had been a great admirer of Dickens since meeting him years before on a previous visit to England, and he had been angling for some time for an invitation to stay with his 'dear Boz.' Having recently taken possession of Gad's Hill Place, Dickens had little choice but to issue the invitation so clearly expected of him. Hans

Andersen accepted with alacrity and stayed for five weeks during most of which time Wilkie was also a guest at Gad's Hill. Sir Henry Dickens, K.C., in his recollections of his father, tells a story which illustrates Andersen's childlike humour. Wilkie appeared one day in an enormous wide-awake hat, which Andersen proceeded to adorn with a garland of daisies, quite unsuspected by the wearer. The Dickens boys then persuaded Wilkie to accompany them on a walk through the village and were delighted by the laughter of the passers-by, the reason for which remained a mystery to Wilkie until he got home and removed his hat. Andersen enjoyed his visit to Gad's Hill enormously; for his host, however, the naïve charm of the author of the fairy-tales had begun to wear thin. On his departure a card was placed on the dressing table of his bedroom which read, 'Hans Andersen slept in this room for 5 weeks which seemed to the family ages.'

Reports of the undoubted success of *The Frozen Deep* at the Gallery of Illustration had spread to the provinces, and by the end of July, Manchester was clamouring to see it. The sum which Dickens had in mind to hand over to Mrs. Jerrold had not yet been reached, and he willingly concurred. The Free Trade Hall was booked and two performances arranged for Friday and Saturday, August 21st and 22nd. Dickens did not wish the female parts to be played on this occasion by the members of his family, for the ostensible reason that their voices and gestures would be lost in so large a hall, but perhaps also on grounds of propriety. He sought the advice of Alfred Wigan, manager of the Olympic Theatre, in the matter of engaging professional actresses and Wigan proposed a Mrs. Ternan and her daughters Ellen and Maria, who were playing at the Royal Princess's Theatre, Oxford Street. Dickens accepted the suggestion and, with no time to lose, the three actresses began to rehearse at Tavistock House.

At the very first rehearsal Dickens fell violently in love with the eighteen-year-old Ellen Ternan. He had met her some months earlier in her dressing-room at the Haymarket, where he had found her in tears because she was forced 'to show too much leg.' Although rehearsing in his own house, Dickens was unable, or made no attempt, to conceal his infatuation and his wife quite naturally felt affronted. Relations were already strained when the company left for Manchester on August 20th, 1857.

Besides Dickens and the author, the cast for the Manchester performance included Mark Lemon, Shirley Brooks, Lemon's successor as editor of *Punch*, Augustus Egg and Wilkie's brother Charles. Stimulated to the highest pitch by the emotional excitement, Dickens gave the performance of his life at the Free Trade Hall, and inspired the whole cast to surpass itself. In a foreword to the MS. copy of *The Frozen Deep*, now in the Victoria and Albert Museum, Wilkie Collins wrote: 'At Manchester this play was twice performed; on the second evening before three thousand people. This was, I think, the finest of all its representations. The extraordinary intelligence and enthusiasm of the great audience stimulated us all to do our best. Dickens surpassed himself. He literally electrified the audience.' A few days later Dickens was able to hand over more than £2,000 to Jerrold's widow.

Reaction set in immediately. Troubled by his passion for Ellen Ternan and aware that soon he must face a crisis in his domestic life, Dickens fell headlong into gloomy introspection. A week after their return from Manchester he wrote to Wilkie:

Partly in the grim despair and restlessness of this subsidence from excitement, and partly for the sake of *Household Words*, I want to cast about whether you and I can go anywhere—take any tour—see anything—whereon we could write something together. Have you any idea tending to any place in the world? Will you rattle your head and see if there is any pebble in it which we could wander away and play at marbles with? We want something for *Household Words*, and I want to escape from myself. For when I *do* start up and stare myself seedily in the face, as happens to be my case at present, my blankness is inconceivable—indescribable—my misery amazing.

Wilkie obediently rattled his head, and produced the idea of a walking-tour in Cumberland. This would remove Dickens from his own surroundings, in which he was feeling so restless; and if they were to collaborate in an account of their experiences, the writing of it might to some extent take his mind off the impending domestic crisis. The proposal was eagerly accepted and they left London in early September.

Their initial excursion ended in misfortune. Dickens was determined to climb Carrick Fell, and with the local inn-keeper—who later confessed he had not set foot on the mountain for twenty years—as guide, they set off in pouring rain. The summit was reached, but on the way down the visibility worsened, the pocket compass broke, and the party lost its way. The final disaster occurred when Wilkie slipped on a stone while crossing a brook, fell down and sprained his ankle. He had to be carried down the rest of the way by Dickens, 'exactly like Richard Wardour in private life,' and it was only after many difficulties that they arrived back at the inn after nightfall.

As the unlucky Wilkie lay immobilised with 'his foot wrapped up in a flannel waistcoat, and a horrible dabbling of lotion incessantly in progress,' they seized the opportunity to start on their narrative, *The Lazy Tour of Two Idle Apprentices*. Within a few days, Wilkie was able to hobble about with the aid of two sticks, but further walking was out of the question for the remainder of the holiday. On the look-out for good 'copy,' they decided to visit Doncaster during St. Leger week. They found rooms at the Angel Hotel, where Wilkie, for whom putting things away in cupboards was no part of a Lazy Tour, provoked his immaculate friend to write, 'I am perpetually tidying the rooms after him, and carrying all sorts of untidy things which belong to him into his bedroom, which is a picture of disorder.' Wilkie was still unable to walk out of doors, but was taken for a couple of carriage rides about the town; he was promised a third upon completion of his part of the current instalment, which was sticking a little. Towards the end of September the two friends parted company, Dickens returning to Gad's Hill and Wilkie going on to Scarborough for a short stay. He returned to 2, Harley Place, which was now the Collins family *pied-à-terre* in London since Mrs. Collins was living mainly in the country.

The Lazy Tour of Two Idle Apprentices which appeared in *Household Words* in five parts during October, 1857, is the record of a fairly uneventful trip, and its general effect is somewhat fragmentary. Each writer pads out his contribution with an essay in the macabre, Wilkie's story of 'The Dead Hand' being later included in *The Queen of Hearts*.

In the reflections of Mr. Idle, which occur in Part III of the *Lazy Tour*, we can detect a substratum of autobiographical truth.

Thomas Idle, *alias* Wilkie Collins, is musing upon disasters which befell him in his youth through engaging in unnecessary activity instead of following his proper instinct towards indolence. He recalls that, as a lazy and popular schoolboy, he was suddenly constrained to try for a prize, and actually won it. From that moment life at school became unbearable; the idle boys shunned him as a deserter, the industrious ones as a new and possibly dangerous competitor, while the masters began to punish him for offences which they would previously have overlooked as inevitable. A further misfortune arose, shortly after he had left school, from his ill-advisedly playing in a cricket match he had intended merely to watch. The strenuous exertions involved in getting out of the way of the ball, he claims, produced a perspiration which in turn brought on a chill which kept him in bed for many weeks. He had been a healthy child since birth and this was his first serious illness. Finally, Mr. Idle reflects upon his brief flirtation with the Law. 'Young men who aspired to the honourable title of barrister, were, very properly, not asked to learn anything of the law, but were merely required to eat a certain number of dinners at the table of their Hall, and to pay a certain sum of money; and were called to the Bar as soon as they could prove that they had sufficiently complied with these extremely sensible regulations.' We are told that, having thus painlessly acquired the status of barrister, he was persuaded to enter a conveyancer's chambers with a view to learning something of his profession. This resolution was short-lived, however, and a fortnight later he bade a permanent farewell to the Law. He had in the meantime made the acquaintance of a very adhesive bore, who took a liking to him and pursued him for a long time. Mr. Idle draws the moral which seems to him incontrovertible, that where the choice lies between inertia and action, the one spells bliss and the other catastrophe.

Wilkie had just completed a year on the staff of *Household Words*, the occasion being marked by a rise of £50 per annum. Dickens wrote to Wills: 'I don't remember whether I have told you that I have made the arrangement with Collins—that he is extremely sensible of the extra Fifty, and was rather unwilling to take it—and that I have no doubt of his being devoted to *H.W.*, and doing great service.'

The Christmas Number was the occasion of a rather more

successful attempt at collaboration than the *Lazy Tour*. The original idea of *The Perils of Certain English Prisoners*, was Wilkie's, which may account for its marking an abrupt departure from the type of fireside story which Dickens' readers had come to expect at the Christmas season. There are three chapters of which Dickens wrote the first and last, Wilkie the second and longest. Each revised the work of the other.

The Perils of Certain English Prisoners, which Dickens read for the first time to a gathering of friends on December 1st, 1857, is a tale of pirates and adventure in Central America, of marches through jungle and escape by rafts, and bears little resemblance to anything else written by either author. It has been said that, in their joint productions, it is often impossible to distinguish Dickens' work from Collins'; in this story, however, there is an unmistakable shift of emphasis at the end of each chapter from character to incident and setting and back again. Wilkie's scene, in 'The Prison in the Woods,' is carefully set—with generous splashes of local colour—and his action moves forward with deliberate tread, while Dickens is content to breathe life into a handful of memorable characters, with no more than a passing glance at the melodramatic situation into which he flings them.

Dickens had the manuscript of the *Perils* bound, and presented it to Wilkie with a covering note dated February 6th, 1858. 'Thinking it may one day be interesting to you—say, when you are weak in both feet, and when I and Doncaster are quiet and the great race is over—to possess this little Memorial of our joint Christmas work, I have had it put together for you, and now send it on its coming home from the Binder.' At the sale of Wilkie's effects after his death, the manuscript realised the sum of £200.

Wilkie Collins had become a regular contributor to *Household Words*, not only of short stories, but of articles dealing with a wide variety of subjects. Some of these he collected a few years later and published as *My Miscellanies*. The topics range from a biography of Balzac to concise accounts of French crimes of the Eighteenth Century (no doubt distilled from his copy of Méjan's *Causes Célèbres*), from 'A Petition to the Novel-Writers' to an amusing discussion of one of the earlier 'Answers to Correspondents' columns of popular journalism.

Now and again he would launch a protest against some injustice or other which had come to his notice. In one such article entitled, 'Highly Proper,' he attacked a schoolmaster who, in refusing to keep Alfred Wigan's son at his school on the ground that Wigan was an actor, had displayed the sort of snobbery which always roused him to anger. The attack was on too wide a front, however, for Dickens, who wrote to Wills: 'I particularly wish you to look well to Wilkie's article, and not to leave anything in it that may be sweeping, and unnecessarily offensive to the middle class. He has always a tendency to overdo that—and such a subject gives him a fresh temptation.'

Wilkie was devoting a good deal of his time to the affairs of *Household Words*, for, apart from his contributions, he was acting as Wills' assistant and in this capacity frequently attended editorial conferences. These would sometimes take the form of dinners at the office when the discussion would be accompanied by the ritual of brewing Gin Punch, an elaborate manœuvre executed with all the showmanship of which Dickens was capable. Of the relative merits of his two closest associates Dickens later wrote to Bulwer-Lytton, 'Wills has no genius, and is, in literary matters, sufficiently commonplace to represent a very large proportion of our readers . . . Wilkie Collins is a partner here for three years, and I can trust him implicitly.' Dickens must have been out of humour with Wills when he wrote this, since it is hardly likely that he would have retained as his sub-editor for twenty years one who was merely commonplace in literary matters, but it was upon Wilkie's judgment that Dickens came more and more to rely.

Three years of journalism did not harm, if they did little to develop Wilkie Collins' talents as a writer. He was versatile and soon learned to strike the particular note that his editor required, but he lacked the flair of a George Augustus Sala and was never quite happy in the journalistic field. His best work resulted from such opportunities as he had to exercise his narrative skill, for instance in the series dealing with French crimes. The humorous articles, in which he was trying to copy Dickens' journalistic style, are for the most part ponderous and exhibit a tendency which he was never able to keep completely under control, perhaps best described as literary archness.

During the winter of 1857–8, he had been working on a new play, this time with an eye on the commercial theatre. In March,

Dickens wrote to Miss Coutts, 'I am engaged to dinner today, to hear Wilkie Collins read a new play (in the construction of which I have held no end of councils with him) which he designs for Mr. Robson.' Wilkie greatly admired Robson's acting and was anxious to provide him with a part at least as good as that of Aaron Gurnock, which he had played in the Olympic production of *The Lighthouse*. The Olympic Theatre, in Wych Street, near the Strand (one of the streets which disappeared to make way for the Aldwych) was steadily acquiring a tradition as the home of well-acted melodrama. It became the fashion to distinguish between 'Olympic drama' and 'Adelphi drama,' the latter being regarded as altogether cruder and more old-fashioned. The Olympic was to be the scene of many a Wilkie Collins first night, and it was here that the new melodrama, *The Red Vial*, was presented in October, 1858. Besides Robson, who played Hans Grimm, a half-wit, the cast included Mrs. Stirling, an actress of considerable reputation.

From the rise of the curtain, *The Red Vial* was an utter failure. The audience at first tittered and then roared with laughter at the most serious moments of a play which was described by one critic as 'two hours of unbroken seriousness.' The loudest outburst came at the climax of the play, the awakening of a supposed corpse in the Frankfurt deadhouse. The sight of a naked arm thrust from the door of a mortuary-cell and clutching at the handle of an alarm-bell was more than even an Olympic audience could swallow. Henry Morley considered the characters 'mere puppets, uttering commonplace sentiments tediously expressed.' Mrs. Stirling's performance was favourably noticed, but about Robson opinion was sharply divided. It was generally agreed that nothing could have saved the play. After a few nights it was withdrawn to be forgotten by all except its author who, twenty years later, refurbished the plot and turned it into a novel. The manuscript of the play bears a note in Wilkie's handwriting: 'On its first night it was damned. Mrs. Stirling and Addison both admirable. Poor little Robson did his best. The rest is silence.'

This was the first time that Wilkie Collins had tasted the bitterness of failure. One effect was to turn his attention once more towards the novel and away from a medium which never lost its fascination for him, but for which he was curiously unsuited. No one who reflects upon Wilkie's contribution to English fiction during the next ten years, can wholly regret the fiasco of *The Red Vial*.

In the spring of 1858 the inevitable separation of Dickens and his wife had taken place; the details are too well-known to need repetition here. One aspect of the matter is, however, relevant. It had been suggested more than once, on the slenderest evidence, that Wilkie Collins' influence played a large part in precipitating the final break. He probably did not, as Forster did, actively dissuade Dickens from taking a step which was the logical outcome of the estrangement between him and his wife. To assume more than that must be mere conjecture, since we know that he remained Mrs. Dickens' friend until her death twenty years later. It is the same with the affair of Dickens' 'Personal Statement,' which appeared in most of the periodicals. Forster again tried to discourage him and Mark Lemon went to the length of refusing to publish the statement in *Punch*—an act which lost him Dickens' friendship. Forster states that Dickens was guided by the advice of 'a certain distinguished man (still living)' but there is little ground for suggesting, as has been suggested, that he was referring to Wilkie Collins. A more likely explanation may be found in Percy Fitzgerald's *Memories of Charles Dickens*: 'Forster suggested that the matter should be submitted to Mr. Delane, and this gentleman unfortunately gave his voice for publication.'

Wilkie Collins' role throughout this domestic crisis and the reaction that followed was rather that of a sympathetic listener. The letters become more intimate in tone. Henceforth it is, 'My dear Wilkie,' instead of 'Dear Collins'; Dickens is no longer 'ever faithfully,' but 'ever affectionately.' On March 21st, he writes:

> The domestic unhappiness remains so strong upon me that I can't write, and (waking) can't rest one minute. I have never known a moment's peace or content since the last night of *The Frozen Deep*.

Two months later, just after the separation, Dickens writes again.

> A thousand thanks for your kind letter. I always feel your friendship very much, and prize it in proportion to the true affection I have for you.
> Your letter comes to me only tonight. Can you come round in

H

the morning (Wednesday) before 12? I can then tell you all in lieu of writing. It is rather a long story—over, I hope now.

In August, 1858, Wilkie, who had been unwell, was recuperating at Broadstairs while Dickens was engaged on a Reading Tour designed, as he wrote to Wilkie, 'to wear and toss my storm away —or as much of it as will ever calm down while the water rolls.' Their correspondence was quite uninhibited, as is shown by Dickens' reply to a letter in which Wilkie had apparently made a jocular allusion to Dickens' frequent changes of address : 'As to that furtive and Don Giovanni purpose at which you hint, that may be all very well for *your* violent vigour, or that of the companions with whom you may have travelled continentally, or the Caliphs Haroun Alraschild with whom you have unbent metropolitanly; but anchorites who read themselves red hot every night are as chaste as Diana . . .' November found them both at Gad's Hill working on the Christmas Number, 'A House to Let,' which was to be the last of the *Household Words* series.

Wilkie's next task was the collection of a number of his short stories for publication in book form, which necessitated the contriving of a chain of narrative upon which to hang them, after the fashion of Dickens' Christmas Stories. When *The Queen of Hearts*, which contains some of his best short tales, was published in the following year by Hurst & Blackett, it received only a brief notice in *The Athenaeum* which described the book as 'a reprint of the author's contributions to *Household Words*.' This called forth an indignant, if slightly disingenuous, reply from the author. He explained in a letter to the editor that 'rather less than one-fourth' of the book was a reprint from *Household Words*, but omitted to state that this fourth represented half the number of stories in the book, or that the remainder were reprinted from other periodicals. The editor, while accepting the rebuke, thought that these explanations might have been given in a preface, but added : 'We make room for them however with hearty goodwill; for we have the highest respect for Mr. Collins as a conscientious cultivator of the art of story-telling.'

Wilkie's brother Charles was also beginning to drift into journalism and had already published several articles in *Household Words*.

As a painter, Charles Allston Collins was a most exacting critic of his own work, and an inordinately slow worker. The inevitable result was that picture after picture was left unfinished, and he began to find the pen a readier means of expression than the brush. Encouraged to write by both Dickens and Wilkie, a year or two later Charles abandoned painting altogether.

Neither his brother's defection nor his own close association with Dickens, a strong opponent of Pre-Raphaelitism, prevented Wilkie from maintaining his old friendship with the founders of the Brotherhood, and Holman Hunt in particular. Writing some 45 years later, Hunt gives an interesting picture of Wilkie Collins about this time.† One was sure, he wrote, of a warm welcome at whatsoever time of day one dropped in upon him. He would rock himself to and fro in his rocking chair, his hands clasping his knees, and 'ask with deep concern where you came from last.' His room was decorated with his father's paintings, including one or two beautiful pictures of the Bay of Naples.

Finding Hunt's gaze wandering, on one occasion, to a painting by another hand, Wilkie exclaimed:

Ah! you might well admire that masterpiece; it was done by that great painter Wilkie Collins, and it put him so completely at the head of landscape painters that he determined to retire from the profession in compassion for the rest. The Royal Academy were so affected by its supreme excellence and its capacity to teach, that they carefully avoided putting it where taller people in front might obscure the view, but instead placed it high up, that all the world could without difficulty survey it. Admire, I beg you, sir, the way in which those colours stand; no cracking in that *chef d'oeuvre*, and no tones ever fail. Admire the brilliancy of that lake reflecting the azure sky; well, sir, the painter of that picture has no petty jealousies, that unrivalled tone was compounded simply with Prussian blue and flake white. It was put on, you say, by a master hand; yes, but it will show what simple materials in such a hand will achieve. I wish all masterpieces had defied time so triumphantly.

We can easily indentify the subject of this panegyric as 'The

† *Pre-Raphaelitism and the Pre-Raphaelite Brotherhood.* W. Holman Hunt. (*Macmillan*, 1905).

Smugglers' Refuge,' which graced the Walls of the Royal Acadamy Exhibition of 1849.

The object of Holman Hunt's visit on the particular occasion he describes, was to seek Wilkie's advice. Having just completed his enormous canvas 'The Finding of Christ in the Temple,' after six years of intermittent work, Hunt was exercised to know how much he should ask for it. 'You must take care and get a thundering big price for it or you will be left a beggar,' advised Wilkie, and asked Hunt if he had any figure in mind. Hunt replied that 5,500 guineas, 'far more than has ever been given in England for a modern picture,' would be no more than a fair reward for the work he had put into it. 'Then,' said Wilkie, 'that is the figure you must ask, and you should be able to get it,' adding that if Hunt felt diffident about it, he should consult Dickens' opinion. 'Dickens is not only a man of genius, he is a good business man. Go to him and ask him.' The story has a happy ending. Wilkie arranged the meeting; Dickens despite his prejudice against the Pre-Raphaelite School, agreed with Wilkie's view, and the picture was ultimately sold to a dealer for £5,500.

Wilkie Collins was, according to Hunt, a generous spender at all times, although prudent in money matters. As a host, 'no one could be more jolly than he as the lord of the feast in his own house, where the dinner was prepared by a chef, the wines plentiful and the cigars of choicest brand. The talk became rollicking and the most sedate joined in the hilarity; laughter long and loud crossed from opposite ends of the room and all went home brimful of good stories.'

Holman Hunt's final observation is, whether intentionally or not, something of an enigma. 'Personally, he was without ambition to take a place in the competition of society, and avoided plans of life which necessitated the making up of his mind enough to forecast the future.'

In July, 1860, Holman Hunt acted as best man at the wedding of Charles Collins to Dickens' younger daughter Kate. Since adopting the profession of literature, Charles had been gathered more closely into the Dickens circle and had seen a good deal of Kate during his visits to Gad's Hill. He was attracted to her from the first and, for her part she found this strange young man interesting and sympathetic. The announcement of their engagement in the spring of this year occasioned no little surprise among their friends, although Wilkie had written to Ward some months before, 'Charley continues to spin madly in the social vortex, and is still trying hard to talk himself into believing that he ought to be married.' That Kate accepted his offer may be partly attributed to the changed atmosphere in the Dickens household since her mother's departure. She never accepted, as did her sister Mamie, the substitution of Aunt Georgina as mistress of the house and looked on her coming marriage as a means of escape.

Dickens must have viewed this link between the Collins family and his own with pleasure but also with some misgivings. Charlie's temperament was too nervous and highly-strung and his health too delicate for him to be an ideal husband. He possessed, however, great charm and sincerity and was well liked by those who knew him best. Forster wrote of Charles Collins that 'no man disappointed so many reasonable hopes with so little fault or failure of his own, that his difficulty always was to please himself, and that an inferior mind would have been more successful in both the arts he followed.' His personal appearance was striking. Hunt described him as 'slight, with slender limbs, but erect in the head and neck, square in the shoulders, beautifully cut features, large chin, a crop of orange-coloured hair (latterly a beard), blue eyes.' On the whole Kate might have done a good deal worse, and so far as is known, Dickens made no attempt to place any obstacles in the way of the marriage.

The wedding, which took place at Gad's Hill, was a great event for the villagers who, turning out in force, formed triumphal arches all the way to the church. A special train from London Bridge was organised for the guests who included Mr. and Mrs. Wills, the Forsters, Frederick Lehmann, Charles Fechter, Edmund Yates, H. F. Chorley, Thomas Beard and, of course, Wilkie. After the ceremony the party played games on the lawn and was then taken to Rochester to inspect the castle and to Chatham to hear a band concert. The programme, being signed 'W. Collins, Band-master,' gave rise to a number of bad jokes at Wilkie's expense. The departure of the bride and bridegroom was a tearful moment, 'Katey crying bitterly on her father's breast, Mamie dissolved in tears, and Charlie as white as snow.'

After the guests had returned to London at eleven o'clock at night, Dickens was discovered by his elder daughter in Kate's room with his face buried in her wedding-gown, murmuring in a broken voice, 'But for me Kate would never have left home.'

Early in 1859, as the result of a quarrel on mainly personal issues, Dickens dissolved partnership with Bradbury and Evans. Such a step entailed, as he fully intended it should, the end of *Household Words*. Taking with him Wills, Wilkie and most of his other 'young men,' he founded a new weekly, *All the Year Round*, similar in appearance and content to its predecessor. He even contrived to have the first number on sale several weeks before the final issue of *Household Words*. Bradbury and Evans, naturally incensed at Dickens' somewhat high-handed behaviour, decided to retaliate. They declared war by launching yet another periodical, *Once a Week*, with which they hoped to entice back into their fold at least some of the readers who had transferred their allegiance to Dickens' new paper.

It was therefore essential, with a subscription war brewing between the two periodicals, for Dickens to get *All the Year Round* off to a good start. His own new novel was sufficiently advanced to begin serial publication with the first issue, a fact which may have influenced his timing in bringing *Household Words* to an end. *A Tale of Two Cities* was a strong enough attraction to ensure the initial success of the magazine, but being considerably shorter than his average would only stretch to six months in serial form. Some worthy successor had to be found without delay. It is characteristic of Dickens that at this crucial point he should turn for his next serial, not to a safe name like Bulwer-Lytton, but to Wilkie Collins, in whose future as a novelist he had an unshakable faith. It was a gamble which succeeded far beyond even Dickens' expectations.

8

Caroline

A T the age of thirty-five Wilkie Collins seemed to have settled down to the life of a bachelor in premature middle-age, or so our limited knowledge of his private circumstances would suggest. Most of his time, apart from an occasional yachting expedition or holiday abroad, had been spent in the comfortable surroundings of his mother's house. He liked to dine out, even more to entertain his friends; he was a keen theatregoer and liked to listen to music. In fact he enjoyed the normal pleasures of Victorian middle-class society, and above all he enjoyed work.

As for his emotional life up to this point, any attempt to outline it must be based largely on conjecture. There is no direct evidence. Mention has been made of a serious attachment some ten years earlier as the possible genesis of *Basil*, but the details remain a mystery. If indeed Wilkie was involved in a love-affair that bore some resemblance to Basil's violent passion for Margaret Sherwin, this would only be consistent with a strange infatuation of his childhood. When he was only twelve years old he conceived a passionate affection for a married woman three times his age. So intense was his jealousy of the woman's husband that he could not bear to be in the same room, and ran away whenever he saw him approaching. The story is told in a brief critical study of Wilkie Collins, published in Germany in 1885.† Since Wilkie was alive at the time and had corresponded with the author, we must assume that he himself was the source of the information. Usually reticent about his private life, he may have regarded this incident as merely humorous and without any particular significance. It

† *Wilkie Collins: Ein biographisch-kritisch versuch.* E. von Wolzogen. (Leipzig, 1885).

does, however, reveal him as one who would be at least inclined to form strong emotional attachments in adult life. All we can say is that, between the *Basil* episode and the year 1859, he seems to have been free of any serious or lasting attachment.

Judged by his expressed opinions, Wilkie seems to have been disinclined towards marriage. In several articles in *Household Words* he stressed, with apparent satisfaction, his own bachelor state, and in more than one letter of the 1850's he referred in faintly derogatory terms to the institution of matrimony. 'Haven't much time for marriage myself,' he told his mother in a letter from Paris; and writing to his brother Charley he described a mutual acquaintance as 'one of those fresh-complexioned men with a low forehead and a meek character who always take kindly to the institution of marriage,' prophesying that he would achieve 'domestic happiness, a large paunch and a numerous family—in the enjoyment of which advantages he will live respected and die happy.' Marriage was all very well for others, one inferred, but for himself the freedom of a bachelor existence was indispensable —at any rate while his affections remained unengaged.

All this was changed with dramatic suddenness. The turning point in human affairs most often comes as a result of the chance encounter, the accident of time or place. So it was with Wilkie Collins. He met, in strange circumstances, a young woman and fell instantly in love with her. Although they now lie buried in the same grave, they never became man and wife.

This association had a marked effect on Wilkie both as regards his development as a novelist and his social environment. Information concerning it is sketchy and it may be useful at this point to depart from the chronological scheme so far followed in order to assemble, as far as possible, the various pieces of evidence into a coherent pattern. This is no simple task since his friends, in writing of him, sought by omitting any reference to his mistress to breathe a fog of respectability over his private life. Most of the details which enable us to trace the course of this relationship have come to light within the last ten or fifteen years; some of them appear for the first time here.

In 1899, ten years after Wilkie's death, there was published *The Life of John Everett Millais*, by his son J. G. Millais, in which the following passage occurs:

One night in the '50's Millais was returning home to 83, Gower Street from one of the many parties held under Mrs. Collins's hospitable roof in Hanover Terrace, and, in accordance with the usual practice of the two brothers, Wilkie and Charles, they accompanied him on his homeward walk through the dimly-lit, and in those days semi-rural, roads and lanes of North London . . . It was a beautiful moonlight night in the summer time and as the three friends walked along chatting gaily together, they were suddenly arrested by a piercing scream coming from the garden of a villa close at hand. It was evidently the cry of a woman in distress; and while pausing to consider what they should do, the iron gate leading to the garden was dashed open, and from it came the figure of a young and very beautiful woman dressed in flowing white robes that shone in the moonlight. She seemed to float rather than run in their direction, and, on coming up to the three young men, she paused for a moment in an attitude of supplication and terror. Then, suddenly seeming to recollect herself, she suddenly moved on and vanished in the shadows cast upon the road.

'What a lovely woman!' was all Millais could say. 'I must see who she is, and what is the matter,' said Wilkie Collins, as, without a word he dashed off after her. His two companions waited in vain for his return, and next day, when they met again, he seemed indisposed to talk of his adventure. They gathered from him, however, that he had come up with the lovely fugitive and had heard from her own lips the history of her life and the cause of her sudden flight. She was a young lady of good birth and position, who had accidentally fallen into the hands of a man living in a villa in Regent's Park. There for many months he kept her prisoner under threats and mesmeric influence of so alarming a character that she dared not attempt to escape, until, in sheer desperation, she fled from the brute, who, with a poker in his hand, threatened to dash her brains out. Her subsequent history, interesting as it is, is not for these pages.

The final sentence can be interpreted as a hint of an association which was not entirely respectable.

The next link is provided by Dickens' younger daughter Kate who, as Mrs. Kate Perugini, lived to a great age and whose reminiscences, edited by her friend Gladys Storey, appeared as recently as 1939. Since Kate's first husband was Wilkie's brother Charles, she was in a position to know the facts concerning her brother-in-law's private life. Unlike the many others who must have known, she was not averse to making them public. She quotes the passage from Millais' life referred to above, and comments 'Wilkie Collins had a mistress called Caroline, a young woman of gentle birth and the original of *The Woman in White*.' Mrs. Perugini had previously asserted, in conversation with friends, that the woman referred to in the Millais story was the same young woman who lived with Wilkie at No. 12, Harley Street and elsewhere.

Millais states explicitly that this strange meeting engendered in Wilkie's mind the basic idea of *The Woman in White*, and readers of the novel will recognise the situation. We shall, however, see in the following chapter that *The Woman in White* is based upon an actual case which had been before the French Courts some fifty years earlier. This does not entitle us to dismiss the Millais story as wholly fictitious, even if it does suggest a parallel too neat for unqualified acceptance. The story is, by inference, accepted by Kate Perugini, who is a credible witness as to other details of the association, and it was not apparently contradicted at the time of publication when there were still persons living who would know the facts. The most likely explanation is that such an encounter did take place in circumstances not unlike those described, and that the facts were subsequently adjusted to fit the theory formed after the event either by Millais or his biographer.

The shadowy figure who was to play so large a part in Wilkie Collins' life was Caroline Elizabeth Graves, née Courtenay. At the time of their meeting she was the wife—or possibly the widow—of George Robert Graves, of whom nothing is known. She was born about the year 1834 and probably married while in her teens. She had one child, a daughter, Harriet Elizabeth (also known as Carrie, or 'little Carrie,' and later as Harriette Elisabeth Laura) born in the early 'fifties. It is not possible to fix precisely Wilkie's first meeting with Caroline but there are indications that it took place in the early part of 1859.

In view of the intimacy existing between Dickens and Wilkie one would expect to find in the former's letters references to his friend's mistress. There are in fact three such references in the Nonesuch Edition of the *Letters* published in 1938, all suppressed in earlier editions. Proper names are carefully omitted. In a letter dated October 30th, 1859, Dickens wrote to Wilkie, 'I am charmed with the Butler.† O, why was she stopped! Ask her flinty mother from me, why, why, didn't she let her convert somebody! And here the question arises—Did she secretly convert the Landlord?' And on July 12th, 1861, 'Love to the Butler from her ancient partner in the card Trade. And kind regards to the Butler's mama.'

In a letter of August 19th, 1850, to a Mrs. Dickinson he is a little more explicit: 'Wilkie has finished his White Woman (if he had done with his flesh-coloured one, I should mention that too) and is in great force.' One might perhaps draw the inference that Dickens did not at that time regard the association as likely to be a lasting one.

No letter from Wilkie to Caroline has survived, so far as is known. Nor was it his practice to refer to her in his own letters, apart from those to Charles Ward. Ward alone receives the normal salutations one might expect, such as 'Caroline sends her kindest regards,' or 'both Caroline and I are delighted to hear that Jane's confinement is over,' and on occasion more extended references which will be alluded to later. The only instance of his even mentioning Caroline to any other correspondent occurs in a letter to Frank Archer in 1875: 'A line to congratulate you (on Mrs. Graves' part as well as on mine) upon your excellent performance.' Although Mrs. Collins must have known of the liaison, there is not even an oblique reference to Caroline's existence in the large number of letters from Wilkie to his mother which have survived. One imagines that either she disapproved of the liaison, or wished to show her son's letters to friends who were not in the secret. Stranger still, perhaps, is a similar omission in letters to his brother. Charley was not only a frequent visitor at Wilkie's house, but spent at least one holiday in company with Wilkie and Caroline Graves. All this would seem to suggest a deliberate intention on Wilkie's part to conceal from all but their intimate friends the fact that a liaison existed. On the other hand, there are repeated entries in the Post Office London Directory, which he must have approved, showing Mrs. Graves as the tenant of successive houses where he was well known to reside.

The first reference to Caroline Graves appears in a letter of May, 1859, to Charles Ward in which Wilkie writes: 'You won't

† Apparently Dickens' pet name for Caroline's small daughter.

mind my going away at eight o'clock (to the Opera), will you?—
and leaving the engagement between us two in every other respect
exactly the same. Dine at six—cigar afterwards—tea—I slip off—
Caroline keeps you company and makes you your grog—and you
stay as long as you feel inclined.' This letter was written from
2a, New Cavendish Street, which was their address for the next
seven months. In December they moved to 12, Harley Street, where
they remained for five years. Their next move at the end of 1864
brought them to 9, Melcombe Place, Dorset Square, where Mrs.
Graves was for the first time shown as the tenant in the Post Office
Directory for 1866. When Wilkie took a lease of 90, Gloucester
Place, in 1867, her name appeared as the occupant continuously
until 1880, when all pretence of concealment was abandoned and
the Directory proclaimed Mrs. Graves and Wilkie Collins as joint
occupants.

On evidence such as this one might justifiably presume a steady
and continuous relationship, indeed a marriage in all but name.
There are, however, further facts which considerably alter the
picture. After the passage in *Dickens and Daughter* already quoted,
Kate Perugini goes on to state that Caroline later married another
man and that Wilkie attended the wedding. After the ceremony
he visited Kate (she was at that time his sister-in-law) and told her
the whole story, saying, 'I suppose you could not marry a man
who had . . .?' to which she replied decisively, 'No, I couldn't!'
and, we may suspect, promptly changed the subject. Official records
corroborate Mrs. Perugini's story of the marriage. On October 4th,
1868, Caroline Elizabeth Graves, described as a widow, and Joseph
Charles Clow, son of a distiller, were married at St. Marylebone
Parish Church, the witnesses to the register being Wilkie's great
friend, Francis Carr Beard, and Caroline's daughter Harriette.

About the same time Wilkie formed a liaison with a woman
named Martha Rudd, later known as Mrs. Dawson. In the course
of the next five years she had three illegitimate children of whom
he was the father, the first, Marian, being born at 33, Bolsover
Street exactly nine months after Caroline's marriage to Joseph
Clow. Another daughter, Harriet Constance, was born at the same
address two years later and a son on Christmas Day, 1874, at 10,
Taunton Place, Regent's Park. They were all given the surname of
Dawson and were acknowledged by Wilkie Collins as his children

in his Will, by which he bequeathed half the residue of his estate to Mrs. Dawson in trust for them. Only the son's birth appears to have been registered; he was given the name of William Charles Collins Dawson. The informant was Martha Dawson and the father's name is shown in the register as William Dawson, Barrister-at-Law. In a letter dated April, 1876, to Frederick Lehmann, Wilkie talks of 'a visit to my morganatic family,' which suggests that the association was no secret from his more intimate friends. For the rest, we know little of Martha Rudd or her progeny. She lived for some years at 10, Taunton Place, and sent a wreath to Wilkie's funeral. She tended his grave for a time after Caroline's death.

Although Martha Rudd became the mother of his children there is little doubt that Caroline Graves was the woman who exercised the greatest influence on his life. As to the nature of that influence there can only be conjecture, but in the absence of direct evidence to the contrary one may assume that their relationship was on the whole a happy one. True, there is the enigmatic sentence in Thomas Seccombe's article on Wilkie Collins in the *Dictionary of National Biography*: 'Intimacies formed as a young man led to his being harassed, after he became famous, in a manner which proved very prejudicial to his peace of mind'; but this could be interpreted to mean almost anything.

Mystery surrounds Caroline's second marriage; from the moment that Joseph Clow signed the register as her husband, his name vanishes from our sight. Less than two years later, Wilkie inscribed a presentation copy of his new novel to 'Mrs. George Graves,' and though there is no record of a divorce it was as 'widow of G. R. Graves,' and not as the wife or widow of Joseph Clow, that Caroline was described at the time of her death. She returned to live with Wilkie early in the 70's and remained with him, as Mrs. Graves, until his death nearly 20 years later.

He adopted her daughter Harriet, who became his amanuensis and attended to all his correspondence whenever he was away. She continued to perform these duties even after her own marriage—to Wilkie's solicitor—in 1878. In his will he provided for Caroline and her daughter as well as for his own three children and their mother. Caroline Graves died in 1895 at the age of 61, and was buried in Wilkie's grave at Kensal Green Cemetery.

9

'The Woman in White'

DESPITE the emotional turmoil of his private life, the latter half of 1859 must have been for Wilkie Collins a time of intense creative activity. The new novel had to be ready to commence serial publication in November and there was much preparation to be done. The basic idea of The Woman in White, was as Clyde K. Hyder pointed out,† almost certainly suggested by a sensational lawsuit in the French Courts some fifty years earlier, the story of which was given in some detail by Méjan in Recueil des Causes Célèbres, the book Wilkie had picked up at a Paris bookstall in 1856.

The facts of the case are briefly these. Adélaïde-Marie-Rogres-Lusignan de Champignelles, Marquise de Douhault, became a widow in 1787 at the age of 46. Her father had died some three years earlier, and her brother, M. de Champignelles, had wrongfully seized the greater part of the estate including property which should have come to his mother and sister. Mme. de Douhault decided to visit Paris in order to try and recover this property for her mother, who was very poor, and for herself. She announced her intentions to her sister and to a Mme. de Polignac, expressing at the same time some misgivings about the proposed journey. Leaving her home at the end of December, 1787, accompanied by two or three servants she intended staying for a few days at Orleans with her nephew, M. Dulude. This gentleman was unable to offer her accommodation and persuaded her to stay instead with another relative, M. de la Roncière, who lived some ten miles away. She remained here several days and, on the eve of her departure for Paris—January 15th, 1788, was taken for a drive along the

† Wilkie Collins and The Woman in White. Clyde K. Hyder (P.M.L.A., 1939).

banks of the Loire by her hostess. After taking a pinch of snuff from Mme. de la Roncière, the Marquise was seized with a violent headache which obliged her to return to the house where she fell into a deep sleep.

This much Mme. de Douhault remembered clearly, but of the events which followed she had only a hazy recollection. She believed that she remained asleep for several days. Upon waking, she found herself in the Saltpétrière in Paris under the name of Blainville. She tried to communicate with her friends, but discovered that all her correspondence was intercepted. After a suitable interval, Mme. de Douhault's death was presumed and her estate passed to her heirs, who included her brother and M. Dulude. In June, she contrived to send a letter describing her plight to Mme. de Polignac, who succeeded in procuring her friend's release. It is mentioned that the white dress she was wearing on her arrival at the Saltpétrière was restored to her. She had no difficulty in establishing her identity among her friends and servants but the villainous brother used every means to prevent her from proving her identity in the eyes of the law. The case dragged on for years and Mme. de Douhault never succeeded in regaining either her property or, legally, her identity. She died in 1817 a poor woman.

When describing to a friend how he had found some of his best plots in Méjan's book, Wilkie expressly cited *The Woman in White* as being one of them. Although he offered other explanations towards the end of his life, of how he first hit upon the central idea, the points of similarity between novel and *cause célèbre* are too marked to be dismissed as mere coincidence. The drugging, the incarceration in an asylum, the obliteration of identity, even the detail of the white dress, all point to this once-famous French case as having provided the basic threads from which Wilkie wove the gloriously intricate plot of *The Woman in White*.

It may be of some interest to examine the skeleton of this remarkable piece of construction. Fortunately we have two sources of first-hand information on the subject. In the late 'seventies he gave an interview to Edmund Yates which was published in the *World*, and in 1887 he contributed an article, in the form of an open letter, to the *Globe* entitled 'How I write my Books.' Both deal specifically with the writing of *The Woman in White*.

The central idea, 'the pivot on which my story rests,' has crystallised as the substitution of persons effected with the help of a private asylum. The first part of the story will deal with the destruction of the victim's identity, the second with its recovery. One or two characters begin to suggest themselves. There must be a villain, and upon reflection he decides that the crime is too ingenious for an English villain. Thus, Count Fosco is born. Wilkie always insisted that, despite the many letters he received from abroad accusing him of 'gross personal caricature or rather too accurate portraiture,' Fosco was not modelled upon any particular person. 'I knew a man who loved canaries, and I had known boys who loved white mice,' he said, 'and I thought the mice running about Fosco while he meditated on his schemes would have a fine effect.' Fosco's obesity was almost an after-thought. 'I had begun my story when it struck me that my villain would be commonplace, and I made him fat in opposition to the recognised type of villain. His theories concerning the vulgar clap-trap that "murder will out," are my own.' As a contrast to Fosco, and as his tool, he believes that a minor villain is required, 'a weak, shabby villain'—Sir Percival Glyde in fact. The nature of the crime is then considered in greater detail; convention dictates that the victim of the substitution shall be a young lady of gentle birth, and for contrast her 'double' must be of poor parentage. Laura Fairlie, the former, materialises almost uninvited but the double presents difficulties.

I try what a walk will do for me—and fail. I devote the evening to a new effort—and fail. Experience now tells me to take no more trouble about it, and leave that other woman to come of her own accord. The next morning, before I have been awake in my bed for more than ten minutes, my perverse brains set to work without consulting me. Poor Anne Catherick comes in to the room and says, 'Try me.'

He has his idea. He now has four characters. Now comes the task of building up the story which involves 'three efforts.'

First effort: to begin at the beginning. Second effort: to keep the story always advancing without paying the smallest attention to the serial division in parts, or to the book publication in volumes. Third effort: to decide on the end. All this is done as my father used to paint his skies in his famous sea-pieces, at one heat. As yet I do not enter into details; I merely set up my landmarks. In doing this the main situations of the story present themselves; and at the same time I see my characters in all sorts of new aspects. These discoveries lead me nearer and nearer to finding the right end. The end being decided on, I go back again to the beginning, and look at it with a new eye, and fail to be satisfied with it. I have yielded to the worst temptation that besets a novelist—the temptation to begin with a striking incident, without counting the cost in the shape of explanations that must and will follow. I get back (as I vainly believe) to the true starting-point of the story. I am now at liberty to set the new novel going; having, let me repeat, no more than an outline of story and characters before me, and leaving the details in each case to the spur of the moment. For a week, as well as I can remember, I work for the best part of every day, but not as happily as usual. An unpleasant sense of something wrong worries me. At the beginning of the second week a disheartening discovery reveals itself. I have not found the right beginning of *The Woman in White* yet.

One of the discarded ideas was to open the novel in Cumberland, with the Limmeridge household awaiting the arrival of the new drawing-master. There follows a frantic but unprofitable search for a better notion. 'I and my manuscript have quarrelled, and don't speak to each other.' Then a brief paragraph in the newspaper catches his eye, and the solution presents itself in a flash. 'From that moment I am done with my miseries. *The Woman in White* begins again; and nobody will ever be half as much interested in it now, as I am.' Much remains to be done in the way of construction. The story must be broken up into a series of personal narratives and carefully rearranged to create the maximum suspense and mystification. We learn nothing more of the ingenious juggling with time and place nor of the manipulation of incident which must have contributed towards what has been described as 'the finest plot-novel in the English language.' He simply tells us: 'For the next six months the pen goes on; it is work, hard work.'

By August 15th, 1859, he had finished the first instalment, and wrote to Wills from Church Hill Cottage, Broadstairs, which he had taken for six weeks.

I send enclosed (and registered—for I should go distracted if it was lost) my first number. Please let me have duplicate proofs as soon as possible, for I want to see something in connection

I

with the story which is not a mass of confusion. It is an awfully long number—between 8 and 9 pages; but I *must* stagger the public into attention, if possible, at the outset. They shan't drop a number when I begin, if *I* can help it.

It was at Broadstairs that a solution was found to the problem of a title. He had thought of many possibilities, many more had been suggested by helpful friends such as Dickens and Forster; all were discarded. If the final choice seems to us obvious and inevitable, the author did not find it so. He has described how, one moonlight night, he wandered over the cliffs towards the North Foreland, smoking cigar after cigar, racking his brain for the right title. In the vicinity of what is said to be the original Bleak House, he threw himself on the grass. Looking across at the white shape of the North Foreland lighthouse, he thought: 'You are ugly and stiff and awkward; you know you are as stiff and as weird as my white woman . . . White Woman . . . Woman in White . . . the title, by Jove!' A roundabout way to the obvious, perhaps, but at least the story carries, in its very inconsequence, the ring of truth.

Dickens liked the title immediately and wrote by return, 'I have not the slightest doubt that the Woman in White is the name of names and the very title of titles.' All his other friends were unenthusiastic. Forster, who regarded himself as an expert in the matter of titles, complained that it was too long and too irrelevant.

The issue of *All the Year Round* for November 26th, 1859, contained the final instalment of *A Tale of Two Cities*, followed by this handsome introduction of the opening chapter of *The Woman in White*':

We purpose always reserving the first place in these pages for a continuous original work of fiction, occupying about the same amount of time in its serial publication as that which is just completed. The second story of our series we now beg to introduce to our readers. It will pass, next week, into the station hitherto occupied by *A Tale of Two Cities*. And it is our hope and aim, while we work hard at every other department of our journal, to produce, in this one, some sustained works of imagination that may become a part of English Literature.

The success of the new serial was immediate. Wilkie Collins had in truth 'staggered the public at the outset.' Nor did they drop a number after he had begun; the circulation, which had already reached a remarkable figure thanks to *A Tale of Two Cities*, continued to rise steadily. In a single month no less than 35,000 'back numbers' were sold. The progress of *The Woman in White* became a dinner-table topic and bets were struck on the outcome of this or that situation. What, for instance, was the nature of the crime which had placed Sir Percival Glyde in Mrs. Catherick's power?

All this makes more surprising the story† of how George Smith (of Smith, Elder) missed his opportunity of publishing what he described as 'the most popular novel of the century.' Learning that Wilkie Collins was at work on a new novel, Smith, Elder had written to say that they would like to make an offer for it. In January, 1860, when perhaps half-a-dozen instalments had appeared, Wilkie received an offer from Sampson Low for the book, and promptly wrote to Smith, Elder to give them the promised opportunity. George Smith had not been following the story in *All the Year Round* and turned to his clerks for their opinions. By an odd chance not one of them had read it either. Smith was, as often, in a tearing hurry, being engaged to dine out, and Wilkie had asked for an early reply. A hasty note was dictated offering the sum of £500. At dinner the lady sitting next to George Smith startled him by asking if he was reading 'that wonderful book, *The Woman in White*,' and was astonished at his reply. 'Everyone is raving about it,' she said. 'We talk "Woman in White" from morning till night!' Smith reached his office much earlier than usual the following morning, only to learn that the letter had been delivered to Wilkie Collins the night before. He wrote in his *Memoirs* that he would have multiplied his offer five-fold, had he heard that piece of gossip a couple of hours earlier, and concluded sadly, 'If my offer had been multiplied tenfold, I should have made a large sum by the transaction; but my hasty original offer cost me the pleasure and profit of publishing *The Woman in White*.'

Edward Marston, discussing the transaction in his reminiscences, *After Work*, does not recollect the exact figure his firm paid for the English rights of *The Woman in White*, but it was far more than Wilkie had ever received before. For the advance proofs, since

† Recounted in *The House of Smith Elder*, by Leonard Huxley (privately printed, 1923).

there was no such thing as American rights, Harper Brothers of New York paid him about £500. His success was due to the sensation which the serial version created from the start. In a letter dated January 7th, 1860 to E. M. Ward, he wrote:

> I do hope and believe that the story *will* be the best I have written yet. It is on a much larger and much more elaborate scale than anything I have done hitherto—and, as far as it has gone, it has certainly made itself felt pretty strongly not only in England but in America as well. The effort of keeping it going week after week is (in the reporter's famous phrase) 'more easily imagined than described.' When I approach the glass in the morning to brush my hair, I am quite agreeably surprised to find that it has not turned grey yet.

And to Charles Ward he wrote about the same time, 'My weekly race with the press is beginning to weigh heavily on me.'

Dickens put his finger on the one serious weakness of the book, a weakness which was perhaps inseparable from the narrative method employed, but which would be unlikely to escape Dickens' eye for character.

> I have read this book with great care and attention. There cannot be a doubt that it is a very great advance on all your former writing, and most especially in respect of tenderness. In character it is excellent . . . The story is very interesting and the writing of it admirable.
>
> I seem to have noticed, here and there, that the great pains you have taken express themselves a trifle too much, and you know that I always contest your disposition to give an audience credit for nothing, which necessarily involves the forcing of points on their attention, and which I have always observed them to resent when they find out—as they always will and do. But on returning to the book again, I find it difficult to take out an instance of this. It rather belongs to your habit of thought and manner of going about the work. Perhaps I express my meaning best when I say that the three people who write the narratives in these proofs have a DISSECTIVE property in common, which is essentially not theirs but yours; and that my own effort would be to strike more of what is got *that way* out of them by collision with one another, and by the working of the story.
>
> You know what an interest I have felt in your powers from

the beginning of our friendship, and how very high I rate them? *I* know that this is an admirable book, and that it grips the difficulties of the weekly portion and throws them in a masterly style. No one else could do it half so well. I have stopped in every chapter to notice some instance of ingenuity, or some happy turn of writing; and I am absolutely certain that you never did half so well yourself. So go on and prosper. And let me see some more, when you have enough (for your own satisfaction) to show me.

In July he was able, weary but elated, to lay down his pen. In a letter to his mother dated 'Thursday, July 26th, 1860, five o'clock p.m.' he wrote: 'I have this instant written at the bottom of the four hundred and ninetieth page of my manuscript the two noblest words in the English language—The End— . . . I must go out and walk off the work and the excitement of winning the battle against the infernal periodical system, at last.' A few days later Dickens wrote: 'Let me send you my heartiest congratulations on your having come to the end of your (as yet) last labour, and having triumphantly finished your best book. I presume the undersigned obedient disciple may read it *now*?'

Despite the intense interest displayed by the public in the serial version, many people prophesied that *The Woman in White* would not succeed in book form. Whilst agreeing that the author had contrived to maintain the tension admirably from one instalment to the next, they professed to see weaknesses in the story which would be fatal to the published novel. Publication was fixed for August 15th, and on the 3rd Wilkie invited some of his closest friends to Harley Street to celebrate. The guests included Holman Hunt, Egg, E. M. Ward, Frederick Lehmann and Henry Bullar, the last-named being a barrister on the Western circuit and an old friend of the family. In his letter to Ward, Wilkie wrote:

I have done! (except my *varnishing days* in respect of proof sheets which publishers and translators are still bothering about). We dine here at half past six on Thursday to drink success to the book in England, America, Germany and Canada, in all which places it will be published this month. Will you come? No evening dress—everything in the rough . . . cast respectability to the winds and write me a line to say you will come.

It is remarkable that both the English and American editions were published on or about August 15th, less than three weeks after Wilkie had completed his manuscript. There was certainly every need for haste on the part of Harpers who, in order to recoup the money they had paid for advance proofs, had to out-distance the American pirate publishers by the largest possible margin. These firms had cut down to a very few weeks the lapse of time between the publication in London of a novel by an established English author, and its appearance under their imprints in the New York bookshops. It is significant that in Harpers' first edition the copious illustrations which decorate most of the text stop short two or three chapters from the end, indicating that no time could be spared for the illustrator once the final instalment of proofs had crossed the Atlantic. Such was the system by which the English novelist received no payment whatever in respect of the greater part of his American sales, a system which the American public relished since it meant cheap books. As Dickens had written from the States in 1842, 'the raven hasn't more joy in eating a piece of stolen meat, than the American has in reading the English books which he gets for nothing.' Years later a New York publisher told a friend of Wilkie's that he had sold 126,000 copies of *The Woman in White*. 'He never sent me sixpence,' was Wilkie's sour comment.

Unwilling perhaps to endure the strain of publication day in London he rushed up to Yorkshire to stay with friends. Passing through London on August 22nd on his way to another house-party in Kent, he learned to his satisfaction that the entire first impression of 1,000 copies had been sold on the day of publication, and that the second impression was selling fast. He was back at 12, Harley Street in early September but stayed only long enough to fix up another yachting cruise with Pigott. After sailing around the Bristol Channel for a week or two in 'a capital safe boat'—the weather frustrated once again their intention to cross to Ireland—he returned home towards the end of the month. It was only then that he began to deal with the letters and newspapers piled high upon his desk. He read first the reviews, which were for the most part sharply critical, and then turned to the letters which 'brimmed over with eulogy.' The experience taught him a long-remembered lesson, he told Hall Caine many years later. 'These letters,' he reflected, 'are nearly all from total strangers, and may be said to represent in some measure the opinion of the general public. These reviews are by professional writers, some of them my intimate friends. Either the public is right and the press is wrong, or the press is right and the public is wrong. Time will tell. If the public turns out to be right, I shall never trust the press again.' There is a very obvious confusion of thought here, which led him in later years to regard popularity and merit as more or less synonymous. No doubt the press was wrong in failing to recognise *The Woman in White* as a masterpiece of its kind. What he failed to appreciate was that the appearance of seven impressions of *The Woman in White* in six months did not in itself constitute proof that the book possessed literary merit. Subsequently he mistrusted reviews, favourable or otherwise, even to the extent of overlooking their effect on public opinion, which he regarded as nearly infallible. The professional critic he came to look upon as a barrier rather than a bridge between himself and the reading public. It was partly in an attempt to eliminate this barrier, real or imagined, that he persisted in addressing the reader directly in prefaces to his novels, contrary to all advice.

On this occasion, there was no lack of tributes from delighted readers. Reporting the book's success, clinical as well as financial, to his mother, Wilkie wrote:

It is soothing the dying moment of a *young* lady—it is helping (by homœopathic doses of a chapter at a time) to keep an *old* lady out of the grave—and it is the first literary performance which has succeeded in fixing the attention of a deranged gentleman in his lucid intervals! The other day I reckoned up what I have got for it thus far. One thousand four hundred pounds—with the copyright in my possession, and the disposal of all editions under the extravagant guinea and a half price in my hands. Cock-a-doodle doo! The critics may go to the devil—they are at the book still as I hear, but I see no reviews.'

That Wilkie Collins was no different from many another writer who pretended to ignore the critics is shown by the postscript. Here he announced the enclosure of *The Spectator*, instructing his mother to turn to 'a review of *The Woman in White* answering the *Saturday Review*.'

The Times did not review *The Woman in White* until October 30th when it was already in its third edition. Apart from observing that too little attention had been devoted to character, the reviewer was on the whole favourably disposed towards the book, which he described as 'a novel of the rare old sort which must be finished at a sitting.' The author's request in his Preface that critics should avoid disclosing the secrets of the plot provoked this one to write:

> We are commanded to be silent lest we should let the cat out of the bag. The cat out of the bag! There are in this novel about a hundred cats contained in a hundred bags, all screaming and mewing to be let out. Every new chapter contains a new cat. When we come to the end of it out goes the animal, and there is a new bag put into our hands which it is the object of the subsequent chapter to open. We are very willing to stroke some of these numerous cats, but it is not possible to do it without letting them out.

Then, stealthily, the reviewer produced the ace from his sleeve. 'If we dared trespass upon details . . . we could easily show that Lady Glyde could not have left Blackwater Park before the 9th or 10th of August.' Whereas the entire plot turns in the final volume upon the date of Lady Glyde's departure, which was stated to be July 26th.

Wilkie lost no time in writing to his publisher, Edward Marston.

> If any fresh impression of *The Woman in White* is likely to be wanted immediately, stop the press till I come back. The critic in *The Times* is (between ourselves) right about the mistake in time. Shakespeare has made worse mistakes—that is one comfort, and readers are not critics who test an emotional book by the base rules of arithmetic, which is a second consolation. Nevertheless we will set it right at the first opportunity. They are going to dramatise the story at the Surrey Theatre, and I am asked to go to law about *that*. I will certainly go and *hiss* unless the manager makes a 'previous arrangement' with me.

Fame had indeed come to Wilkie Collins. While the novel was still selling in its thousands, manufacturers were producing *Woman in White* perfume, *Woman in White* cloaks and bonnets, and the music-shops displayed *Woman in White* waltzes and quadrilles. Even Dickens had hardly known such incidental publicity. In America the book's success was phenomenal; both Harper Brothers and the pirates made large sums of money out of it. Among Wilkie's colleagues, Dickens was not alone in his enthusiasm. Thackeray sat up all night reading it. Edward Fitzgerald read it three times, and named a herring-lugger he owned *Marian Halcombe*, 'after the brave girl in the story.' The Prince Consort admired it greatly and sent a copy to Baron Stockmar. On the other side of the account Bulwer-Lytton described it as 'great trash.'

With *The Woman in White*, Wilkie Collins' art reached maturity at a single leap. There is an assurance, an authenticity about it which sets it quite apart from his earlier novels, and indeed from much that he wrote afterwards. As an example of sustained story-telling it is unsurpassed. From Walter Hartright's meeting with the mysterious woman in white in the Finchley Road, a scene which Dickens bracketed with the march of the women to Versailles in Carlyle's *French Revolution* as the two most dramatic moments in English literature, to the final gruesome glimpse of Fosco lying in the Paris morgue, the suspense is maintained in masterly fashion. Andrew Lang wrote in the *Contemporary Review* within a few months of Wilkie's death :

> *The Woman in White* is a masterpiece of excitement and ingenuity. There is hardly a page but lives with its own mysterious life, and beckons you to follow till the end. It is a rare thing among novels of incident, of secret and of adventure, to find one that you can read several times . . . Though it is a work which we can never forget, we can often return to it; and it made Mr. Collins for long the most popular favourite in English fiction.

This typical Collins plot has been likened to a game of chess. Walter de la Mare has called him 'a literary Capablanca.' It would perhaps be more apposite to describe *The Woman in White* as a chess tournament, so many are the games simultaneously in progress. Count Fosco, on his own account, conducts two or three with such brilliance and bravado that we are almost sorry when in the end he faces checkmate at the hands of his plodding opponents. The master game between author and reader is conducted with scrupulous fairness on Wilkie's part. He is able to do this largely through the method he adopts in telling his story, the use of a series of personal narratives written by various characters of the plot. Each narrator is allowed to tell the whole truth as he knows it at the time of writing, but it is by an ingenious arrangement of the narrative that the author is enabled to guard his secrets, quite legitimately, until the proper time for disclosure.

The plot is one of the most tortuous and perfectly dovetailed in all fiction, and yet it is unfolded with complete lucidity.

The admirable carpentry of the book has sometimes tended to obscure other merits less commonly associated with the name of Wilkie Collins. He was always able to produce a telling character-sketch, the likeness done in a few vivid strokes. In the more difficult art of creating characters out of their speech and actions, and of developing them in their mutual relationships, he had been less successful. *The Woman in White*, however, marks a great advance in this respect, and is rich in what may be termed three-dimensional characters.

Most remarkable perhaps is Marian Halcombe, who has more in common with Ibsen's Nora than with the typical heroine of Victorian fiction. Courage and a lively and intelligent mind compensate for the beauty which her creator was bold enough to deny her.

> Never was the fair promise of a lovely figure more strangely and startlingly belied by the face and head that crowned it. The lady's complexion was almost swarthy, and the dark down on her upper lip was almost a moustache. She had a large, firm, masculine mouth and jaw; prominent, piercing, resolute brown eyes; and thick, coal-black hair growing unusually low down on her forehead. Her expression—bright, frank, and intelligent—appeared, while she was silent, to be altogether wanting in those feminine attractions of gentleness and pliability without which the beauty of the handsomest woman alive is beauty incomplete.

We watch with admiration the prolonged battle of wits with Count Fosco, in which she displays a tenacity and a resourcefulness worthy of her cunning opponent. In the long gallery of Collins' characters, Marian Halcombe represents his most deeply felt tribute to the qualities he admired in woman. We believe in her absolutely, and it is small wonder that Wilkie was inundated with letters from bachelors begging him to divulge her real name and address in order that they might seek her hand in marriage.

Into the subtly humorous portrait of Frederick Fairlie, hypochondriac and dilettante, Wilkie, who could always smile at his own weaknesses, projected something of himself. Fairlie lives his life of claustrophobic seclusion in a world of half-light and whispers, and describes himself as 'nothing but a bundle of nerves dressed up to look like a man.' Then there is Mrs. Catherick, as proud of her newly-acquired respectability as she is obsessed by her disreputable past.

Memorable as these characters are, Count Fosco is quite unforgettable. From the moment of his appearance, one-third of the way through the novel, he dominates the scene. He is admittedly a grotesque, larger than life, a creature of carefully conceived eccentricities and fustian humour; and yet, by some curious alchemy, Wilkie Collins contrives to fuse these qualities together to produce, not the stock villain of melodrama, but a figure of flesh and blood. However diabolical his schemes may be, however inordinate his suavity, however arrogantly he may strut across the stage, Fosco seldom steps beyond the bounds of credibility. Like Marian, recording her first impressions, we feel a 'strange, half-willing, half-unwilling liking for the Count.' The author gives us no direct portrait of Fosco, preferring that his impact upon the various narrators of the story should be communicated to us in their own words. It is an effect which oddly foreshadows Proust's masterly presentation of that other fascinating monster, M. de Charlus.

A contemporary journalist once described Wilkie as a master of 'the creepy effect, as of pounded ice dropped down the back.' No better example of this could be found than the moment when Marian's diary, in which she has set down all her suspicions of the conspiracy being woven by Fosco around the helpless Laura, is continued during her illness in a different handwriting—the characteristic flourish of Fosco himself.

It is not surprising that Sir Percival Glyde, the 'mean and shabby villain' cast in more conventional mould, is acted off the stage by his mentor and fellow-conspirator, Fosco. The roles least adequately filled are those of hero and heroine, if one may thus describe Walter Hartwright and Laura in a book where the interest is more or less equally divided among so many characters. Like many another novelist, Wilkie is at his weakest when depicting the good and the innocent, and neither character excites more than our superficial interest; if we notice at all Walter's disappearance from the scene during a large part of the story, his absence hardly disturbs us. Ann Catherick, the Woman in White, suffers from an infirmity of mind, which, while appealing to our sympathies, nevertheless limits our interest in her and her fate, and she misses the tragic stature intended for her by the author. Mention must also be made of Pesca, whose tedious chatter in the opening pages must have deterred many readers, but whom we forgive when he reappears at the close as the surprising instrument of Fosco's destruction. It has been said that his character was suggested by Gabriele Rossetti, father of the painter, who was himself a well-known teacher of Italian and had been, in his youth in Italy, a member of the secret society of patriots known as the Carbonari.

The novel of sensation must depend to a large extent upon the creation of a convincing atmosphere, in which the melodramatic incidents of the plot are made to appear almost inevitable. In *The Woman in White* he succeeds for the first time in harnessing his talent for scenic description to the dramatic requirements of the story, and induces in the reader that mood of suspended disbelief essential to the full enjoyment of melodrama. Who would not expect sinister events in a setting so forlorn as this?

The ground, shelving away below me, was all sand, with a few little healthy hillocks to break the monotony of it in certain places. The lake itself had evidently once flowed to the spot on which I stood, and had been gradually wasted and dried up to less than a third of its former size. I saw its still, stagnant waters, a quarter of a mile away from me in the hollow, separated into pools and ponds by twining reeds and rushes, and little knolls of earth. On the farther bank from me, the trees rose thickly again, and shut out the view, and cast their black shadows on the sluggish, shallow water. As I walked down to the lake, I saw that the ground on its farther side was damp and marshy, over-grown with rank grass and dismal willows. The water, which was clear enough on the open sandy side, where the sun shone, looked black and poisonous opposite to me, where it lay deeper under the shade of the spongy banks, and the rank overhanging thickets and tangled trees. The frogs were croaking, and the rats were slipping in and out of the shadowy water, like live shadows themselves, as I got nearer to the marshy side of the lake. I saw here, lying half in and half out of the water, the rotten wreck of an old overturned boat, with a sickly spot of sunlight glimmering through a gap in the trees on its dry surface, and a snake basking in the midst of the spot, fantastically coiled, and treacherously still. Far and near, the view suggested the same dreary impressions of solitude and decay; and the glorious brightness of the summer sky overhead, seemed only to deepen and harden the gloom and barrenness of the wilderness on which it shone.

Incidentally, this description of the lake at Blackwater Park brought him a most indignant letter from a property-owner who recognised in every detail the picture of his own estate, which lack of money prevented him from adequately maintaining. He charged the novelist with trespassing on his property and with advertising its owner's impecuniousness. It so happened that Wilkie was able to assure the gentleman that his estate was situated in one of the few English counties in which he had never set foot.

Among other letters he received was one from a lady, in the main laudatory, but complaining that Count Fosco was 'a very poor villain.' She offered to provide the author with first-hand material for the presentation of a villain who would eclipse all others in the whole range of fiction. 'The man is alive,' she wrote, 'and is constantly under my gaze. In fact he is my husband.' The lady was the wife of Bulwer-Lytton.

The Woman in White represents one of the twin summits of Wilkie Collins' achievement. *The Moonstone* is possibly the more flawless in construction, and affected more profoundly the stream of English fiction, but for sheer story-telling the earlier novel stands supreme. Authors are notoriously poor judges of their own work, but we might exclude from this generalisation the man whose tombstone is inscribed, in accordance with his own explicit instructions, 'author of *The Woman in White* and other works of fiction.'

IO

'No Name'

THE next twelve months or so were among the happiest of Wilkie Collins' life. At the age of 36 he was no longer, as many had regarded him, just one of 'Mr. Dickens' young men,' but a celebrity in his own right. He had learned to enjoy success without losing his balance. His domestic life was happy and seemed relatively stable, if unconventional. He had no monetary cares and for a brief period his health was better than for some time past. He lived, as he liked to do, a full social life, and invitations to public functions, musical evenings and private dinner parties showered upon him. In the winter of 1860 we find him staying for the first time with those literary lion-hunters, the Monckton Milnes, at Fryston, in Yorkshire. He also came into touch with George Eliot and G. H. Lewes, and frequently attended their musical 'Saturday afternoons' at their house near Regent's Park.

The musical evening—or afternoon—was an established feature of social life in the London of the Sixties, and Wilkie was known to be a keen music-lover. His understanding of the subject was not particularly profound and we have Dickens' word, for what it is worth, that he was virtually tone-deaf, but at least it is to his credit that his favourite composer was Mozart. If music appears in one of his novels, it is almost sure to be Mozart. Laura Fairlie and Walter Hartwright play Mozart piano-duets; Uncle Joseph's musical box plays—rather too often, one must confess—'Batti, batti,' the air from *Don Giovanni*; the blind Lucilla in *Poor Miss Finch* plays a Mozart sonata on the piano. He liked Italian opera, particularly Rossini, Donizetti, Bellini and Verdi, and shared the fashionable enthusiasm for Meyerbeer. For Wagner, whose music-dramas were soon to make their impact on the London opera-goer, he conceived a violent dislike. Neither did he apparently appreciate Beethoven, to judge from a letter written in 1861 to the Lehmanns:

> In *one* respect only, I have been the worse for the delightful party at Hallé's—the 'Great Kreutzer Sonata' has upset me about classical music. I am afraid I don't like classical music after all —I am afraid I am not the Amateur I once thought myself. The whole violin part of 'The Great K.S.' appeared to me to be the musical expression of a varying and violent stomach-ache, with intervals of hiccups.

Wilkie Collins' first reported appearance as an after-dinner speaker dates from the same year. He had always hesitated to make public speeches and envied Dickens' fluency in this field. George Dolby recounts the story of an evening in the fifties, when he, Wills, Wilkie and Dickens were discussing the technique of public speaking. Dickens, to illustrate his point, made a brilliant extempore speech proposing the health of the president of an imaginary rowing-club. Called upon to respond, neither Wills nor Wilkie felt equal to the task, and Dickens was left to reply to his own toast, a feat he performed with the same aplomb. On May 23rd, 1861, Wilkie was Chairman at the Newsvendors' Benevolent Institution Dinner and managed to acquit himself as a speaker rather better than he had expected. Wills was present and gave an account of the proceedings to Dickens who replied:

> Many thanks for your report of Wilkie, which amused and interested me very much. His quality of taking pains, united to a natural quickness will always get him on.

To Wilkie he wrote:

> I am delighted to receive so good an account of last night, and I have no doubt it was a thorough success. Now it is over, I may honestly say that I am glad you were (by your friendship) forced into the Innings, for there is no doubt that it is of immense importance to a public man in our way to have his wits at his tongue's end.

The nine months following the completion of *The Woman in White* were a period of comparative inactivity. Apart from collaborating with Dickens on the Christmas Story for 1860, he wrote nothing beyond an occasional article for *All the Year Round*. In October, 1860, he took Caroline to Paris for a short visit. He told his mother of his plan to travel 'first class all the way, with my own sitting-room at the best hotel when I get there—and every other luxury that the Capital of the civilised world can afford.' At last he could travel in the style of Dickens without having to weigh the chances of wheedling a loan out of his mother. He pressed Charles Ward to accompany them, but without success. 'Change your mind,' he wrote, 'and come to Paris. Only £4 there and back 1st class, £4 more for expenses—and there you are. *Sell a child*— terms £10 down! Slawkenbergins would fetch more if disposed of *by weight*, but I think him too amiable to be parted with. Try the baby, and let us devour the proceeds at the Trois Frères.' It amused him to tell, in connection with this trip, the story of a Parisian gentleman who had been reading *The Woman in White* in translation and had written to the author to complain that Count Fosco was an absolute likeness of himself. Having described how he flung the book to the other end of the room, the irate French-man proceeded to demand satisfaction, leaving to the author the choice of weapons. He had learned that Wilkie intended to visit Paris on a certain day during the following week and concluded with the chilling words, 'J'attendrai Monsieur Vilkie avec deux témoins à la gare.' No Fosco-like Frenchman turned up, however, at the Gare du Nord, and one cannot avoid a suspicion that the letter may have been a practical joke perpetrated by Dickens with the help of one of his many friends resident in Paris.

On his return to England, Wilkie set off with Dickens for a short visit to the West Country seeking local colour for the Christ-mas Story. They spent the first night in a 'beastly hotel' at Bideford, where they 'had stinking fish for dinner' and could not get a drink of any kind. Dickens wrote to Georgina, 'No adventure whatever. Nothing has happened to Wilkie,' doubtless recalling the disastrous beginning to the Idle Tour. From Bideford they posted to Liskeard visiting Clovelly en route; and Clovelly, lightly disguised as Steepways, provides the setting of the opening chapter of *A Message from the Sea*. Their collaboration in this story is more closely knit than usual, and it is hard to detect the precise division of labour. The opening chapter seems unmistakably Dickens, and Chapter IV 'The Seafaring Man,' can be attributed with reasonable certainty to Wilkie; both writers shared in the remaining chapters. It would be a bold critic who asserted the authorship of any particular paragraph, since they deliberately attempted, from time to time, to imitate each other's style. 'It is amusing,' declared Wilkie on one occasion, 'to see reviewers point out a passage of mine as an example of Dickens' peculiar vein, and in the next sentence comment on a paragraph of Dickens' as a sample of Wilkie Collins' sensational style.' *A Message from the Sea* was one of the most popular Christmas stories, more than a quarter of a million copies being sold.

A pirated dramatic version of *A Message from the Sea* was announced for presentation at the famous Britannia Saloon, Hoxton, within a few weeks of the story's publication.† The two authors visited the theatre on the first night and threatened the manager, Lane, with legal proceedings if the production were not withdrawn. Lane was sufficiently impressed by the force of their argument to comply with the request for that night at least. He sent an emissary to Gad's Hill the following day but failed to induce Dickens to change his mind. Dickens wrote to *The Times* the same day explaining his action and announcing his intention to deal likewise with any similar breach of the rights of authors. The subsequent history of the affair is somewhat confused. The Britannia continued to announce nightly performances of *A Message from the Sea* for the next four weeks, and these almost certainly took place. Lane had probably decided, after taking legal opinion, to call the author's bluff. In a letter to a friend Dickens claimed to have instituted proceedings in Chancery, at the same time expressing doubts as to the strength of his case, but no action appears to have come before the court.

In the same month, January, 1861, Wilkie resigned from *All the Year Round*, having been on the staff of Dickens' periodicals for more than five years. He no longer needed a regular salary and was doubtless relieved to be free from the trammels of weekly journalism. Dickens wrote to him: 'I am very sorry that we part company (though only in a literary sense) but I hope we shall work together again one day.' Not until six years later did they collaborate again, and for the last time, upon *No Thoroughfare*,

† The dramatisation is wrongly attributed to Wilkie Collins by Professor Allardyce Nicoll in *XIXth Century Drama*. A synopsis of the plot for a dramatic version was published for the authors by *All the Year Round* in 1861, no doubt to protect the dramatic copyright, but the play itself was never written.

K

although Wilkie did contribute one story to the 1861 Christmas Number, 'Tom Tiddler's Ground.'

Publishers were now competing for the right of Wilkie Collins' work, and he was in the happy position of being able to play one off against the other. In so doing he was scrupulously fair, as Edward Marston of Sampson Low testified. Hurst and Blackett were keen to reprint his novels in their Standard Library, and Blackett called upon him offering a substantial sum for the copyrights. Thereupon Sampson Low were given a similar opportunity and made an identical offer. Since they had already reprinted *The Woman in White* in the cheaper one-volume form, Wilkie, regarding them as having a prior claim, accepted their offer. He had, according to Marston, a perfect knowledge of his own value and stood in no need of a literary agent to make bargains for him.

The first reference to a successor to *The Woman in White* comes in a letter from Dickens dated April 28th, 1861, to Bulwer-Lytton concerning the latter's *A Strange Story*, shortly to succeed *Great Expectations* in *All the Year Round*. 'Wilkie Collins will be at work to follow you.' A few weeks later, Wilkie was 'slowly—very slowly—building up the scaffolding of the new book.' Dickens had hurried his own novel on to the scene earlier than intended, in order to offset the disastrous fall in circulation occasioned by Charles Lever's *A Day's Ride*. The final instalment of *Great Expectations* appeared in August and an editorial note announced that its successor would be *A Strange Story*, to be followed in its turn by a new novel from Wilkie Collins' pen. Unfortunately the circulation again began to diminish, and with it the high hopes Dickens had entertained of the Bulwer-Lytton novel. This time he had no *Great Expectations* to stop the rot and had to be content with advertising Wilkie's forthcoming novel at the end of each number, during the last three months of *A Strange Story*'s weary course.

It is a difficult moment in any writer's career when he is faced with having to follow up his first great success. The easiest, if often fatal method, is of course to repeat the successful formula, but Wilkie was seldom attracted to the line of least resistance. 'I think I can hold the public fast with an interest quite as strong as in *The Woman in White*, and with a totally different story,' he wrote in July, 1861, when he had completed the outline of the new novel; and six months later, 'I lay great stress on my originality this time—for the first element of success is not to repeat the other book.' Although widely regarded as a pure sensation-novelist, he became increasingly affected by a seriousness of purpose which did credit to his social conscience as certainly as it impaired his literary virtues. He expressed strong views on the novelist's duty to his public, which in his opinion went far beyond the mere provision of entertainment. He once stated that his principle in writing fiction was threefold, 'Make 'em cry, make 'em laugh, make 'em wait,' but he could also have claimed, on occasion, a laudable desire to 'make 'em think' as well. Aware that a sermon is the more acceptable, to the public at which he aimed, for being sandwiched between the covers of a sensation-novel, he began to cast about for serious themes around which to spin his incomparable web of narrative. Earlier novels had touched here and there upon a social problem, conditions in fever hospitals in *Basil*, the abuse of religious instruction in *Hide and Seek*, the lack of public control over private asylums in *The Woman in White*. In none of these books, however, was the problem more than incidental to the plot. Possibly inspired by Dickens' example he now came to believe more and more in the social functions of the novel; what he failed to appreciate was that his own talents were unsuited to this purpose and could only suffer by being forced into the uncongenial channel of the propaganda-novel. Later on his zeal for reform, for exposing injustice and castigating cruelty took an even stronger grip upon him until, like ivy on a tree, it all but strangled his natural gifts. In the eighteen-sixties, however, he was at the height of his powers, and by carefully co-ordinating his theme, the social and legal implications of illegitimacy, with the demands of the plot, he produced, in *No Name*, his one satisfactory 'purpose-novel.'

The August heat drove Wilkie and Caroline out of London just as he had begun the new novel. They spent most of the month at the Royal Hotel, Whitby, where he had a pleasant private sitting-room with three bow-windows overlooking the harbour and its fishing-boats. There were inconveniences, however. 'Among the British matrons established in the hotel,' he wrote, 'is a Rabbit with *fourteen* young ones. She doesn't look at all ashamed of herself—nor her husband either.' These and dozens of other children combined with 'a brass band hired by the proprietor to play four hours a day' to distract him from work. 'Working against noise is the hardest work of all,' he decided, and made his way back to London in leisurely stages, 'studying localities' for the new book on the way. He found it particularly hard to squeeze into the periodical instalments, but finished the first two by mid-September, six months before they were due to appear. Indeed by the time the story began in *All the Year Round* on March 15th, 1862, the entire first volume was in print. This time he clearly intended to keep well ahead of schedule.

Dickens was again most encouraging. He was 'immensely struck' by the outline of the story, and communicated his enthusiasm to Wills, 'whose eyes rolled in his head with astonishment.' After reading the first volume Dickens wrote to Wilkie: 'I find in the book every quality that made the success of *The Woman in White*, without the least sign of holding on to that success or being taken in tow by it. I have no doubt whatever of the public reception of what I have read. You may be quite certain of it. I could not be more so than I am.' In the same letter Dickens suggested no fewer than twenty-seven possible titles, some of them almost unbeliev-ably banal, as for instance, 'Through Thick and Thin,' 'Changed, or Developed?' 'Playing out the Play,' 'Nature's Own Daughter,' and 'Which is Which?' The final choice, *No Name*, was once again Wilkie's own.

His plans for steady and unhurried work on the new novel were upset by a serious decline in his health, which became apparent about this time. As we have seen, from being a normally robust child he had become, not exactly a sick man, but one of uncertain health rather too much at the mercy of wind and weather. By 1862 Wilkie's recurring ailment had taken on some of the aspects of gout, and was ultimately diagnosed as 'rheumatic gout,' a convenient name for a complaint which possessed symptoms of both rheumatism and gout. Many eminent physicians, however, declared that there was no such thing.

Gout was then—and is to some extent still—something of an enigma to the medical profession. A fairly recent textbook describes it as 'that riddle of the ages upon which so many physicians from time immemorial have expended their dialectic skill.' Once the disease had taken a firm hold there seemed little hope of a permanent cure, and treatment was largely negative in character. The patient was advised to eschew rich food and alcohol, a form of treatment unlikely to appeal to a devout lover of wine and food such as Wilkie Collins. Rudolf Lehmann, who painted his portraits during the 'eighties, remarked upon his peculiar theories that nothing the palate relished could be harmful and nothing the palate disliked could be wholesome, adding wryly that the state of Wilkie's health hardly bore out the validity of his theory. He would follow his doctor's instructions regarding diet as long as an acute attack lasted, but was much too fond of good living to regard abstinence as more than a temporary expedient. Inevitably recurrences became more frequent as the years went by.

Even in its ordinary manifestations gout is an extremely painful complaint and hardly deserves the lightly humorous allusions it so often provokes. It may be confined to the legs and feet but can attack almost any part of the body; in Wilkie's case the eyes became seriously affected and gave rise to the most excruciating pain. Again physicians are divided as to whether there is such a condition as 'gout of the eyes,' which was the description used by Wilkie and his doctor, but they agree that gout is not uncommonly associated with, and may be the cause of acute ocular inflammation such as iritis or conjunctivitis. A friend of Wilkie's, Charles Kent, said after visiting him during one of these attacks, 'his eyes were literally enormous bags of blood!'

It was to alleviate the pain during these attacks of gout that he began about this time to take opium, usually in the form of laudanum. The laudanum proved of course a potent anodyne, but soon the effect would wane, the agony would return and the dose would have to be repeated until the attack subsided. References to laudanum in his books reflect Wilkie's intense feeling of gratitude for its powers. Miss Gwilt, in *Armadale*, writes in her diary: 'Who was the man who invented laudanum? I thank him from the bottom of my heart, whoever he was. If all the miserable wretches in pain of body and mind, whose comforter he has been, could meet together to sing his praises, what a chorus it would be! I have had six delicious hours of oblivion; I have woke up with my mind composed.' Dr. Ezra Jennings, in *The Moonstone*, expresses views on the virtues of opium, 'all-powerful and all-merciful drug.' which are the author's own.

Wilkie became a chronic sufferer from gout. There would be a few weeks, a few months perhaps, of freedom from pain, and then another attack would seize him. The drug would become necessary once more, but each time, as the patient gradually acquired a tolerance for it, the dose had to be imperceptibly increased. As his general health deteriorated, so his reliance upon the drug became more absolute. Then he began to need more opium to counteract the effect of opium itself and soon the faithful servant had become the tyrannical master. So Wilkie Collins came with tragic inevitability to join the company of Coleridge and de Quincey. The process naturally took some time. Perhaps twenty years elapsed between the first medicinal doses and the nightly wineglassful of laudanum which he found necessary in later years merely to ensure sleep. What is extraordinary is that so apparently frail a constitution could stand up to excessive drug-taking for so long, and that he was able to earn a good living by his pen right up to the end.

There is frequent mention of ill-health in his letters of 1862, and as early as January, Dickens, who did not hesitate to include among his many roles that of amateur physician, wrote:

> It is pretty clear to me that you must go in for a regular pitched battle with that rheumatic gout. Don't be satisfied with Frank Beard's patching you, now that you have leisure, but be set up afresh. I don't like that notion of the eight and forty hours. It's not a long enough time and the treatment *in* the time must be too ferocious. Nature does not proceed in that way, and is not to be proceeded with in that way. With all respect for my hon. friend M.R.C.S., I think it a demonstrable mistake, and I hope you will arrive at the same conclusion.

The Frank Beard mentioned was Francis Carr Beard, younger brother of Thomas Beard, who was one of Dickens' oldest friends. He carried on practice at 44, Welbeck Street and became not only Wilkie's medical adviser but also one of his most intimate friends. Beard had prescribed, among other forms of treatment, a course of Turkish Baths.

During the first half of the year Wilkie was fighting a running battle against sickness. In April he sought a change of air on the East Coast and probably stayed at Aldeburgh, which is the scene of much of the second volume of *No Name*. When he returned to London a few weeks later he was a little better, and decided to spend the whole summer by the sea. The place he chose was Broadstairs, for which his affection outweighed even the extortions of the inhabitants. 'No moderate income can cope with their demands,' he had written a year or two earlier. 'A skinny little chicken is three and sixpence—meat equally dear—vegetables three times the London price—my landlord won't draw me a bucket of water without being paid for it—the cook I have engaged sends me up my dinner at the small charge of ten and sixpence a week and her keep, tea and beer besides . . . And the Broadstairs people complain of the shortness of their season! It is a wonder they have a season at all.'

A long search for a cottage at a reasonable rent ended in his taking The Fort House, where Dickens had often stayed, for four months. Caroline and he moved in at the end of June, 1862. In this pleasant cottage, with its view of the sea from every room, his health began to rally. The tonic effect of the sea air was aided by tepid salt-water baths, of which treatment he wrote: 'I swear by tepid salt-water baths—they soothe while you are in them and they invigorate afterwards.'

Though working at some pressure he was able to entertain a succession of visitors. His brother Charley, Frank Beard, Henry Bullar, Piggott and Charles Ward came down to stay at different times. Dickens came over from Folkstone on August Bank Holiday for a few days. The Lehmanns were unable to accept his invitation because Frederick was about to sail for America on a business trip. In a letter from Broadstairs wishing him *bon voyage*, Wilkie somewhat surprisingly revealed himself as a supporter of the Southern States in the Civil War then raging:

> The one chance for that miserable country on the other side of the Atlantic is that those two blatant impostors, Lincoln and McClellan will fail to get the 300,000 new men they ask for. If I thought it would be the least use, I would go down on both my knees and pray with all my might for the total failure of the new enlistment scheme.†

† The issues of the American Civil War were widely misunderstood in England. Even our leading statesmen made errors of judgement which appear astonishing in the light of subsequent history.

Wilkie was always most anxious to have the factual details of his novels correct. Writing against time, separated from books of reference, he is constantly importuning his friends to supply topographical details and information on a variety of subjects needed for *No Name*. Charles Ward is bombarded with requests to discover and report how long a letter took to reach Zurich in 1847; what is the average length of a round voyage to Hong Kong; what day of the week was March 4th, 1846; whether a letter posted in Dumfries can reach London the following morning; how many days' notice are required for a marriage by licence; and how often the mail leaves for Shanghai. Wills is invited to provide local information about Dumfries and thus spare him a visit to Scotland. Is it a thriving manufacturing town and what does it manufacture? Is the neighbourhood hilly or flat, barren or cultivated? Can he furnish the name of a suitable village on the banks of the Nith where a couple on their honeymoon might hide themselves? If he cannot get the facts he will have to write from pure imagination. 'And won't the letters come pouring in *then* to correct my mistakes! There is nothing the British reader enjoys so much as catching his author in the wrong.'

His publishers had been pressing him to finish *No Name* in time for publication in December, and by mid-September there is a desperate note in his references to the book. 'I shan't have done before the end of the year,' he told Wills, 'perhaps not before the end of January. They seem to like the story and be d——d to them. The women write me letters begging for more each week. I wish they may get it!' Domestic difficulties of one kind and another had added to his worries. Caroline had been unwell. Both their servants had left. Inviting Wills to visit them, he wrote: 'If you don't mind waiting on yourself, *I'll* black your boots.' A month later, just before their return to Harley Street, he said: 'I am sadly fagged with my work—I hope to God I shall finish in six weeks' time.'

Dickens took an even closer interest than usual in the progress of *No Name*. He found the second volume 'wonderfully fine' and made many suggestions for improvements of detail, even to correcting the grammar. As soon as Wilkie returned to London in late October, his health broke down completely. Dickens, who was about to leave for Paris, heard of his friend's plight at the last moment and dashed off this letter:

My dear Wilkie,—Frank Beard has been here this evening, of course since I posted my this day's letter to you, and has told me that you are not at all well, and how he has given you something which he hopes and believes will bring you round. It is not to convey this insignificant piece of intelligence, or to tell you how anxious I am that you should come up with a wet sheet and a flowing sail (as we say at sea when we are not sick), that I write. It is simply to say what follows, which I hope may save you some mental uneasiness—for I was stricken ill when I was doing *Bleak House* and I shall not easily forget what I suffered under the fear of not being able to come up to time. Dismiss that fear (if you have it) altogether from your mind. Write to me at Paris at any moment, and say you are unequal to your work, and want me, and I will come to London straight, and do your work. I am quite confident that, with your notes, and a few words of explanation, I could take it up at any time and do it. Absurdly unnecessary to say that it would be a makeshift! But I could do it, at a pinch, so like you as that no one should find out the difference. Don't make much of this offer in your mind; it is nothing except to ease it. If you should want help, I am as safe as the bank. The trouble will be nothing to me, and the triumph of overcoming a difficulty great. Think it a Christmas Number, an Idle Apprentice, a Lighthouse, a Frozen Deep. I am as ready as in any of these cases to strike in and hammer the iron out.

You won't want me. You will be well (and thankless) in no time. But there I am; and I hope that the knowledge may be a comfort to you. Call me, and I come.

Such a generous and timely gesture, coming from one who was already working at high pressure, must have warmed Wilkie's heart. Although it so happened that he was able to do without the promised help, he long remembered this demonstration of true friendship on the part of the man he loved and respected above all others.

Writing to his mother, who was apt to worry about his health, on November 6th, he made light of his illness: 'The weather has upset me . . . cold in the head, cold in the throat, cold in the chest —internal upset as well. I am getting used to it, and I laugh like a fiend over my own maladies. There is only one true friend to the afflicted in body—and his name is Brandy and Water—and he comes with particular healing in his wings when he is *Hot.*' He struggled on, writing when he could, and six weeks later was able to write to Lehmann, 'I have got downstairs today—very, very weak but decidedly, I hope, on the road to recovery.' The novel was finished in December. There is a marked falling off in the closing chapters which show all too clearly the strain and fatigue under which they were written.

No Name, dedicated to Francis Carr Beard 'in remembrance of the time when the closing scenes of this story were written,' was published on 31st December, 1862. A first edition of four thousand copies was printed and by five o'clock only four hundred remained. Thanks to the remarkable sales of its predecessor he had been able to make a very good bargain with Sampson Low, who paid £3,000 for the rights—£500 in cash and the balance in notes at three, six and nine months. 'Low has outbidden everybody,' he wrote triumphantly to his mother, 'and has offered the most liberal price that has ever been given for the *reprinting* of a work already published periodically—no less a sum than Three Thousand Pounds! Add to this the receipts from *All the Year Round* and from America, and the amount reaches Four thousand, six hundred. Not so bad for story-telling!' Edward Marston, of Sampson Low, admitted that it was a great risk forced upon them by a very vigorous competition, but added that the book had a considerable sale and they came off without loss. Charles Reade, at the time little more than an acquaintance of Wilkie, told Marston, 'The *Woman in White* was a great book. *No Name* is not. The independent public bought the former largely because it was well worth buying. *No Name* you forced in even greater numbers on the libraries, and the libraries forced it on their slaves the genteel public. But the great public are not crushed under machinery, and they have a judgement and a will of their own.' Despite Reade's assertion, the author of *No Name* had already obtained even better terms for his next novel.

No Name is the most unjustly neglected of all Wilkie Collins' novels. Unlike its predecessor, it breaks no new ground; it is at once a less sensational and a simpler story than *The Woman in White*. This time there is no intrinsic mystery to beckon the reader on to the end—the only 'secret,' as the author remarks in his Preface, is revealed midway through the first volume—and yet the progress of Magdalen Vanstone's fortunes stimulate almost as much excitement as the unfolding of Fosco's intrigues or the search for the lost Moonstone. It is an example of plain, straight-forward story-telling at its best.

The book opens with a carefully observed picture of a middle-class household in the West Country. We are introduced to the Vanstone family and their servants one by one as they descend the stairs to begin their daily routine. All is apparently solid, comfortable and conventional. Then follows a series of events which sweep away the very foundations of their happiness and security. The father is killed in a railway accident, the mother dies of grief, and the two daughters learn with brutal suddenness that they are illegitimate and almost penniless.

It was perhaps permissible to present the situation, if essential to the plot, of a couple living in sin; it was unpardonable to depict them as having lived together for years in perfect concord, loved by the family and respected by the friends they had deceived. Wilkie was careful to provide mitigating circumstances which went some way towards redressing the moral balance of the situation, but the Vanstones show no trace of that sense of shame and guilt which might have appeased the guardians of morality in literature. It was not to be supposed that his audacity would go unchallenged. Nor was it surprising that one of the louder protests should appear in the pages of the *Quarterly Review*, by whose standards even Dickens was deemed vulgar. To this journal Mrs. Oliphant contributed an article on 'Sensation Novels' in the form of a review of some two dozen such books recently published, including *No Name*. In the course of her generally disparaging remarks on this debased form of literature, she took Wilkie severely to task on the moral issue. '*No Name* is principally a protest against the law which determines the social position of illegitimate children. But the prosecution of this main purpose involves, as a subordinate purpose, a plea in behalf of the connexion to which such children owe their existence.' She then quotes an admittedly unfortunate sentence in which Wilkie speaks of 'the accident of their father having been married when he first met their mother'—meaning the accident of his having been unable to obtain a divorce—and comments acidly: 'We have often heard an illegal connexion and its result euphemistically designated as a "misfortune"; but this is the first time, so far as we are aware, in which a lawful marriage has been denominated an "accident".'

Unluckily Mr. Vanstone dies intestate and the fortune which he has intended for the daughters passes to his elder brother from whom he had long been estranged. Neither Michael Vanstone, nor his son Noel who succeeds to the inheritance shortly afterwards, is prepared to make any provision for the two unhappy girls. The main story concerns the flight from home of the younger daughter, Magdalen, and her campaign of vengeance against cousin Noel, a shifty, weak-kneed valetudinarian.

Magdalen Vanstone is perhaps Collins' most ambitious portrait of a young woman. She is a younger, more beautiful, and more headstrong Marian Halcombe, equally brave and resolute, but with a streak of ruthlessness, almost of cruelty, entirely foreign to Marian's nature. Wilkie would have us regard her as a personification of the struggle between Good and Evil, but his powers were hardly of that order. It is as individuals playing out their own particular drama, and not as symbols, that his characters command our attention.

He places himself under an unnecessary handicap in insisting upon his heroine's extreme youth. It is not easy to accept, in a girl of twenty brought up in a sheltered middle-class home, quite the measure of self-reliance and singleness of purpose with which he endows Magdalen. None the less, this central situation of a young girl alone against the world, turning her back on home and family, no doubt caused a flutter of excitement in the breasts of readers accustomed to the more fragile heroines of the period.

At the outset of her adventures Magdalen enlists the dubious support of Captain Wragge, charlatan, trickster, and petty black-mailer—and the one really successful comic character in the pages of Wilkie Collins. 'His manners were distinguished by a grave serenity. When he opened his lips, he spoke in a rich bass voice, with an easy flow of language, and a strict attention to the elocutionary claims of words in more than one syllable. Persuasion distilled from his mildly-curling lips; and, shabby as he was, perennial flowers of courtesy bloomed all over him from head to foot.'

Captain Wragge will always deserve a disreputable place in the long line of engaging rogues who have enriched English fiction. from Peregrine Pickle to Christopher Isherwood's Mr. Norris.

That huge, trembling mass of flesh, Mrs. Wragge, is a figure equally of comedy and of pathos. Slow-witted, untidy, forgetful, she is the constant butt of her husband's raillery, and is forever offending against his passionate sense of order. She cannot help sleeping 'crooked,' slipping off her shoes in the presence of company, or perpetrating some other misdemeanour that provokes the Captain's waspish tongue. To overcome her 'constitutionally torpid' nature, he persists in shouting at her; it is 'a necessary stimulus to her ideas.' 'Shout at her—' explains the Captain, 'and her mind comes up to time. Speak to her—and she drifts away from you directly.' And to demonstrate the point he roars, 'Mrs. Wragge! Put your cap straight!'

The Fourth, and longest, Scene takes place at Aldeburgh. Its flat and desolate surroundings provide a perfect background for what is in effect the climax of the book. How vividly he conveys the isolation of the Suffolk landscape:

It was a dull airless evening. Eastward was the grey majesty of the sea, hushed in breathless calm; the horizon line invisibly melting into the monotonously misty sky; the idle ships shadowy and still on the idle water. Southward, the high ridge of the sea dyke, and the grim massive circle of a martello tower, reared high on its mound of grass, closed the view darkly on all that lay beyond. Westward, a lurid streak of sunset glowed red in the dreary heaven—blackened the fringing trees on the far borders of the great inland marsh—and turned its little gleaming water-pools to pools of blood. Nearer to the eye, the sullen flow of the tidal river Alde, ebbed noiselessly from the muddy banks; and nearer still, lonely and unprosperous by the bleak waterside, lay the lost little port of Slaughden; with its forlorn wharfs and warehouses of decaying wood, and its few scattered coasting vessels deserted on the oozy river-shore. No fall of waves was heard on the beach; no trickling of waters bubbled audibly from the idle stream. Now and then, the cry of a sea-bird rose from the region of the marsh; and at intervals, from farmhouses far in the inland waste, the faint winding of horns to call the cattle home, travelled mournfully through the evening calm.

It is at Aldeburgh that the fascinating duel of wits between Captain Wragge and Mrs. Lecount, Noel Vanstone's faithful housekeeper, is fought. This provides the opportunity for a display, both brilliant and amusing, of Wilkie's chess-game methods. Mrs. Lecount, whose Achilles heel is the memory of her late husband, a biologist, and her consequent reverence for Science, is almost a match for the unscrupulous Captain. He has been studying a popular work entitled *Joyce's Scientific Dialogues*, and insinuates himself into her confidence by pouring out a farrago of elementary Science culled from its pages.

Here too occurs the dramatic scene in which Magdalen, overcome with horror and remorse now that her long-sought revenge is at hand, contemplates suicide by poison. Grasping a bottle of laudanum she watches the coasting vessels glide slowly past her window, determined to leave to blind chance the decision she cannot make for herself. If an even number of ships pass within half-an-hour she will live; if an odd number she will die.

This bottle of laudanum, as Dorothy L. Sayers has pointed out, is something more than a mere accessory to a 'sensation-scene.' It becomes, on its reappearance later in the story, a vital element in the development of the plot. It is certainly true of his best work to say: 'He never wastes an incident; he never leaves a loose end; no incident, however trivial on the one hand or sensational on the other, is ever introduced for the mere sake of amusement or sensation.'†

The pattern of *No Name*, divided as it is into eight 'scenes,' suggests that the author had in mind from the first the idea of a stage adaptation. Two separate dramatic versions were in fact made by him, but neither, so far as we know, reached the stage. This is in some ways surprising when one recalls that he successfully adapted for the theatre three far more complex novels, *The Woman in White*, *The Moonstone* and *Armadale*. He remarked, however, towards the end of his life that he could never get the dramatic version of *No Name* to come right.

The first attempt, made in collaboration with W. B. Bernard, was published in 1863 by the Office of *All the Year Round*, soon after the appearance of the novel, which it follows fairly closely. It was in five acts and offered formidable difficulties in performance. Seven years later a second version, the work of Wilkie alone, was published privately. This time the ending was completely altered and two important characters omitted. Still he was dissatisfied and refused an Edinburgh Repertory Theatre permission

† Dorothy L. Sayers. Introduction to *Great Short Stories of Mystery, Detection and Horror.* (Gollancz, 1928).

to produce the play. Finally he invited his friend Wybert Reeve, the actor-manager, to try his hand, giving him *carte blanche*. Wilkie was so pleased with Reeve's adaptation that he abandoned all idea of further tinkering with his own versions, and gave it his blessing. Wybert Reeve spent much of his theatrical life touring Australia and the United States, and it was in Melbourne that the only recorded performances of *No Name* took place.

II

'Armadale'

APART from the fact that *No Name* was selling well the year
1863 began badly for Wilkie. He had thought he would
either 'go mad with the sudden emptiness of head' that
followed the completion of his book, or seek oblivion in Paris, that
city of dissipation.' A renewed attack of gout, making it difficult
for him even to get up and down one flight of stairs, settled the
problem. His mother had been seriously ill, but was slowly mend-
ing, and to her he made light of his own trouble. 'It is not a
violently inflammatory attack. The pain in the foot is easily kept
under by a simple poultice of cabbage leaves covered with oiled
silk.' None the less he determined to try and rid himself of the
complaint once and for all. Dickens, ever ready with medical
advice, had suggested spa-treatment, and Wilkie began to collect
information about Continental spas from a fellow-sufferer. In
March he told his mother of his plan to try Aix-la-Chapelle 'when
I am strong enough for the hateful railway travelling, which
disgusts and depresses me even when I am in health.' If Aix-la-
Chapelle did not suit him he would try a famous spring at Wildbad
in the Black Forest. Taking with him a German travelling-servant
supplied from Coutts' register of couriers he left England in early
April. He travelled via Lille ('a good hotel, and no drawback but
a fiercely-snoring Frenchman in the next bedroom'), and Ghent,
where he 'hobbled out' to inspect the Prince Bishop's Palace,
celebrated in *Quentin Durward*, and reached Nuellen's Hotel, Aix-
la-Chapelle, on April 17th.

Aix suited him admirably at first. It was not gay, but if he
could only get well there he was 'willing to think it Paradise.' He
drove out every day to the hills and exercised his legs in the
bracing air. He found himself as well known as in London, with

German, French and American readers 'all vying in civilities and attention,' and demanding autographs. Recounting this to his mother he added, characteristically, 'Keep this to yourself—it would look like vanity to other people, but I know you will like to hear it.'

The details of the cure are contained in a lighthearted letter to Nina Lehmann:

As for me, I am all over sulphur, inside and out; and if ever a man felt fit for the infernal regions already, I (in respect to the sulphurous part of the Satanic climate) am that man. The invalid custom here is to rise at seven in the morning, to go out and drink the water hot from the spring, and to be entertained between the gulps with a band of music on an empty stomach. You who know me will acquit me of sanctioning by my presence any such uncomfortable proceeding as this. I have an excellent courier. I send him to the spring with a stoppered bottle, and I drink my water horizontally in bed. It was nasty enough at first, but I have got used to it already. The next curative proceeding discloses me, towards the afternoon, in a private stone-pit, up to my middle in the hot sulphur spring; more of the hot water is pouring down on me from a pipe in the ceiling; a worthy German stands by my side, directing the water in a continuous shower on all my weak points with one hand and shampooing me with the other. We exchange cheerful remarks in French (English being all Greek to him and German all Hebrew to me); and, oh, don't we massacre the language of our lively neighbours! In mistakes of *gender*, I am well ahead of the German—it being an old habit of mine out of my love and respect for the fair sex, to make all French words about the gender of which I feel uncertain, feminine words. But in other respects my German friend is far beyond me. This great creature has made an entirely new discovery in the science of language—he does without verbs. 'Trop fort? Bon pour vous fort. Trop chaud? Bon pour vous chaud. Promenade aujourd'hui? Aha! bon pour vous promenade. Encore la jambe—encore le dos—frottement, ah, oui, oui, frottement excellent pour vous. Repos bon pour vous—à votre service, monsieur—bon jour!' What an excellent method! Do think of it for your boys—I would practise it myself if I had my time to begin over again. The results of all these sulphurous proceedings—to return to them for the last time before I get to the end of my letter—are decidedly encouraging in my case.

L

So far I can't wear my boots yet, but I can hobble about with my stick much more freely than I could when I left London; and my general health is benefiting greatly by the change. As for the rest of my life here, it is passed idly enough. The hotel provides me with a delightful open carriage to drive out in, contains a cellar of the best Hock and Moselle wines I ever tasted, and possesses a Parisian cook who encourages my natural gluttony by a continuous succession of entrées which are to be eaten but not described.

The water, he informed his brother Charley, tasted like 'the worst London egg you ever had for breakfast in your life,' and he went on to describe how his doctor, 'a jolly German with a huge pair of gold spectacles and a face like an apple,' smoked a cigar with him every morning after breakfast. Since, besides displaying a reverence for tobacco, the doctor allowed 'all wines provided they are of the best vintages, and all cookery provided it is thoroughly good,' we can recognise without much difficulty the original of Herr Grosse, the ophthalmic surgeon of *Poor Miss Finch*.

Wilkie's stay at Aix was clouded by news of the death of his great friend Augustus Egg. Egg's health had long been giving cause for anxiety and his friends had persuaded him to spend the winter in the milder climate of Algeria. Wilkie now learned that he had died just before he planned to return, and lay buried on a hillside overlooking Algiers. To Holman Hunt, who brought the news, Wilkie exclaimed: 'So I shall never any more shake that dear hand and look into that beloved face!' Dickens, too, was deeply affected and sent Wilkie a long letter recalling their happy association with the 'Kernel,' concluding, 'We must close up the ranks and march on.'

After a month, though somewhat better in health, he was far from cured, and decided to move on to Wildbad. Situated by a mountain stream in the heart of the Black Forest, this little town, hardly more than a village, was dominated by palatial hotels and 'a Bath House as big as Buckingham Palace, and infinitely superior to it in architectural beauty.' It was strange, he reflected, to see all this magnificence, 'and stranger still to think that some of the acutest forms of human misery represent the dismal foundation on which the luxury and grandeur are built up. Paralysis comes here and pays the bills which encourage the enterprising landlord to add to the size of his palace of an hotel. Rheumatism puts its aching hand in its pocket with a groan, and justifies the Town Council in keeping up the splendour of the Bath-House.' Here he underwent a month's course of a bath a day, which roused every lurking ache and pain. The result of this martyrdom, he was persuaded, would be to drive out the gout from its very sources. He left for home about the middle of June, 1863, 'unquestionably better and on the road, I hope, to recovery at last.' It was a vain hope.

Since completing *No Name* he had written nothing at all. In ordinary circumstances this would have mattered little since he had earned sufficient money to enable him to take a prolonged rest. There were, however, other considerations. As long ago as July, 1861, he had been approached by George Smith, who had never ceased to regret having missed the chance of publishing *The Woman in White*. Deciding that there would be no mistake this time, Smith put in a pre-emptive bid of £5,000 for the copyright of 'a work of fiction a little longer than *The Woman in White*,' to follow *No Name* and to be published serially in *The Cornhill*. Telling Charles Ward of the offer Wilkie wrote: 'No living novelist (except Dickens) has had such an offer as this for one book.† If I only live to earn the money, I have a chance of putting something by against a rainy day, or a turn in the public caprice, or any other literary misfortune.' A week later, he was able to write in triumph to his mother:

> 'The five thousand pound negotiation is settled. I signed the agreement on Saturday morning. The first monthly part of the new book to be delivered in manuscript on the 1st of December, 1862—the fifteen remaining parts to follow regularly each month—and the five thousand pounds to be paid, as the novel is written, in monthly instalments—no bills at long dates, and no difficulties or complications of any kind. Smith & Elder have dealt with me like princes.'

As George Smith intended, the figure was beyond all possibility of competition from *All the Year Round*. Dickens, though disap-

† At the time of writing (August, 1861) this was probably correct. A few months later, however, Smith, Elder offered George Eliot £10,000 for the rights of *Romola*. When the book turned out to be less than the stipulated length she accepted a figure of £7,000.

pointed at losing his most successful serial-writer, was very reasonable and fully approved his going to *The Cornhill*. Smith stated that he was also prepared to bid for the book rights of *No Name* and although these were secured by Sampson Low, Smith's elder's intervention was certainly responsible for pushing up the price to £3,000. Well might Wilkie invite his mother to consider him '(if life and health last) in the light of a wealthy novelist.'

By the summer of 1862 it had become clear that *No Name* could not be finished before the end of the year, and he was forced to ask Smith for a postponement. Nor did the state of his health in the New Year encourage him to embark on a long serial. On March, 19th, 1863, he wrote: 'The Smith & Elder's book is put off again—not by any means given up. They have behaved most kindly and considerately about it'; and three months later he received a letter from Smith allowing him until December 1st to send in the first number. On his return from Wildbad he was in high hopes of being able to get down to work again, and at last had a basic idea for the new novel. Patient George Smith merely asked him to state in the coming October whether he might advertise the book as beginning in *The Cornhill* in the New Year—more than twelve months late.

It was desirable during this hiatus in his writing that Wilkie's name should be kept before the public, and he accordingly arranged for Sampson Low to publish a selection of his articles from *Household Words* and *All the Year Round*. A letter written in August, 1863, to his publishers, in referring to 'the liberal promptitude with which you have met my wishes' and confirming acceptance of 'terms suggested by myself,' makes it clear that he had again driven a good bargain. The two volumes of *My Miscellanies* appeared the following November.

His reputation as a journalist had brought him some months earlier an offer from a new quarter. Strahan, the publisher, was about to establish the magazine *Good Words* and approached Wilkie through John Hollingshead with a view to his taking on the editorship. Two considerations led him to decline the offer, his obligations to Smith, Elder and the state of his health. Replying to Hollingshead on the 15th January, 1863, he considered that it would be unfair to *The Cornhill* if he were to divide his labours in the manner proposed. The letter continues:

'I could not consent, in justice to Messrs. Strahan and in justice to my own sense of responsibility, to undertake the conductorship of the new journal unless I exercised a regular supervision over the contents of each week's number before publication, and unless I rendered such assistance to my fellow-labourers in the way of suggestion (where suggestion was wanted) as might assist in giving the journal a character and position of its own in the public estimation. In the present state of my health—which is very far from satisfactory or assuring—I should not be equal to meet such a demand on my resources as this (and I know, by experience, that the demand would certainly come), at a time when the mental strain of writing a long serial story, in a form of publication out of my customary practice, would be laid on me for many months together. The necessity of husbanding my energies for the present is a necessity which I have good reason to know is not to be trifled with.'

He nursed himself carefully through the summer, with a week at Gad's Hill, a visit to the Lehmanns, and a trip to Cowes with Pigott to hire a yacht for a month. Part of the new story was to be set in the Isle of Man and he wanted to sail there if possible. The boat was hired, but they got no further than Torquay. 'All my nervous pains and susceptibilities to changes in the temperature increased as soon as I left the shore. For ten days and nights I stuck by the vessel in spite of them. But time did nothing to acclimatise me to the penetrating dampness of the sea-air.' The laborious spa-treatment had achieved nothing after all. It was a bitter disappointment. There was nothing for it but to ask Smith for yet another postponement and 'to run for it before the winter sets in,' to Naples and perhaps to Sicily. Any delay was preferable to another breakdown. As for the book, he was still under forty and reckoned that he could afford to wait.

He was, however, determined to see the Isle of Man, 'the one inaccessible place left in the world.' Accompanied by Caroline and 'little Carrie,' he reached Douglas at the end of August. The steamer trip had been tiresome—'rain half the way across, and no room below, if I had been inclined to venture there. Tide out when we got there—disembarkation in boats—fearful noise and confusion—an old lady tumbled into the water, and fished up again by her venerable heels.' The Douglas hotels were 'crammed with

12. Harley Street. W,
21st April 1864

Gentlemen

On the other side, I return
you the notice of my life for the
new edition of "Men of the Time".
I have made certain alterations
and additions — but by removing
two sentences at the end (which
it is not absolutely necessary to retain)
I have avoided increasing the
length of the notice, while I have
I hope added to its fulness and
accuracy.

Faithfully yours
Wilkie Collins

To
Messrs. Routledge Warne & Routledge

SPECIMEN OF COLLINS' HANDWRITING
Autograph letter to Messrs. Routledge

thousands of rough and ready visitors from the manufacturing districts'; every third shop was a spirit-shop and every second inhabitant drunk. It was, he decided, too late in the year to be visiting northern islands in his rheumatic condition. He especially wished to see the Calf of Man, and the Sound separating it from the main island. After an unsuccessful attempt to reach the place by boat, he travelled across country in the hotel's jaunting-car and found the scene 'wild and frightful, just what I wanted—everything made for my occult literary purposes.' He was prepared to go to immense trouble to have his local colour accurate, and always preferred to rely on his own experience. Having obtained his objective he hurried back to London, only to find that the penalty for this ill-advised excursion was another sharp attack of gout.

It was with a sigh of relief that he left England early in October, with Caroline and her daughter, bound for a warmer climate. From Marseilles they travelled by 'vetturino' to Genoa, following the route he had taken with his parents nearly thirty years before. Nice, in the meantime, had grown thrice as large and was unrecognisable. Mentone and San Remo were carefully inspected as possible havens in the event of disturbances in Southern Italy driving them northward again. Nothing was threatening yet, but in a newly-established kingdom whose lazy population was being conscripted to serve in the Italian army, anything could happen. Wilkie believed in looking ahead, and in securing his line of retreat. By the time they reached Genoa his health was already improving in the mild climate. He could walk up the hills on the road faster than the horses could follow, and he no longer got into bed at night 'with the infirm deliberation of a man of seventy or eighty years old.' Indeed the mosquitoes were proving more troublesome than the pangs of rheumatism. Intent on proving that his ingenuity embraced more than the construction of plots, he devised a 'protective night-dress' for himself.

I have got a small muslin balloon which ties under my beard, and encloses my whole head and face—without touching nose, eyes or mouth, and I have the sleeves of my nightgown sewn up with a couple of old cambric pocket handkerchiefs. In this extraordinary costume I can hear the mosquitoes humming all round me with the most supreme indifference. When I wake, in the grey of the morning, I see them crawling over my muslin balloon and my cambric mufflers, trying hard to find a way in—failing at every point—stopping to consider in 'indignation-meetings' of twos and threes—expressing their sentiments in a sound like a very small wind at a very great distance—and then flying away in disgust.

From Genoa they took a coasting steamer to Civita Vecchia en route for Rome. The sea-trip was a mistake. At Pisa the sirocco descended and with it rain, fog and damp which brought on sciatica 'in both hams at once.' Then the wind blew up and 'the two Carolines suffered sea-martyrdom.' The elder Caroline was so ill that she could not be moved from the deck all night, and was feeling the effects a week later. A promise was extracted from Wilkie that he would avoid night-voyages in future. After only a week in Rome they went on to Naples, a city he loved dearly, with every intention of remaining there for some months. Naples proved another disappointment. Though the weather was glorious he found it too relaxing: 'My appetite is beginning to fail me,' he wrote, 'I don't sleep as well as I did, and my foot . . . is getting stiff and painful again.' A fortnight was enough to convince him that Naples was doing him harm instead of good. He was warned against Sicily as being still more relaxing and though recommended to visit Cairo, decided to turn northwards. He would try Florence because he felt that he needed 'stringing up with a little brisk bracing cold air.' When they reached Rome, however, he discovered that Rome could supply just the dry, cold air that he needed, and here they stayed for nearly three months.

It seems to have been on the whole a happy three months. They lived in great comfort in a five-room apartment on the first floor of the Hotel des Iles Britanniques. Rome was full of English folk with whom he politely exchanged cards, pleading illness 'when there is a threatening of anything more serious than cards.' Thus he was able to avoid their dances and dinner-parties and to live his life in Rome in his own way. The Opera, for which he was full of praise, provided most of the entertainment he wanted. For two shillings he could hear the finest performances of Verdi from the best stall in the house, and there was 'no infernal fuss and expense of evening costume.' It was a great advance on London where, he complained, they would not let him in unless he spent a guinea and put on a pair of black trousers. The one drawback of Rome was the presence of the French garrison which shattered 'with incessant martial noises' on drums and bugles the quiet of the ancient city. 'Nothing is serious to a Frenchman,' he wrote, 'except soldiering—and nothing astonishes him but the spectacle of his own bravery.'

As his health improved so his spirits rose. On his birthday, 'January 8th, 1864 (Feast of St. Collins),' he wrote to his mother:

If your reckoning is right—which I have a melancholy satisfaction in doubting—I am now writing to you at the mature age of *Forty*. Mercy on us! Who would ever have thought it? Here is forty come upon me—grey hairs springing fast, especially about the temples—rheumatism and gout familiar enemies for some time past—all the worst signs of middle-age sprouting out on me—and yet, in spite of it all, I don't *feel* old. I have no regular habits, no respectable prejudices, no tendency to go to sleep after dinner, no loss of appetite for public amusements, none of the melancholy sobrieties of sentiment, in short, which are supposed to be proper to middle-age. Surely there is some mistake? Are you and I really as old as you suppose?

The letter goes on to describe a visit to one of Rome's smaller churches where, to his surprise and delight, he found children preaching:

Children of five, six and seven years old, who had learnt their little sermons, and their little gesticulations and genuflexions and crossings, and let them off at the congregation with perfect solemnity and composure. As each child ended, the congregation cried 'Bravo!' and the next child (male and female indiscriminately) popped up into the temporary pulpit like a Jack-in-the-Box. I ventured on asking a Priest near me (I am on excellent terms with the Priests as we all take snuff together) what it meant. He said—'You read the New Testament, my dear Sir? You remember the passage, "Out of the mouths of Babes and Sucklings, etc., etc."? Very good! There *are* the babes and sucklings! And what have you got to say against *that*?' I had nothing to say against it—and I cried 'Bravo!' with the rest of the congregation.

The same letter makes reference to Thackeray's sudden death, of which he had just learned: 'I, as you know, never became intimate

with him—but we always met on friendly and pleasant terms. He
has left a great name, most worthily won, and he has been spared
the slow misery of a lingering death-bed.' At the same time he
mentions a personal loss he has suffered in the death, from gastric
fever, of his travelling-servant, to whom he had become very
attached.

Wilkie could hardly avoid interesting himself in Italian politics,
and exchanged views with Dickens on the immediate prospects of
the new regime. The main phase of the Risorgimento was over, and
only the Papal State of Rome and the Austrian-held province of
Venice stood in the way of the complete unification of Italy. The
Pope, supported by French arms, was to defy Garibaldi successfully for another six years. In Rome the political situation was
reflected in a bewildering confusion of currencies, of which Wilkie
wrote to Charles Ward: 'There is one price for the Pope's gold
and another for Victor Emanuel's and another for Louis Napoleon's
and another for silver—and I have opened an account with Free-
born, and have got a primitive Roman cheque-book—and when
I don't make mistakes (which I generally do) I get paper-money to
pay in, and paper-money is at par, and I save I don't know how
much.'

Caroline had apparently been unwell for he adds:

My little domestic landscape begins to look brighter at last.
Caroline is very much better—able to walk out, and beginning
to show some faint signs of colour in her cheeks. She wants to
be at home again (how like cats women are!) and bids me tell
you with her kind regards that she wishes she was pouring you
out a glass of dry sherry on a nice gloomy English Sunday afternoon. Caroline junior has had a dirty tongue, but we threw in
a little pill and fired off a small explosion of Gregory's Powder,
and she is now in higher spirits than ever, and astonishes the
Roman public by the essentially British plumpness of her cheeks
and calves. As for me, I go on thriving in the cold.

It is of some interest that, whereas he had often in the past asked
Ward to send on his letter for Mrs. Collins to read, on this occasion
he appended a brief note to be cut off the foot of the letter and
forwarded to her, merely saying that he was well. Most probably
he did not wish her to see the references to Caroline and her
daughter.

At last he felt well enough to begin the rough outline of his book for George Smith, to be called *Armadale*. Ideas were coming to him 'thicker and thicker' and he was satisfied that he had a fine subject. By the time he returned to England in March most of the important preliminary work was done and on April 20th, 1864, he told his mother: 'After much pondering over the construction of the story I positively sat down with a clean sheet of paper before me, and began to write it on Monday last. So far my progress is slow and hesitating enough—not for want of knowing what I have to do, but for want of practice. After a year and a half of total literary abstinence, it is not wonderful that my hand should be out. Patience and time will I hope soon give me back my old dexterity—and meanwhile it is something to have begun.' He advised Smith that *Armadale* could be announced as beginning in the November issue of *The Cornhill*—almost two years after the date first proposed—and made the pleasant discovery that one monthly part for *The Cornhill* was only the equivalent of two weekly parts for *All the Year Round*.

During the spring and summer he made fairly good progress with the new novel, determined this time to have a substantial portion written before the serial commenced. He found time to visit Stratford-on-Avon with Dickens and Browning for the tercentenary of Shakespeare's birth, and once or twice went down to stay with Dickens at Gad's Hill. In August he was in Norfolk 'studying localities' for the book, and taking time off to go sailing with Charles Ward and Pigott. About this time he was contemplating the purchase of a boat of his own, but never in fact acquired one.

He had made his mind up to leave Harley Street. For one thing it was noisy, and he was becoming more and more sensitive to noise. In a short time he had lost 'five working days through nothing but pianos at the back of the house and organs, bagpipes, bands and Punches in front.' Although at one time he thought there was nothing for it but the Temple, they managed to find a reasonably quiet flat a 9, Melcombe Place, off Dorset Square, to which they moved about Christmas, 1864, 'for the time being.' In fact they remained for nearly three years. This was the first of his addresses at which Mrs. Graves openly resided according to the London Directories.

With the onset of winter he began to worry about his health again and persuaded Frank Beard to call in a brain and nerve specialist. He was told that nothing was seriously wrong, only a 'gouty irritation' which had upset his nerves. The doctor placed him on a new regimen, which he detailed in a letter to his mother: 'Dine lightly at two—work from four to seven or eight o'clock—go out—come back for supper at half past nine or ten. Bed between eleven and twelve. Light breakfast—read and idle between breakfast and two o'clock. Eat light things—game poultry—eggs, farinaceous puddings—*no lean meat*—claret and hock to drink—and for the present no exerting myself with society and dinner parties.'

Armadale began in serial form in November as scheduled and made a good impression from the start. The following month it opened in America in *Harper's Monthly*, and probably saved that magazine from extinction. Its sales had fallen disastrously during the period following the Civil War and Harper Brothers were considering bringing it to an end. There was, however, a great increase in demand for the issue containing the first instalment of *Armadale*, and before the story was completed the magazine had regained its former circulation. Dickens, who had read the proofs during a week-end they spent together at Dover, 'prognosticated certain success,' and Wilkie was almost more pleased to learn from George Smith that the printers were highly interested in the story; for to them, he wrote, 'all books represent in the first instance nothing but weary hard work.' He had hoped to persuade Millais to do the illustrations, but Millais was swamped with work and he fell back upon George Housman Thomas, a bank-note engraver who also illustrated Trollope's *Last Chronicle of Barset*.

The following year, 1865, was uneventful. He took Caroline to Paris for a week or two in February and went to the theatre every night. In April, he was invited to take the chair at the Twentieth Anniversary Festival of the Royal General Theatrical Fund, where he spoke at some length. E. M. Blanchard, the dramatic critic, reported that he was a good chairman and made an excellent speech. Not long afterwards Rossetti invited him to join a committee which was organising a testimonial to George Cruikshank. It may be remembered that Cruikshank, previously a heavy drinker, had been converted some twenty years earlier to total abstinence.

As with many such converts it had been a case of substituting intolerance for intemperance, and he became one of teetotalism's most violent advocates; at a dinner he was apt at any moment to make a vehement attack on any fellow-guest who was drinking anything but water. It is hard to see why Rossetti imagined that such a *bon viveur* as Wilkie would wish to be associated, however indirectly, with the Temperance Movement. He cannot have been altogether surprised when Wilkie declined in somewhat sharp terms. He had a general objection to Testimonials, he said, and as for this particular one, 'I cannot honestly say that I feel the necessary respect for Mr. Cruikshank's use of his abilities, during the period in which he has been before the public in connection with the "Temperance Movement." '

In the meantime *Armadale*, to which he devoted infinite care, was proceeding on its course and most of his time was occupied with keeping three months ahead of instalments, the minimum safe period in his view. Even the month of August was spent at home, and he discovered the delights of London in August. 'It is wonderfully quiet—all the people who interrupt me are away . . . and I roam the empty streets and inhale the delightful London air (so much healthier than those pretentious humbugs the seaside breezes!) and meet nobody, and come back with the blessed conviction that I have *not* got to dress to go out to dinner.'

Armadale was finished early in April, 1866, after two years in the writing, a good deal longer than he took over any other book. 'I was never so excited myself,' he wrote, 'when finishing a story as I was this time. Miss Gwilt's death quite upset me.' He had managed to save a certain amount of money out of Smith, Elder's substantial monthly payments, and informed Charles Ward that he now had £1,500 invested in 'the Funds. About as much saved from *Armadale* as Marshal & Snelgrove make in a quarter of an hour by the brains and industry of other people. If I live I will take a shop—and appeal to the backs or bellies (I have not decided which) instead of the brains of my fellow creatures.' His other news is that he is reported dead in France, and is requested to deny the rumour by a Frenchman who has 'betted ten bottles of champagne' that it is false. He celebrated the completion of his labours by going to Paris for ten days with Frederick Lehmann, where he was quite happy to idle in the open air and enjoy the comfort of his favourite small hotel. 'And yet,' he told his mother, 'such is the perversity of mankind, I am half sorry to have parted from my poor dear book.'

The novel was published in two volumes about the end of May, 1866, and dedicated to John Forster 'in affectionate remembrance of a friendship which is associated with some of the happiest years of my life.' Since Wilkie was incapable of irony, at least in his personal relationships, this gesture towards one whose hostility he must have recognised was somewhat generous. Though Forster brought himself to pay a handsome tribute to the book, there is no sign of his having grasped the olive-branch. On the contrary his jealousy of Wilkie Collins continued to smoulder for the rest of his life.

Armadale is Wilkie Collins' longest and in some respects his most ambitious novel. If the plot of *The Woman in White* is complex, that of *Armadale* is labyrinthine. The success of the earlier book told him that the reading public had an appetite for sensation, and in *Armadale* he set out to provide a banquet. Although there is little actual mystery it is an exciting, well-told story. About it hangs that tense, thundery atmosphere of sensationalism which Wilkie Collins could so effectively conjure up. And yet the book is a failure. The fact is that he had deliberately set himself the task of eclipsing *The Woman in White*, a task that proved beyond his powers. In the end the very surfeit of sensation antagonises the reader, and the unbridled use of coincidences, especially when they contribute nothing to the plot, goes far to destroy his receptiveness. It is, however, a failure which comes near to success; if Wilkie had not over-reached himself in his search for the last word in sensationalism, if he had brought himself to discard one or two improbable situations and to simplify the plot slightly, what a book *Armadale* might have been!

The mainspring of the story is the idea of fatality. Wilkie's obsession with Doom is given full rein. The course of the plot is foreshadowed in a Dream which the hero, Allan Armadale, dreams aboard a stranded wreck. This dream is carefully noted down by him on waking, in true Collins fashion, and even subdivided into seventeen sections. The earlier sections represent a hint of things past, as yet unknown to the dreamer, the remainder a forewarning of things to come. There is a characteristic of melodrama, cited by

T. S. Eliot as typical of Wilkie Collins, that of 'delaying longer than one would conceive it possible to delay, a conclusion which is inevitable and wholly foreseen.' No better example could be found than the plot of *Armadale*, in which each of the prophecies of the Dream is fulfilled in its turn.

The book is prolific in incident, rich in character and atmosphere. No summary of the plot of this most tortuous of romances could do justice to its author's inventiveness. It opens with a Prologue in which Allan's father makes his dying confession, at some length, in the bedroom of an inn in the Black Forest. It is typical of Wilkie's prodigality in the matter of plot and incident that there would be in this prologue alone material enough for a whole sensation-novel whereas it provides little more than the background to the story proper. In his essay on Wilkie Collins, Swinburne wrote: 'The prologue is so full of interest and promise that the expectations of its readers may have been unduly stimulated; but the sequel, astonishingly ingenious and inventive though it is, is scarcely perhaps in perfect keeping with the anticipations thus ingeniously aroused.'

In Lydia Gwilt he presents a full-dress portrait of the '*femme fatale*,' unscrupulous, fascinating, vicious. It is a difficult thing to do convincingly, and it would be idle to pretend that Miss Gwilt, memorable and striking though she be, is an entirely satisfactory figure. If he was inhibited to some extent by the literary conventions of the time, many critics held that in his handling of this vicious creature, he had in fact overstepped the limits of good taste. None the less, Miss Gwilt does succeed in dominating the book, as he intended she should, and her half-unwilling love for Midwinter is strangely real and moving. She is a figure, said Swinburne, who would have won the deepest sympathy from English readers had her creator possessed a French instead of an English name.

With the lesser characters Wilkie's touch is surer, and if they are mostly unpleasant they entertain no less on that account. The Pedgifts, father and son, country solicitors, pit their wits against Miss Gwilt's in a manner which recalls those other duels between Fosco and Marian, and between Mrs. Lecount and Captain Wragge. Their clerk, Bashwood, seedy and downtrodden, nurses a hopeless passion for Lydia Gwilt which, from being at first merely comic, develops almost in spite of the author into something deeply pathetic. Here is our first glimpse of him:

> He was a lean, elderly, miserably respectable man. He wore a poor old black dress-coat, and a cheap brown wig, which made no pretence of being his own natural hair. Short black trousers clung like attached old servants round his wizen legs; and rusty black gaiters hid all they could of his knobbed ungainly feet. Black crêpe added its mite to the decayed and dingy wretchedness of his old beaver hat; black mohair in the obsolete form of a stock, drearily encircled his neck and rose as high as his haggard jaws. The one morsel of colour he carried about him, was a lawyer's bag of blue serge as lean and limp as himself.

Finally there is Mrs. Oldershaw, Lydia Gwilt's confidante and accomplice, a Hogarthian figure who carries on the Ladies Toilette Repository in Diana Street, Pimlico. It was S. M. Ellis who discovered† that Wilkie had based this character upon a certain Madame Rachel Leverson, who had a flourishing business at her Beauty Parlour at 47a, New Bond Street. Here large sums of money were extracted from gullible women whose beauty she claimed to be able to preserve, or enhance, by means of various cosmetic preparations with romantic names, and a wide range of remedial treatments such as the 'Arabian bath.' At this time Madame Rachel, to whom blackmail and procuring did not come amiss, was at the peak of her prosperity, occupying her own box at the Opera and advertising herself as 'Purveyor to the Queen.' It was not until two years after the publication of *Armadale* that she was convicted of fraud after a sensational trial, and sentenced to five years' penal servitude. Unabashed, she re-opened her shop on her release and continued to prosper for another six years, at the end of which she again found herself at the Old Bailey. At this trial it was revealed that the Arabian baths consisted of bran and hot water, and that the wildly expensive 'Jordan Water' came from the pump in the backyard of her shop. Madame Rachel received a further five-year sentence and died before completing it in Woking Prison.‡

† *Wilkie Collins, le Fanu and others.* S. M. Ellis. (*Constable*, 1931).
‡ A detailed account of Mme. Rachel Leverson's career is included in *Six Criminal Women* by Elizabeth Jenkins. (*Sampson Low*, 1949).

Mrs. Oldershaw was certainly no more fantastic than her counterpart in real life.

Collins the scene-painter is much in evidence, always ready with his careful brush-strokes to lend realism and colour to the happenings of melodrama. Here he sets the scene for *Armadale*'s famous Dream :

It was past two; the moon was waning; and the darkness that comes before dawn was beginning to gather round the wreck. Behind Allan, as he now stood looking out from the elevation of the mizen-top, spread the broad and lonely sea. Before him were the low, black, lurking rocks, and the broken waters of the channel, pouring white and angry into the vast calm of the westward ocean beyond. On the right hand, heaved back grandly from the waterside, were the rocks and precipices with their little table-lands of grass between; the sloping downs, and upward rolling heath solitudes of the Isle of Man. On the left hand rose the craggy sides of the Islet of the Calf—here, rent wildly into deep black chasms; there, lying low under long sweeping acclivities of grass and heath. No sound rose, no light was visible on either shore. The black lines of the topmost masts of the wreck looked shadowy and faint in the darkening mystery of the sky; the land-breeze had dropped; the small shoreward waves fell noiseless; far and near no sound was audible but the cheerless bubbling of the broken water ahead, pouring through the awful hush of silence in which earth and ocean waited for the coming day.

If *Armadale* falls short of his best work in certain respects, it remains a powerful contribution to the fiction of the Victorian age.

As might have been expected it caused a considerable flutter on its appearance. Wilkie himself had foreseen something of the kind when he wrote in his brief preface : 'Readers in particular will, I have some reason to suppose, be here and there disturbed—perhaps even offended—by finding that *Armadale* oversteps in more than one direction, the narrow limits within which they are disposed to restrict the development of modern fiction—if they can.' If he hoped by these words to disarm criticism on moral grounds, he failed, as he failed on other occasions. In the *Athenaeum* H. F. Chorley, veteran music-critic and reviewer, wrote :

M

It is not pleasant to speak as we must speak of this powerful story; but in the interest of everything that is to be cherished in life, in poetry, in art, it is impossible to be over-explicit in the expression of judgment.

He could hardly have been more explicit than the strident reviewer of *The Spectator*:

The fact that there are such characters as he has drawn, and actions such as he has described, does not warrant his over-stepping the limits of decency, and revolting every human sentiment. This is what *Armadale* does. It gives us for its heroine a woman fouler than the refuse of the streets, who has lived to the ripe age of 35, and through the horrors of forgery, murder, theft, bigamy, gaol and attempted suicide, without any trace being left on her beauty . . . [This] is frankly told in a diary which, but for its unreality, would be simply loathsome, and which needs all the veneer of Mr. Wilkie Collins's easy style and allusive sparkle to disguise its actual meaning.

Five years or so later, when the hubbub had died down, an article in *Vanity Fair* described *Armadale* as 'perhaps his finest work.' An admirer of our own day was T. S. Eliot, who wrote:†

The one of Collins' novels which we should choose as the most typical, or as the best of the more typical, and which we should recommend as a specimen of the melodramatic fiction of the epoch, is *Armadale*. It has no merit beyond melodrama, and it has every merit that melodrama can have. If Miss Gwilt did not have to bear such a large part of the burden of revealing her own villainy, the construction would be almost perfect. Like most of Collins' novels, it has the immense—and nowadays more and more rare—merit of being never dull.

After some ten years on the shelf, his play *The Frozen Deep* was accepted in September, 1866, by the Wigans for production at the Olympic about Christmas. Soon afterwards he made arrange-ments for a trip to Rome with his friend Edward Pigott in October, intending to return at the beginning of December in time to see the final rehearsals. Then the opening production of the Olympic season failed, and the management decided to put on *The Frozen*

† *Selected Essays, 1917-1932* (Wilkie Collins and Dickens). T. S. Eliot (*Faber and Faber*).

Deep in October instead of Christmas. In an effort to save time and money he approached Dickens with a view to procuring the scenery of the amateur production, only to learn that it had been cut down into small panels and was virtually useless. Though he would be abroad on the first night—since Pigott could not postpone his holiday—he read the play to the cast and supervised the earlier rehearsals. To make matters worse he caught a bad cold which seized him 'by the nose, teeth, face, throat and chest in succession.'

Finally, after dashing down to Tunbridge Wells to say goodbye to Mama Collins and coming back 'to sketch the play-bill and hear the Manager's last words,' he contrived to leave with Pigott as planned. They stayed a day in Paris where he was able to discuss a dramatic version of *Armadale* which his friend Regnier, of the Théâtre Français, was preparing for the French stage. They travelled through Switzerland and over the Splügen Pass to Milan. From Milan he wrote a long letter to Nina Lehmann—henceforth invariably addressed as 'the Padrona'—who was wintering at Pau.

. . . I have been living in a whirlwind, and have only dropped out of the vortex in this place. In plain English the first quarter of an hour which I have had at my disposal since you wrote to me, is a quarter of an hour tonight, in this very damp and dreary town. Last night my travelling companion (Pigott) and I went to a public ball here. We entered by a long dark passage, passed through a hall ornamented with a large stock of fenders, grates, and other ironmongery for sale on either side, found ourselves in a spacious room lit by three oil lamps, with *two* disreputable females smoking cigars, ten or a dozen depressed men, about four hundred empty chairs in a circle, one couple polking in that circle, and nothing else, on my sacred word of honour, nothing else going on! Tonight I am wiser. I stay at the hotel and write to you.

After an account of his feverish activities before leaving England, he presents the Padrona with the latest morsel of gossip from literary circles, concerning Anthony Trollope's brother:

We were to have gone and stayed with Thomas Trollope in his new villa at Florence. But a woman has got in his way. A charming person of this sex was governess to the daughter of Thomas Trollope, widower—and Thomas Trollope is going to marry her tomorrow at Paris—and so, there is an end of the

Florence scheme. I don't complain—I am all for Love myself—
and this sort of thing speaks volumes for women, for surely a
man at a mature age, with a growing daughter, doesn't marry
again without knowing what he is about, and without remem-
brances of Mrs. Number One which surround as with a halo
Mrs. Number Two? But this is mere speculation.

The letter concludes with a word of advice, and some incidental
observations on the subject of fashion:

Cultivate your appetite, and your appetite will reward you.
Purchase becoming (and warm) things for the neck and chest.
Rise superior to the devilish delusion which makes women think
that their feet cannot possibly look pretty in thick boots. I have
studied the subject, and I say they *can*. Men understand these
things; Mr. Worth, of Paris, dresses the fine French ladies who
wear the 'Falballa,' and regulates the fashions of Europe. He is
about to start 'comforters' and hobnail boots for the approaching
winter. In two months' time it will be indecent for a woman to
show her neck at night, and if you don't make a frightful noise
at every step you take on the pavement you abrogate your
position as woman, wife and mother in the eyes of all Europe.
Is this exaggerated? No! a thousand times no! It is horrible—but
it is the truth.

While *The Frozen Deep* was being given for the first time at the
Olympic, 'and the respectable British Public is hissing or applaud-
ing me, as the case may be,' Wilkie was at Bologna on his way
to Rome. In fact the public applauded with some enthusiasm.
Charles Reade, who was present at the first night in a box, wrote
in his diary: 'The play poorly acted. It is a pretty play but wanted
a head at rehearsal. Too much narrative; but after all, original and
interesting, and the closing scene great and pathetic.' After two
or three weeks in Rome, Wilkie had just completed plans to return
to England via Pau, where he had promised to stay for a few
days with Mrs. Lehmann, when he received serious news from
the manager of the Olympic. In spite of the first night reception
and a moderately favourable press, *The Frozen Deep* was failing
to attract audiences, and Wigan wanted to discuss with the author
what was to be done. There was nothing for it but to cancel his
arrangements and get back to London as quickly as possible.
Accordingly he and Pigott caught the next steamer from Civita

Vecchia to Marseilles, continuing by rail to Paris. They stayed the night at Macon ('to rest after ten hours' shaking on the railway') and in Paris Wilkie had another talk with Regnier. The day after his arrival in London he went to the theatre and examined the accounts, which showed that the play had not even covered its expenses. There was no alternative but to take it off before Christmas after a run of about six weeks. For the author there was 'not a sixpence.'

He wrote to the Padrona to tell her of his disappointment:

The play is (I am *told*, for I have not yet had the courage to go and see it) beautifully got up, and very well acted. But the enlightened British Public declares it to be '*slow.*' There isn't an atom of slang or vulgarity in the whole piece from beginning to end; no female legs are shown in it; Richard Wardour doesn't get up after dying and sing a comic song; sailors are represented in the Arctic regions, and there is no hornpipe danced, and no sudden arrival of 'the pets of the ballet' to join the dance in the costume of Esquimaux maidens; finally, all the men on the stage *don't* marry all the women on the stage at the end, and nobody addresses the audience and says, If our kind friends here tonight will only encourage us by their applause, there are brave hearts among us which will dare the perils for many a night yet of—'The Frozen Deep.'

For these reasons, best of women, I have failed. Is my tail put down? No—a thousand times no! I am at work on the 'dramatic' *Armadale*, and I will take John Bull by the scruff of the neck, and force him into the theatre to see it—before or after it has been played in French. I don't know which—but into the theatre John Bull shall go. I have some ideas of advertising next time that will make the public hair stand on end. And so enough, and more than enough, of theatrical matters.

Oh, I wanted you so at Rome—in the Protestant cemetery— don't start! No ghosts—only a cat. I went to show my friend Pigott the grave of the illustrious Shelley. Approaching the resting-place of the divine poet in a bright sunlight, the finest black Tom you ever saw discovered at an incredible distance that a catanthropist had entered the cemetery—rushed up at a gallop, with his tail at right angles to his spine—turned over on his back with his four paws in the air, and said in the language of cats: 'Shelley be hanged! Come and tickle me!' I stooped and tickled him. We were both profoundly affected.

Is this all I have to tell you about Rome? By no means. Then why don't I go on and tell it? Because it is five o'clock—the British muffin-bell is ringing—the dismal British Sunday is closing in. I have promised to dine with the Benzons† (where I shall meet Fred), and to take Charley and Katie (who is in the doctor's hands again) on my way. I must walk to keep my horrid corpulence down, and the time is slipping away . . .

The 'dramatic *Armadale*' to which he refers, did not achieve an English stage production, although Regnier's adaptation may have been produced in Paris. Wilkie had sent the manuscript to Dickens some months earlier for his comments, which were frankly given. He considered the play technically brilliant, but feared that almost every situation was dangerous and likely to be unacceptable to an English audience. It was a radically different version of the novel which eventually reached the London stage under the title of *Miss Gwilt*.

† Frederick Lehmann's sister and brother-in-law.

12

'The Moonstone'

THE year 1867 provides the first evidence of a growing friendship between Wilkie and Charles Reade, which was to have its effect upon the subsequent work of both novelists. Since most writers of the period found their way to Gad's Hill sooner or later, they had almost certainly been acquainted for several years, and we know that Reade had a great respect for both Dickens and Collins. One of Reade's most powerful novels, *Griffith Gaunt*, had been published the year before and had created even more of a stir than *Armadale* on both sides of the Atlantic. In some quarters the greatest exception had been taken to Reade's handling of sexual relationships and he was thought to have infringed the accepted code of decency and good taste. Surprisingly, the most violent criticism came from America, where one publication, *The Round Table*, attacked the novel in terms which, in Reade's opinion, transgressed the limits of fair comment. He retaliated, first with one of those vitriolic pamphlets for which he was famous, entitled *The Prurient Prude*, and secondly with a writ for libel against the proprietors of the magazine. In canvassing his literary colleagues he obtained from Wilkie Collins not only a promise of his support but also an offer to enlist that of Dickens if possible. Accordingly Wilkie sent a copy of *Griffith Gaunt* to Dickens and asked for his considered opinion as soon as possible. A week later the opinion arrived. Neither Reade nor Collins could have derived much satisfaction from it from the standpoint of the forthcoming lawsuit. After a generous tribute to the sincerity and accomplishment of the story, Dickens proceeded to cross-examine himself in the capacity of Editor of a popular magazine concerning the various situations which had given offence. Would he or would he not, as an editor, have passed this or that passage? In every case he came down reluctantly on the side of the critics. In the event neither Dickens nor Wilkie was required to testify in court, and Reade won his suit, being awarded as damages the derisory sum of six American cents.

There is little doubt that Wilkie's sympathetic attitude over the *Griffith Gaunt* affair brought the two novelists closer together. In many ways it was a curious friendship. In temperament they were poles apart. Reade, with his aggressiveness, his erratic disposition and his inability, or unwillingness, to cope with everyday affairs must have been a strange contrast to the quiet, well-mannered, business-like Wilkie Collins. Years later Augustin Daly, the American 'pirate' playwright, described Reade as 'a surly old gentleman,' contrasting him with 'dear, gentle Wilkie Collins.' And yet they had many things in common. They were both prodigious workers, even if their methods differed fundamentally. They shared a certain contempt for the conventions of their day, for the current coin of morality, and each showed his disregard in the open non-conformity of his domestic life. Like Dickens, Reade shared Wilkie's passionate enthusiasm for the theatre. Finally, they shared a zeal for reform which Wilkie had hitherto kept in check, but which, under Reade's influence, was soon to change the whole direction of his work, and to contribute to his steady decline as a novelist.

He devoted the first few months of 1867 to the planning of a new novel, his only relaxation being a brief visit to Paris at the end of February. By June, the first three instalments were complete and on the 30th Dickens wrote to Wills:

> I have heard read the first three numbers of Wilkie's story this morning and have gone minutely through the plot of the rest to the last line. It gives a series of 'narratives,' but it is a very curious story, wild, and yet domestic, with excellent character in it, and great mystery. It is prepared with extraordinary care, and has every chance of being a hit. It is in many respects much better than anything he has done.

He mentions that they have discussed the best time to begin serial publication—for with *The Moonstone* Wilkie returned to *All the Year Round*—and agreed upon mid-December; in fact the opening instalment appeared on January 4th, 1868.

In the meantime there was other work to be done. A few weeks before, on May 1st, Dickens had written to him: 'Of course I know nothing of your arrangements when I ask you the following question: Would you like to do the next Xmas No. with me —we two alone, each taking half? Of course I assume that the money question is satisfactorily disposed of between you and Wills. Equally, of course, I suppose our two names to be appended to the performance. I put this to you, I need hardly say, before having in any way approached the subject in my own mind as to contrivance, character, story, or anything else.'

It was more than six years since they had last worked in collaboration, and Wilkie readily agreed, despite the claims of his own novel. On July 2nd Dickens wrote: 'This is to certify that I, the undersigned, was (for the time being) a drivelling ass when I declared the Christmas Number to be composed of Thirty-two pages. And I do hereby declare that the said Christmas Number is composed of Forty-eight pages, and long and heavy pages too, as I have heretofore proved and demonstrated with the sweat of my brow.' Towards the end of August, Dickens had written the Overture and was passing on to Wilkie, who had just returned from a brief trip to Switzerland with Lehmann, his ideas of the general outline of the plot. Already the rough division of responsibility appears to have been agreed between them:

I have a general idea which I hope will supply the kind of interest we want. Let us arrange to culminate in a wintry flight and pursuit across the Alps, under lonely circumstances, and against warnings. Let us get into all the horrors and dangers of such an adventure under the most terrific circumstances, either escaping from or trying to overtake (the latter, I think) some one, on escaping from or overtaking whom the love, prosperity, and Nemesis of the story depend. There we can get ghostly interest, picturesque interest, breathless interest of time and circumstance, and force the design up to any powerful climax we please. If you will keep this in your mind, as I will in mine, urging the story towards it as we go along, we shall get a very Avalanche of power out of it, and thunder it down on the readers' heads.

The ensuing letters—no less than eight dealing with *No Thoroughfare* are included in *The Letters of Charles Dickens to*

Wilkie Collins—afford a good insight into their method of working together. The next one, dated September 9th, 'requires no answer, and is merely thrown out to be taken up into your meditations'; he suggests one or two minor changes in the plot and notifies a new twist in the section he is working on. The following day he proposes a meeting:

> I don't think I shall have done Wilding's death by that time (I have been steadily at work, but slowly, laying ground); but the Obenreizer-reproduction chapter will be ready to run over. All the points you dwell upon are already in it. It will be an immense point if we can arrange to *start you for a long run, beginning immediately after Wilding's death,* and if I can at the same time be told off to come in, while you are at work, with the Alpine ascent and adventures. *Then,* in two or three days of writing together, we could finish . . . Have you done—or are you doing —the beginning of the chapter 'Exit Wilding'? I shall very soon want it.

Another week and Dickens is 'jogging on (at the pace of a wheelbarrow propelled by a Greenwich Pensioner) at the doomed Wilding,' and a few days later, 'Like you I am working with snail-like slowness . . . But I think I have a good idea. I send it to you with a view to your at odd times Thinking-out of the last Act.' There follows a snatch of dialogue intended for the climax of the story. By October 5th the end is in sight:

> I have brought on Marguerite to the rescue, and I have so left it as that Vendale—to spare her—says it was an accident in the storm, and nothing more. By the way, Obenreizer has received a cut from Vendale, made with his own dagger. This in case you want him with a scar. If you don't, no matter. I have no doubt my Proof of the Mountain adventure will be full of mistakes, as my MS. is not very legible. But you will see what it means. The *Dénouement* I see pretty much as you see it— without further glimpses as yet. The Obenreizer question I will consider (q'ry Suicide?). I have made Marguerite wholly devoted to her lover. Whenever you may give me notice of your being ready, we will appoint to meet here to wind up.

In the middle of all this Wilkie and Caroline had to leave Melcombe Place and find another house. The search is unlikely to have carried him beyond the boundaries of St. Marylebone, to which neighbourhood he remained faithful to the end. Eventually he bought the lease of No. 90, Gloucester Place, near Portman Square, which was to be his home for almost the rest of his life. The house still stands, one of a pleasant Georgian row, distinguished from its neighbours by a chequer-board flight of steps but unadorned as yet by any commemorative plaque.† They moved in early in September and on the 10th he wrote to Lehmann from his mother's cottage:

> When your letter reached me, I had an old house to leave— a new house to find—that new house to bargain for, and take —lawyers and surveyors to consult—British workmen to employ —and, through it all, to keep my own literary business going without so much as a day's stoppage . . . Come and see me on my new perch. My dining-room is habitable, and the drawing- rooms are getting on.

Further progress is announced a day or two later in a letter to his mother: 'A certain necessary place has got the most lovely new pan you ever saw. It's quite a pleasure to look into it.'

The writing of *No Thoroughfare*, which they obviously enjoyed, brought Wilkie and Dickens closer together than they had been for some years. Almost as soon as it was finished, Dickens left for a Reading Tour of the United States, and Wilkie's engage- ment book was filled with 'dinners public and private, to Dickens on his departure.' As part of the farewell celebrations Dickens dined with him at Gloucester Place 'to warm the house.' On November 8th, 1867, Wilkie travelled to Liverpool in company with his brother Charles, Wills, Charles Kent and various members of Dickens' family to see him off. They had a farewell party aboard s.s. *Cuba*, on which Dickens sailed the next day.

The period of Dickens' absence in America was for Wilkie one of the busiest of his life. First, there was *The Moonstone* which had been more or less shelved during the writing of *No Thorough- fare*; secondly, he had undertaken to assist Wills in the day-to-day affairs of *All the Year Round*; lastly there was the task, which

† Since this was written the London County Council has made good its long-standing omission. A plaque was unveiled by Mr. Michael Sadleir on 23rd May, 1951. The house is now No. 65, Gloucester Place.

Dickens had entrusted to him, of adapting *No Thoroughfare* for the stage. It was only natural that the idea of a dramatic version should occur to two such theatre-minded authors, and by the time Dickens sailed for New York they had made arrangements for the play, as yet unwritten, to be produced at the Adelphi Theatre at Christmas, with Charles Fechter playing the villain, Obenreizer.

They had both known Fechter for some years, and had a high regard for him as an actor and as a friend. Wilkie saw him first on the stage of the Vaudeville Theatre in Paris during the early 'fifties, and met him in 1860 when he came to London to play in Victor Hugo's *Ruy Blas*. In his *Recollections of Charles Fechter*† Wilkie wrote: 'By common impulse we dispensed with the tentative formalities of acquaintance, and became friends from that day to the day of his death.' Fechter, born in London in 1822 of a German father and an English mother, was taken to France as a small child and brought up there. He chose London as his home shortly after his first success here, though the last years of his life were spent in the United States. He possessed great personal charm, but was cursed with an ungovernable temper. As a man of business he was hopeless for, according to Wilkie, 'I have met with many children who had a clearer idea than he possessed of pecuniary responsibilities.' Like his friend, Fechter was something of a gourmet and entertained frequently, if unconventionally, at his house at St. John's Wood. No one dressed for dinner and in summer the guests would more often than not find their host in the garden attired in dressing-gown and slippers. Wilkie recalled that no servants waited upon them and each guest was expected to choose the bottle he liked best and place it beside him on the table. Anyone who wished went into the kitchen to help the French cook, whose tolerance must have equalled his acknowledged artistry. 'We had every variety of French cookery, and twice we put the inexhaustible resources of gastronomic France to the test by dining on one article of food only, presented under many different forms. We had a potato dinner in six courses, and an egg dinner in eight courses.'

When Wilkie and Dickens resigned from the Garrick Club for

† A chapter contributed by Collins to *Charles Albert Fechter*, by Kate Field. (*J. R. Osgood & Co.*, Boston, 1882).

the second time† in March, 1865, as a protest against the black-balling of Wills who had been proposed by Dickens and seconded by Wilkie, Fechter resigned too. He informed the committee that he had acted thus 'because they had blackballed Mr. Wills, and he would trust himself to no community of men in which such things were done.'

Of Fechter's ability as an actor opinion varied considerably. The theatre public took him readily to its bosom as a romantic stage-lover, but his aspirations went beyond such roles. He played Hamlet and Othello in London, on unconventional lines, and was taken to task by many of the critics. His Hamlet in particular, played in a blonde wig and with a foreign accent which he never completely lost, aroused fierce controversy. Clement Scott, writing of the performance many years afterwards, recalled being carried away by Fechter's interpretation and confessed that it was the first time he really understood the play. Dickens had no reservations where his friend's acting was concerned, and spoke of his 'unmistakable genius.' He went so far as to provide financial backing for a Fechter season at the Lyceum in 1863.

Fechter in his turn was a great admirer of Dickens and in January, 1865, presented him with a Swiss châlet which arrived at Gad's Hill from Paris in ninety-four sections. With much effort and at considerable expense it was erected on a plot of ground on the far side of the Dover Road, and connected with the garden of Gad's Hill Place by means of a tunnel under the road. It was in the châlet that Dickens and Wilkie wrote much of No Thorough-fare, and in drawing the character of Obenreizer they had Fechter in mind for the role from the beginning. The proofs were sent to Fechter who 'fell madly in love with the subject,' and prepared a dramatic scenario under the authors' supervision. After Dickens' departure, Wilkie co-opted Fechter to advise on details such as stage directions and costume, and to assist generally. Confident of the play's success, he said to Wilkie: 'Dickens has gone away for six months: he will find No Thoroughfare still running when he comes back.' So, in the event, it turned out.

The Extra Christmas Number of All the Year Round, containing

† The first occasion arose from Dickens' championship of Edmund Yates in his famous quarrel with Thackeray in 1860, which culminated in Yates' expulsion from the Garrick.

No Thoroughfare, appeared as usual in early December, and the public flocked to buy it, as usual, in their thousands. Dickens had built up over twenty years a regular public for his Christmas Numbers, and *No Thoroughfare*, although not a particularly good specimen, contained all the ingredients the readers demanded, crime, love-interest and excitement.

News that a dramatic version was in the offing reached New York even before the publication of the story in London. Two managements approached Dickens on his arrival in America in the belief that he had the play in his pocket. He hurriedly wrote to Wilkie asking for a copy of each act as it was finished, having 'little doubt of being able to make a good thing of the Drama.' A day or two later he wrote:

> *I find that if the Play be left unpublished in England*, the right of playing it in America can be secured by assigning the MS. to an American citizen. That I can do at once by using my publishers here for the purpose. I can make an arrangement with Wallack, in New York, to have it produced at his Theatre (where there is the best company), on a sharing agreement after a certain nightly allowance for expenses, and I have arranged to see Wallack next week.

By Christmas Eve he had received a letter from Wilkie enclosing a copy of the play complete, to which he replied from Boston:

> The play is done *with great pains and skill*, but I fear it is too long. Its fate will have been decided before you get this letter, but I greatly doubt its success . . . There are no end of *No Thoroughfares* being offered to Managers here. The play still being in abeyance with Wallack, I have a strong suspicion that he wants to tide over to the 27th, and get a Telegram from London about the first night of the real version. If it should not be a great success, he would then either do a false one, or do none. Accordingly, I have brought him to book for decision on the 27th. Don't you see?

Dickens was beginning to smell pirates.

The first performance in London was given on Boxing Day, with Carlotta Leclerq, Henry Neville and, of course, Fechter in the leading parts. The Adelphi audience found the melodrama very much to their taste and its success was immediate, contrary to

Dickens' fears. Of the critics, Dutton Cook, editor of the *Pall Mall Gazette*, thought it a skilful adaptation which would be improved by cutting—the play lasted four hours on the first night—but did not consider it a production of very high class; E. M. Blanchard was much pleased by the play, whilst Shirley Brooks, of *Punch*, went home 'howling at myself for sitting through such unmitigated wrott.' Everyone spoke well of Fechter's performance, with Wilkie loudest of all in his praise.

On first nights Fechter used to suffer from appalling stage-fright, and Wilkie describes how he saw him on this occasion an hour or two before the show. 'Pale, silent, subdued, he sat in a corner of the room and looked like a man awaiting the appearance of the sheriff to conduct him to the scaffold.' He had been unable to eat for hours, and could not even smoke his pipe. When Wilkie confessed that his own nerves would not permit him to go in front to watch the performance, Fechter begged him to come along to his dressing-room before the curtain rose. Wilkie found him 'half-dressed, sitting helplessly staring into a white basin, held before him by his attendant in the attitude of a sailor on a channel steamer comforting a suffering lady.' Wilkie did his best to encourage him, and proposed a few drops of his own panacea, laudanum. 'Unable to speak, Fechter answered by putting out his tongue. The colour of it had turned, under the nervous terror that possessed him, to the metallic blackness of the tongue of a parrot. When the Overture began—easily audible in the dressing-room—another attack made the basin necessary.' To the horror of everyone around, this continued right up to the moment in the wings immediately prior to his first entrance. Fechter then walked on the stage and gave one of the performances of his life.

Hopes of golden rewards from American productions of *No Thoroughfare* were not fulfilled. The arrangement with Wallack fell through and on January 12th, 1868, Dickens wrote: 'Pirates are producing their own wretched versions in all directions.' Wherever he read in America the theatre cashed in by producing makeshift dramatic versions of his books, in respect of which he received not one cent. In accordance with his intention, he registered *No Thoroughfare* as the property of Ticknor and Fields, his Boston publishers. Instantly the manager of the Museum Theatre, Boston, announced his version of the play. Its quality can be gauged by the fact that it was actually playing within ten days of the original story's arrival in the States. Ticknor and Fields threatened an injunction, but the manager, well knowing that if they proceeded there would be a public outcry against Dickens, called their bluff and carried on. 'Then,' wrote Dickens, 'the noble host of pirates rushed in, and it is being done, in some mangled form or other, everywhere.'

The London production was well set for a run, and Dickens' tune had changed from that of a fortnight before. 'I am truly delighted to learn that it made so great a success, and I hope I may yet see it on the Adelphi boards. You have had a world of trouble and work with it, but I hope will be repaid in some degree by the pleasure of a triumph.' *No Thoroughfare* ran for 200 nights.

Early in the New Year came the news that Mama Collins, now well over seventy years old, was seriously ill. Wilkie always had the greatest affection for his mother and she obviously adored her son, of whom she was very naturally proud. Although for many years she had lived in the country, mainly at various addresses in the vicinity of Tunbridge Wells, he was in the habit of visiting her several times a year. Moreover, such visits were clearly a pleasure to him rather than a mere filial duty, and he seldom went abroad without first going down to her cottage to say goodbye over a game of cribbage. He also maintained a frequent correspondence over a number of years in which he kept her informed of all his social and literary activities.

These letters, humorous, kindly and candid, suggest that there was a real sympathy between them. Sometimes he would indulge in gentle banter at the expense of some foible of his mother's. For instance she was in his opinion far too economical. 'I have—as I wish to encourage you to spend money—bought you a purse at Paris which it is quite a luxury to open,' he wrote on one occasion; and on another, 'Take care of yourself and live well, and don't save money at the expense of your comfort.' He teased her now and again about her reverence for titles, and took care to inform her that among his congratulatory letters on *The Woman in White* was one from a French duke. Since she was an admirer of Tennyson he was delighted to retail a remark which 'the great T.,' had made to a friend of his: 'My misfortune is that I have not got anything *in* me. If I had only got something *in* me, I could write as well as Shakespeare.'

She was inclined to worry, like most mothers, about her sons. Wilkie once took the trouble to write specially, following a skating disaster in Regent's Park, to reassure her that he was not involved, so that the letter should arrive with the report of the incident in her morning newspaper. Sometimes he took her fears less seriously, as in his reply to a motherly injunction to be careful when travelling in trains: 'Danger in railways from murdering men is nothing —if you don't carry a banker's bag. But danger from virtuous single ladies whose character is "dearer to them than their lives," *is* serious. I won't travel alone with a woman—I promise you that. The British female, judging by her recent appearances in the newspapers, is as full of snares as Solomon's "strange woman"—a mixture of perjury and prudery, cant and crinoline, from whom (when we travel in railways) may the Guard deliver us!' He followed this up with some advice of his own: 'If you feel hot, try a bottle of Sauterne from Hastings—four pinches of snuff—and a mild cigar.' Wilkie appointed himself her supplier of wines and spirits and would usually take down with him a case of brandy or claret or hock.

It was therefore with the deepest distress that he learned that his mother's condition was serious. He hurried down to her cottage near Tunbridge Wells, and very soon realised that she was dying. On January 21st, 1868, he wrote to a friend. 'You will be grieved, I know, at the miserable news which I have to tell you. My dear old mother is dying. She is perfectly conscious, perfectly clear in her mind. But the internal neuralgia, from which she has suffered so long, has broken her down—and, at her present age, there is now no hope. Charley is with me here. All that *can* be done to soothe her last moments is done. The end may be deferred for a few days yet—but it is only a question of time. I can write no more.' The doctor only permitted them to see her for brief spells, and in the intervals Wilkie carried on with *The Moonstone* as best he could. As she lingered on, week after week, he had to divide his time between Tunbridge Wells and London. The strain of the last few months, combined with the worry of his mother's illness, had its effect at last on his own health. In February he was stricken with the most acute attack of rheumatic gout he had yet suffered. As he lay on his sick-bed at Gloucester Place, crippled in every limb, his eyes tortured with pain, the news came on March 19th that his mother was dead. It was, he said, the bitterest affliction of his life.

All this time *The Moonstone* had to be kept going somehow or other. Not more than a third of the story was written and serial publication had started not only in *All the Year Round* but also in *Harper's Weekly*. A letter written to his American publishers from his mother's cottage on January 30th, shows the meticulous care with which he tackled the business side of his work, and also the cordial relations which existed between him and Harper Brothers:

> You will receive with this a corrected revise of the twelfth weekly part of *The Moonstone*, and a portion of the thirteenth weekly part. The completion of the thirteenth weekly part will follow, I hope, by Tuesday's mail. But for the inevitable delay in transmitting the manuscript and receiving the proofs by post, caused by my absence from London, you would have received the whole weekly part by the mail of February 1st. I will arrange to send slips (for the convenience of your artist) by every mail so long as my mother's critical condition obliges me to remain here. And I will be careful—as I have hitherto been careful—to forward the duplicates regularly, in case of accidents by the post. After the next two or three weekly portions, I shall hope to be able to send you, beforehand, a list of subjects for the artist, referring to a part of the story which is already settled in detail, and in relation to which he may feel secure against any after-alterations when I am writing for press. The two numbers of the *Weekly* have reached me safely. The illustrations to the first number are very picturesque—the three Indians and the boy being especially good, as I think. In the second number there is the mistake (as we should call it in England) of presenting 'Gabriel Betteredge' in *livery*. As head-servant, he would wear plain black clothes—and would look, with his white cravat and grey hair, like an old clergyman. I only mention this for future illustrations—and because I see the dramatic effect of the story (in the first number) conveyed with such real intelligence by the artist that I want to see him taking the right direction, even in the smallest technical details.

You may rely on my sparing no effort to study *your* convenience, after the readiness that you have shown to consider
mine. I am very glad to hear that you like the story, so far. There
are some effects to come, which—unless I am altogether mistaken
—have never been tried in fiction before.

Lying prostrate in bed, racked with pain, Wilkie was quite
unable to write and had to dictate to an amanuensis. Recalling
these grim days in the Preface to a later edition of *The Moonstone*
he wrote:

My good readers in England and in America, whom I had never
yet disappointed, were expecting their regular weekly instalments of the new story. I held to the story—for my own sake
as well as for theirs. In the intervals of grief, in the occasional
remissions of pain, I dictated from my bed that portion of *The
Moonstone* which has since proved most successful in amusing
the public—the 'Narrative of Miss Clack.'

In later years he told the story in greater detail to Mary Anderson,
the actress, and an American friend, William Winter, both of whom
have recorded it in their reminiscences.† At first a young man was
engaged to take down the dictation, but whenever the pain became
so intense that Wilkie had to cry out, the amenuensis would rush
to his assistance instead of carrying on with his work. The young
man found it all so distressing that he had to leave. Several other
men were engaged, each time with the same result; all found their
employer's cries and groans unendurable. Finally he engaged a
young woman, 'stipulating that she must utterly disregard my
sufferings and attend solely to my words.' To his astonishment—
for the worst attacks of all followed her arrival—the young woman
was able to do precisely that. Such were the conditions under
which he dictated many chapters of *The Moonstone*. Although there
is no evidence to support such a speculation, it would be interesting
to know whether the young woman was Martha Rudd, who
became the mother of his three children. All we do know is that
Wilkie and Martha must have met before September of the year
1868.

† *A Few Memories*. Mary Anderson (Mme. de Navarro). (*Osgood, McIlvaine*,
1896); *Old Friends*. William Winter. (New York, 1909).

The attack seems to have lasted for some months. During the day concentration on the intricacies of his novel helped him to endure the suffering. The nights were made bearable by larger and still larger doses of laudanum. Indeed he confessed to Mary Anderson that the last part of *The Moonstone* was written largely under the effects of opium. 'When it was finished,' he told her, 'I was not only pleased and astonished at the finale, but did not recognise it as my own.' Certainly opium plays a big part in the story. There is a hint, if nothing more, in the original Preface that he tried out on himself the famous narcotic experiment which forms the main clue to the mystery: 'Having first ascertained, not only from books, but from living authorities as well, what the result of that experiment would really have been, I have declined to avail myself of the novelist's privilege of supposing something which might have happened, and have so shaped the story so as to make it grow out of what actually would have happened—which, I beg to inform my readers, is also what actually does happen.'

By the middle of May he was on the way to recovery, although in a letter to the Padrona he still refers to his 'exhausted state' and 'shattered nerves.' He tells her that he is having a hard fight to finish his book but hopes to be through next month. If she comes to see him it should be before four o'clock because 'I am carried out to be aired *at* 4.'

Early the same month, Dickens returned from his American Reading Tour. Not only was *No Thoroughfare* still running at the Adelphi but negotiations were in train for a Paris production. Fechter fell ill about this time and had to leave the cast, but he obtained his doctor's permission to go to Paris and supervise the rehearsals of *L'Abîme*, as the French translation was called. Dickens was not entirely satisfied with the London production which had 'excellent things in it, but it drags to my thinking,' and he complained that Wilkie and Fechter had missed many pieces of stage-effect. Nothing would satisfy him but to visit Paris himself 'and try my stage-managerial hand at the Vaudeville Theatre.' On June 4th, he reported by letter to Wilkie, who was still unfit to travel, that the piece was a great success. Both he and Fechter had been too nervous to attend the first night and had driven round the Paris streets repairing at intervals to the Café Vaudeville, where Didier, the translator, had furnished them with an act-by-act report.

It is difficult to avoid a belief that shortly after this there occurred some kind of personal estrangement between Dickens and Wilkie. In a letter to Wills dated July 26th, 1868, when *The Moonstone* was nearing the end of its course in *All the Year Round*, Dickens wrote, 'I quite agree with you about *The Moonstone*. The construction is wearisome beyond endurance, and there is a vein of obstinate conceit in it that makes enemies of readers.' In other circumstances these two sentences might be dismissed as no more than dispassionate adverse criticism. But in view of his earlier opinion of the same novel—'in many respects much better than anything he has done'—and his fervent admiration for almost everything Wilkie had previously written, and having regard to the actual words used, it is hard to suppress a notion that personal animosity entered into the matter. There is the further point that Dickens was clearly concurring with a disparaging criticism which Wills had expressed on paper, something Wills would have been most unlikely to do had relations between his editor and Wilkie been normally friendly. It is easy to make unduly heavy weather of this isolated stricture on Dickens' part, but it seems strange that it should concern a book which is almost unanimously regarded as one of the two really outstanding novels written by Wilkie Collins.

Had there been evidence of a falling off in sales of *All the Year Round* Wills and his chief might have attributed the decline to lack of interest in the current serial, and might indeed have persuaded themselves on that account that their first opinion of the story was wrong. Such an explanation would however conflict with the facts as given by William Tinsley in his *Random Recollections of an Old Publisher*. Tinsley, who published the first three-volume edition of *The Moonstone* in July, 1868, wrote: 'The Moonstone and The Woman in White were two of the very few exceptions of the many serials in *All the Year Round* which increased the circulation to any great extent. *The Moonstone* perhaps did more for it than any other novel, not excepting *Great Expectations*. During the run of *The Moonstone* as a serial there were scenes in Wellington Street that doubtless did the author's and publisher's hearts good. And especially when the serial was nearing its ending, on publishing days there would be quite a crowd of anxious readers waiting for the new number, and I know of several bets that were made as to where the moonstone would be found at last. Even the porters

and the boys were interested in the story, and read the new number
in sly corners, and often with their packs on their backs.'

Exactly why Tinsley, whose firm was then little known, was
chosen to publish *The Moonstone* in book-form is obscure; apparently he told Dickens he would like to handle it, and Dickens
introduced him to Wilkie who entered into negotiations. The
copyright of all Wilkie's published works had recently been
acquired by Smith, Elder, but on Dickens' advice he had excluded
the new novel from the deal in the hope of making a better bargain
for it separately. According to Tinsley, the number of subscribers
to three-volume novels had been falling off noticeably in the last
year or so, and this made him unwilling to issue more than 1,500
copies of *The Moonstone* in the first instance, although Wilkie's last
three novels had sold many more copies in their original editions.
He was even doubtful of being able to dispose of 1,500 copies.
Wilkie drove a very hard bargain with him and his solicitors sent
Tinsley a draft agreement which he described as 'a regular corker';
it would, he said, 'pretty well cover the gable of an ordinary-sized
house.' The first edition sold out quickly and Tinsley admitted that
he did very well out of the agreement. Since the type was still
standing, Wilkie was anxious for a further edition of 500 copies
to be printed and proposed that Tinsley should pay him a flat sum
down on a proportionate basis to the original arrangement. Tinsley
countered with an offer to pay so much per hundred copies as they
were sold. Wilkie refused these terms, and negotiations appeared
to be at an end when, to Tinsley's surprise, the printer approached
him to ask if he would allow an edition to be printed off the type
for another publisher. He was willing to agree to this provided
that the second publisher paid a proportion of the original cost of
setting the type. Before anything could be done, however, an excellent review of *The Moonstone* appeared in *The Times* and Wilkie
instructed his solicitors to accept Tinsley's offer; the latter claims
that he deducted £50 to compensate him for his trouble. Wills
commiserated with him and admitted that Wilkie had driven an
equally hard bargain with *All the Year Round* over the serial
rights.

Some twelve years later, Edmund Downey, one of Tinsley's
assistants, was in the Gaiety Bar with his chief one afternoon when
they saw Wilkie Collins, whom Downey describes as 'a plump,

spectacled man, wearing something of a country-squireish air.'†
He made some remark to his chief to the effect that Wilkie looked
harmless enough, to which Tinsley replied, 'My boy, you'd be much
more awed if you had to negotiate a book with him. He's as shrewd
as they make 'em,' and went on to describe the business of *The
Moonstone*. He concluded by admitting that 'the little breeze cost
me the loss of further business with Master Wilkie.'

Across the Atlantic, all the precautions that Harper Brothers
could take failed to prevent the simultaneous appearance of four
separate editions. Wilkie was now in the front rank of American
best-sellers and, as the demand for *The Moonstone* steadily increased
many more publishers hastened to bring out editions of their own.

The Moonstone is from many points of view Wilkie Collins'
most remarkable performance. In this, above all his books, he
achieved precisely what he set out to do, and more—for it is
unlikely that he intended to produce the archetype of a new
branch of English fiction. To the modern reader *The Moonstone* has
the special interest of being the first, and indeed the classic,
example of the English detective-novel. In support of such a claim
no more expert witness need be called than Dorothy L. Sayers,
who wrote in her introduction to the Everyman edition: 'Judged
by the standard of seventy years later, and across a great gap which
acknowledged no fair-play standards at all, *The Moonstone* is
impeccable. What has happened, in fact, is that *The Moonstone* set
the standard, and that it has taken us all this time to recognise it.'

If, in this book, Collins' art reached its zenith, the reason is not
difficult to determine. He chose, consciously or otherwise, a subject
fully within his limitations, a subject unentangled with social
themes and problems better suited to the talents of a Reade or the
genius of a Dickens. The canvas, though crowded, is smaller than
that of *Armadale* or *The Woman in White* and, compared with
the complexities of the earlier books, the plot of *The Moonstone* is
in essence simple. The ingenuity which he brings to bear on its
unfolding could hardly be surpassed, and the construction stands
as a model. Within this smaller compass the flame of his imagination burned the more brightly, penetrating deep into human

† *Twenty Years Ago*. Edmund Downey. (*Hurst and Blackett*, 1905).

emotions and shedding upon the story in places a strange almost magical glow.

The Diamond itself, as large as a plover's egg, seems almost a living thing:

> The light that streamed from it was like the light of the harvest moon. When you looked down into the stone, you looked into a yellow deep that drew your eyes into it so that they saw nothing else. It seemed unfathomable; this jewel, that you could hold between your finger and thumb, seemed as unfathomable as the heavens themselves. We set it in the sun, and then shut the light out of the room, and it shone awfully out of the depths of its own brightness, with a moony gleam, in the dark.

Wilkie acknowledges in the Preface that he was in part inspired by stories of two famous gems, the Koh-i-Noor and the stone that adorned the Russian Imperial sceptre. There may have been other sources, however. Lady Russell† records that he used to be a frequent guest of Sir George Russell at Swallowfields and that the idea of *The Moonstone* arose from stories he heard there of the family heirloom, the famous Pitt diamond. Walter de la Mare, on the other hand, in a footnote to his essay on Collins' Early Novels, claims that the story was suggested by a moonstone which used to belong to Charles Reade, having been brought from India by his brother, and which is still in the possession of the Reade family.

The other main source of *The Moonstone* is less romantic. The newspapers of 1861 had given great prominence to the sensational Road Murder, in which a young woman named Constance Kent murdered her small brother in particularly brutal circumstances. She did not confess until four years after the murder, and at her trial two important pieces of evidence were a blood-stained shift and a washing-book. Although the crime itself plays no part in *The Moonstone*, there is much ado about a washing-book and a paint-stained nightdress. More important is the undoubted fact that Wilkie's detective, Sergeant Cuff, is founded upon the Scotland Yard detective in charge of the Road case, Inspector Whicher. Certain of Whicher's earlier cases were described in a series of articles in *Household Words*, where he is thinly disguised as 'Sergeant Witchem,' and he was in all probability known personally

† *Swallowfields and its Owners.* Lady Constance Russell (1901).

to Wilkie. Similarly, Superintendent Seegrave, the stupid local policeman, had his real-life counterpart in Inspector Foley, who played an even more inept part in the Road case when supposed to be helping Whicher.

Since Sergeant Cuff has fathered such a multitudinous progeny in the literature of detection, he is worth examining at close quarters.

A grizzled, elderly man, so miserably lean that he looked as if he had not got an ounce of flesh on his bones in any part of him. He was dressed all in decent black, with a white cravat round his neck. His face was as sharp as a hatchet, and the skin of it was as yellow and dry and withered as an autumn leaf. His eyes, of a steely light grey, had a very disconcerting trick when they encountered your eyes, of looking as if they expected something more from you than you were aware of yourself. His walk was soft; his voice was melancholy; his long lanky fingers were hooked like claws. He might have been a parson, or an undertaker—or anything else you like, except what he really was.

Thus he struck Betteredge, the house-steward, on his arrival to investigate the disappearance of the moonstone. But Cuff's disagreeable appearance hides some very human qualities, such as his dry, salty humour and his passion for rose-growing. His most endearing quality, however, to those of us who may be satiated with detectives of super-human intellect, is his fallibility. Brilliant as are Cuff's deductions, he makes mistakes; he is a human creature after all.

For our part, we follow the detective happily along his false trails, drawing with faultless logic our wrong conclusions while all the essential clues to the mystery are, if not staring us in the face, at least within our knowledge. The secret is well kept until the moment when the author decides to enlighten us; and even then, with the main mystery solved, he contrives by sheer ingenuity to sustain, and perhaps heighten, our interest in the ultimate fate of the moonstone.

The narrative method follows the pattern of *The Woman in White*. The book comprises a similar series of 'narratives' by different hands, but here they reflect more the personalities of their respective 'authors' and less that of Wilkie himself. Admittedly, in the case of Betteredge's story and of Rosanna's letter to Blake, there is a convention to be accepted in that these two characters are permitted a fluency of expression they would hardly have attained in reality, but the feelings they express are essentially their own.

Gabriel Betteredge, whose narrative is the first and the longest, combines the functions of Greek chorus and amateur detective. As the house-steward, he is both in the midst of, and outside the drama, which he records with a solid, earthy humour. 'A drop of tea,' he tells us, 'is to a woman's tongue what a drop of oil is to a wasting lamp.' If one can forgive his untiring reverence for *Robinson Crusoe*, the book which is his oracle and friend, and some of his more arch 'asides' to the reader, he proves an entertaining companion. Not only is Wilkie's choice of a family retainer as his narrator a device of some subtlety, but it shows once again his genuine interest in the lives of those who lived 'below stairs,' a world which he, unlike nearly all his contemporaries, could describe faithfully, and without either condescension or embarrassment. We can recognise Collins' signature, too, in the portrait of Rosanna Spearman, the deformed housemaid with a prison record. He brings to it real understanding and compassion. Nothing in all his work is more moving than the growth of her hopeless love for Franklin Blake, which leads ultimately to her suicide; it is handled with rare sensitivity and with a complete absence of sentimentality.

Miss Clack, authoress of the 'narrative' that follows, is pure caricature, and caricature with a touch of malice. Always repelled by ostentatious piety, Wilkie had doubtless suffered in many a drawing-room at the hands of evangelistic females. For one such lady he found himself in the position of trustee, a duty which he discharged with less than his usual courtesy, as the following peevish letter to Charles Ward indicates.

'Is the Jones-fund (may "the Lord" soon take her!) paid into *my* account regularly? . . . If it only rests with *me* to decide the matter, pay this pious bitch the two quarters together—so that we may be the longer rid of her . . . Tell me whether (by the help of the Lord) Mrs. Jones's dividends are now regularly paid into my account only. I don't want to pay Mrs. Jones (and the Lord) out of my own pocket.'

The ridiculous Miss Clack, indiscriminately scattering her religious tracts, indefatigable in the exercise of 'Christian duty', was his revenge. His armoury lacked the equipment for effective satire, and the satire is here applied with a heavy hand. As broad comic relief, however, Drusilla Clack serves her turn.

Of the heroine, Rachel Verinder, Betteredge tells us: 'She judged for herself, as few women of twice her age judge in general; never asked your advice; never told you beforehand what she was going to do; never came with secrets and confidences to anybody, from her mother downwards. In little things and great, with people she loved, and people she hated (and she did both with equal heartiness), Miss Rachel always went on a way of her own, sufficient for herself in the joys and sorrows of her life.' Rachel is no ordinary heroine, to whom events just happen, as for example Laura Fairlie; she is a young woman of intelligence and spirit, fully in command of the situation. Similarly Franklin Blake is far removed from the modern hero of so many novels of the period. His experience of the world, and of women, is frankly acknowledged. Among a host of minor characters, most of whom are sketched with a deft and imaginative touch, mention must be made of Ezra Jennings. Into this striking portrait of a man haunted by past misfortune, torn by pain and kept alive by opium, Wilkie put much of his own suffering. There is a terrible authenticity about Jennings' confession:

> To that all-potent and all-merciful drug I am indebted for a respite of many years from my sentence of death. But even the virtues of opium have their limit. The progress of the disease has gradually forced me from the use of opium to the abuse of it. I am feeling the penalty at last. My nervous system is shattered; my nights are nights of horror. The end is not far off now.

Who can doubt that Wilkie had endured many a night such as that described in Ezra Jennings' Journal?

> June 16th—Rose late, after a dreadful night; the vengeance of yesterday's opium, pursuing me through a series of frightful dreams. At one time I was whirling through empty space with the phantoms of the dead, friends and enemies together. At another, the one beloved face which I shall never see again, rose at my bedside, hideously phosphorescent in the black darkness, and glared and grinned at me. A slight return of the old pains, at the usual time in the early morning, was welcome as a change. It dispelled the visions—and it was bearable because it did that.

The *mise-en-scène* is done with all Wilkie's flair for creating atmosphere. The closing pages in particular linger in one's memory long after the book is put aside. The diamond has been restored at last to the sacred Indian city of Somnauth where its story began; a vast throng of pilgrims have gathered from afar to witness the ceremony, and the scene culminates in our final glimpse of the moonstone:

> There, raised high on a throne—seated on his typical antelope, with his four arms stretching towards the four corners of the earth—there soared above us, dark and awful in the mystic light of heaven, the god of the Moon. And there, in the forehead of the deity, gleamed the yellow Diamond, whose splendour had last shone on me in England, from the bosom of a woman's dress.

There is imaginative power too in his conception of the Shivering Sand, and the uncanny spell it cast upon poor Rosanna whose life it claimed.

> The last of the evening light was fading away; and over all the desolate place there hung a still and awful calm. The heave of the main ocean on the great sand-bank out in the bay was a heave that made no sound. The inner sea lay lost and dim, without a breath of wind to stir it. Patches of nasty ooze floated, yellow-white, on the dead surface of the water. Scum and slime shone faintly in certain places, where the last of the light still caught them on the two great spits of rock jutting out, north and south, into the sea. It was now the time of the turn of the tide: and even as I stood there waiting, the broad brown face of the quicksand began to dimple and quiver—the only moving thing in all the horrid place.'

When we recall the circumstances in which the greater part of this novel was written, we can only marvel at the courage and endurance with which he conquered afflictions that would reduce almost any man to utter helplessness. *The Moonstone* has held, and deserved, its special place in fiction as, to quote T. S. Eliot, 'the first, the longest, and the best of the modern English detective novels.'

13

Turning Point

WHATEVER rupture may have taken place between Dickens and Wilkie, friendly relations seem to have been re-established by the time the latter's next play was produced. *Black and White*, a melodrama concerned with slavery and the colour question in Trinidad, was written in collaboration with Fechter during the latter part of 1868. The plot was suggested by Fechter, who was to play the lead, and Wilkie made himself responsible for the conception and development of the characters, and for the dialogue. It is a curious fact that Wilkie, with his far greater experience of writing for the stage, invariably submitted his plays to Dickens for his advice and practical help, whereas, after *No Name*, he apparently ceased to consult him over his novels. Accordingly, the script of *Black and White* was sent to Dickens who replied on February 25th, 1869: 'I have read the play with great attention, and with a stage eye: and I think it will be *a great success*. It is highly interesting, admirably constructed and carried through, and very picturesque.' He added some suggestions concerning stage 'business,' and at Wilkie's invitation spent several hours at the dress rehearsal. And so the hatchet, if there was a hatchet, was buried.

Black and White was first produced at the Adelphi Theatre on March 29th, with Carlotta Leclercq, the Marguerite of *No Thoroughfare*, in the leading woman's role opposite Fechter. The entire Dickens family attended the first night in the lower omnibus-box by the stage, 'full of affectionate partisanship—trying to believe it was a success,' to quote Percy Fitzgerald. Writing to Wills the next day Dickens said: 'You will be glad to hear that Wilkie's play went brilliantly last night. It was extremely well played throughout, and I have rarely seen Fechter to greater advantage. It was more like a fiftieth night than a first . . . There is no doubt that it ought to run, for it has real merit.' The play did not, however, fulfil the promise of a six-months' run, which the tumultuous applause of the first night had seemed to indicate. Wilkie thought Fechter's playing of Maurice de Layrac even finer than his Obenreizer, and many critics shared his view. Dutton Cook praised faintly: 'It is not a work of high order, but it is certainly a commendable specimen of its class.' It ran for about six weeks at the Adelphi, and a short provincial tour followed. Fechter left for America the following year and in January, 1871, he and Carlotta Leclercq appeared in their original roles in a production of *Black and White* at Boston. Wilkie attributed its comparative failure in England to the fact that the public was tired of slavery as a theme after the spate of dramatic *Uncle Tom's Cabins*. It was said in France at the time that the English had developed a mania of 'Oncle Tommerie.'

This was the beginning of a particularly unsettling period of his life. The year 1868 had been a difficult one in many ways. First there had been his mother's death, then the strain of a long and painful illness. Even the great success of *The Moonstone* must have been offset to some extent by the wrangle with Tinsley, perhaps also by a break in his friendship with Dickens. Finally there was the serious upheaval in his domestic life which resulted in Caroline Graves leaving him to marry another man. It is unlikely that we shall ever know the circumstances which led up to Caroline's marriage to Joseph Clow in October, 1868, whether it was a straightforward case of Wilkie's losing her to a rival, or the outcome of some tacit understanding between them. All we do know, on the evidence of his sister-in-law, is that he was present at the wedding ceremony. We may, however, assume that his liaison with Martha Rudd was in some way associated with Caroline's departure, but whether as cause or effect can only be conjecture. Caroline's daughter, then about sixteen years old, remained with Wilkie at Gloucester Place.

On April 24th, 1869, he wrote a strange letter to Frederick Lehmann:

Thank you, from the bottom of my heart, for your kind letter. No man—whatever his disappointments may be—can consider himself other than a fortunate man, when he has got such a friend as you are.

But, for the present, my head is 'well above water.' I have few debts unpaid—I have three hundred pounds or so at my bankers —and a thousand pounds in Indian and Russian railways, which I can sell out (if the worst comes to the worst) at a gain instead of a loss. I may also, in a few months, sell another edition of *The Moonstone* (cheap edition) and get two or three hundred pounds in that way. So, thus far, the money anxieties are not added to the other anxieties which are attacking me. If my health gives way and my prospects darken as this year goes on—you shall be the first man who knows it. Till then, thank you, most sincerely, once more.

I am coming to take pot-luck on Monday next at seven—if you and the Padrona have still arranged to dine alone on that day. Don't trouble to write—unless there is an alteration. I am refusing all invitations on the plea of being 'out of town.' It is necessary to 'lay the keel' of something new—after this disaster —and I am trying to keep myself as quiet as I can.

Yours ever,

W.C.

I shall pay the Arts. Damn the Arts!

There is no means of identifying the 'disaster' mentioned at the end of the letter. It could hardly refer to Caroline's departure which had occurred six months before. It seems too strong a word to describe the comparative failure of *Black and White*, then approaching the close of its brief run. The letter suggests that it is unconnected with money—which Lehmann had clearly offered, or with a breakdown in health. Something else had happened to him that seriously disturbed his peace of mind.

The keel of his next book, *Man and Wife*, was duly laid, but not even hard work could allay his restlessness. It was not easy to adjust himself to the profound change which, after ten years, had come over his private life, and he found it impossible to remain at 90, Gloucester Place, for more than short periods. The Lehmanns came to his rescue in offering him the hospitality of 'Woodlands,' their house in Southwood Lane, Highgate, for as long as he liked. It was here that he spent many months of 1869 and 1870 and wrote much of *Man and Wife*. He was allotted his own study and the household received the strictest injunctions against disturbing him.

The Lehmanns' wide circle of friends, to entertain whom was one of their chief delights, included Reade, George Eliot and G. H. Lewes, Forster, Browning and Millais. Another frequent guest was H. F. Chorley, the critic who had attacked *Armadale* so vehemently in the pages of *The Athenaeum*. Always a trifle eccentric, he was now getting old and his mind was beginning to wander. He still enjoyed dining out, but was apt to suffer from the embarrassing delusion that he was dining in his own home, and used to address the servants of the house by his own servants' names. R. C. Lehmann describes a dinner-party at Woodlands where Chorley rose from the table, asked his hostess to look after his guests for him and in particular to see that Mr. Collins got the wine he liked, and tottered off to bed on the arm of what he imagined to be his own valet. On another occasion when Wilkie lighted his cigar after dinner, Chorley immediately upbraided him, saying that he never allowed smoking in his dining-room. During a lucid interval he apologised profusely to Wilkie, and for a moment all was well; a few minutes later, however, he was off again ringing the bell and giving instructions to the Lehmanns' servants as if they were his own. He died a year or so later, in February, 1872

In his reminiscences, R. C. Lehmann describes Wilkie as he remembers him during these months at Woodlands:

> A neat figure of a cheerful plumpness, very small feet and hands, a full brown beard, a high and rounded forehead, a small nose not naturally intended to support a pair of large spectacles behind which his eyes shone with humour and friendship.

We are told that his conversation was easy and delightful in both English and French. 'I don't care a fig for the accent,' he used to say. 'The French are a polite people, and they don't trouble to think about the accent if they understand you. They understand me.' He had one or two peculiarities of English speech, such as pronouncing 'real' as 'rail,' and 'obliged' as 'obleeged.' If one would hesitate to describe Wilkie as fond of children, in the general sense, there is no doubt that he had a great affection for certain children, among whom were the young Lehmanns. They, in their turn, adored him and never called him by any more formal name than

Wilkie. He seems to have possessed to a high degree the knack of making children feel at ease, and of treating them as equals instead of patronising them. They used to listen breathless to his tales of Tom Sayers, the prizefighter, whom he had often met. 'He hadn't any muscle to speak of in his forearm,' he told them, 'and there wasn't any show of biceps; but when I remarked on that, he asked me to observe his triceps and the muscle under his shoulder, and then I understood how he did it.' No doubt his popularity with the Lehmann boys lost nothing by the help he used to give them with their homework. One evening Rudy was struggling with a Horace Ode which he had to translate into English verse. Wilkie, picking up the Bohn 'crib,' said, 'I'm no good at the Latin, I'm afraid; but I'll see what I can do with the English.' He thereupon started to dictate, as fast as Rudy could write down, a set of couplets beginning:

> *What man or hero, Clio, dost thou name,*
> *On harp or lute, to swell the role of fame?*
> *What God whose name doth sportive Echo sound*
> *On Haemus cold or lofty Pindus' mound?*
> *Or Helicon whence followed Orpheus' strain*
> *The winds and rivers, flowing to the main?*

And so forth for fifty-six lines.

There is a story from another source† which confirms his instinctive understanding of children. Frank Beard's son, Nathaniel, was often entrusted with messages from his father to Wilkie, who lived close by. On one occasion he was told to bring back an answer, and on reaching Wilkie's study, discovered that he had left the note at home. Without thinking, the boy said: 'Never mind, you write the answer while I go back and fetch the letter.' instead of roaring with laughter, Wilkie replied gently: 'Very well, but it will be rather difficult; perhaps you had better bring the note round first.' A trivial incident, but also one that the boy remembered with gratitude years after Wilkie's death.

In October, 1869, he wrote from Gloucester Place a long account of his doings to Frederick Lehmann, who was then in the United States on his way round the world:

† 'Some Recollections of Yesterday.' Nathaniel Beard (*Temple Bar Magazine*, Vol. *cii*).

o

The Stoughton bitters arrived this morning from Liverpool. At the same time appeared a parcel of country sausages from Beard. I sent him back a bottle of the bitters with instructions to drink your health in brandy and bitters, and to meditate on the innumerable virtues of intoxicating liquors for the rest of the day. On my part I suspended an immortal work of fiction, by going downstairs and tasting a second bottle properly combined with gin. Result delicious! Thank you a thousand times! The first thing you must do on your return to England is to come here and taste gin and bitters. May it be soon!

Have I any news? Very little. I sit here all day attacking English institutions—battering down the marriage laws of Scotland and Ireland and reviling athletic sports—in short, writing an *un*-popular book which may possibly make a hit, from the mere oddity of a modern writer running full tilt against the popular sentiment instead of cringing to it. The publishers are delighted with what I have done—especially my American publishers, who sent me an instalment of £500 the other day, on receipt of only the first weekly part. I call *that* something like enthusiasm. Produce me the English publisher who treats his author in this way . . .

Reade has been here, and has carried off my book about the French police ('mémoires tirées des archives'). He begged me to go and see him at Oxford. I said, 'Very well! write and say when.' Need I add that he has *not* written?

I had a friend to dinner at the Junior Athenaeum the other day. Our remonstrance has produced its effect. I declined to order *any*thing after our experience. 'A dinner at so much a head. If is isn't good I shall personally submit myself for examination before the committee, and shall produce specimens of the dishes received by myself.' The result was a very good dinner. When you come back let us try the same plan. Nothing like throwing the whole responsibility on the cook.

I had a day at Gad's Hill a little while since. Only the family. Very harmonious and pleasant—except Dickens's bath, which dripped behind the head of my bed all night . . . Fechter has refused what appears to everybody but himself to be an excellent offer from America. He seems determined to go 'on his own hook' in December next, and will find the managers whom he has refused his enemies when he gets there. I am afraid he has made a mistake.

Mrs. John Wood has made the St. James' Theatre a perfect fairy palace, and is playing old English comedy with American actors. Scenery and dresses marvellously good. A great success. The other great success I am going to see on Wednesday—monkeys who are real circus riders, jump through hoops, dance on the horse's back, *and* bow to the audience when they are applauded. We shall see them in Shakespeare next—and why not? They can't be worse than the human actors, and they *might* be better. Where will you be when this reaches you? I am told you have got to San Francisco. That will do. Come back. Leave well alone, and come back. I will describe Japan to you, and take you to see the manufacturers afterwards at the Baker Street Bazaar.

Man and Wife had been accepted for serial publication by *Cassell's Magazine* and *Harper's Weekly*, and instalments began in January, 1870, and November, 1869, respectively. Harpers, who were clearly doing very well out of him despite the multiplication of their rivals, offered him £750—the same sum that they had paid for his last two or three books—but added that if he received a better offer 'from any *responsible* house, from whom you are sure of getting your money' they would match it. Several letters concerning *Man and Wife*, written to Cassell, Petter & Galpin, proprietors of *Cassell's Magazine*, have been preserved. The first refers to expletives in literature, a subject about which he felt strongly :

The expletive is not essentially necessary at the place which you point out to me—and I am very ready to make what concessions I can to your ideas of what is due to your constituency, at the outset of our literary connection. The objectionable 'Damn it' shall therefore disappear. But I must at the same time beg that this concession may not be construed into a precedent. Readers who object to expletives in books, are—as to my experience— readers who object to a great many other things in books, which they are too stupid to understand. It is quite possible that your peculiar constituency may take exception to things to come in my story which are essential to the development of character, or which are connected with a much higher and larger moral point of view than they are capable of taking themselves. In these cases, I am afraid you will find me deaf to all remonstrances —in those best interests of the independence of literature which are *your* interests (properly understood) as well as mine.

It is to be hoped that Messrs. Cassell appreciated the concession. At a later date, another publisher found him less accommodating on a similar point:

> The other alteration I cannot consent to make. The 'damns' (two 'damns' only, observe, in the whole story) mark the characters at very important places in the narrative. The 'compromise' which you suggest is simply what they would *not* say . . . My story is *not* addressed to young people exclusively—it is addressed to readers in general. I do not accept young people as the ultimate court of appeal in English literature. Mr. Turlington must talk like Mr. Turlington—even though the terrible consequence may be that a boy or two may cry 'Damn' in imitation of him. I refer your friends to Scott and Dickens—writers considered immaculate in the matter of propriety. They will find damn where damn ought to be in the pages of both those masters. In short, I am damned if I take out damn!

The remainder of the Cassell correspondence refers to the thorny question of international copyright, a subject in which Wilkie, as one of the most popular English writers beyond the shores of his own country, was especially interested. His work was now regularly translated into French and German, and often into Dutch, Polish, Italian and Russian. Publication for European circulation in English by his friend Baron Tauchnitz of Leipzig had become more or less simultaneous with London publication. By 1870 reciprocal copyright was the rule in most European countries, but Holland and Switzerland refused to conform. It was not to be expected that a profitable author like Wilkie Collins would escape the attentions of publishers in Holland, nor that a man of his temperament and business acumen would quietly acquiesce in what he considered to be plain theft. In November, 1869, a Dutch firm, Belinfaute Brothers of The Hague, approached Cassells with an offer, as between publishers, for the electrotypes of *Man and Wife*. Although Wilkie's consent was unnecessary, Cassells considerately informed him of the approach. Here, he thought, was the chance for which he had been waiting, the opportunity 'of taking some public notice of the dishonesty of the publishers in Holland—and of contrasting it with the honourable conduct of Tauchnitz, who is also not bound by any treaties to pay English authors, but who does pay them nevertheless.' In a letter to

Cassells announcing his intention of joining battle, he complained, with some justification: 'In this matter everybody in Holland gains something—the printer, the papermaker, the translator, the publisher. I, who set the whole thing going, get nothing.'

He tried writing to The Hague, 'good-humouredly and strongly,' but got nowhere. His blood was now up. Having sent copies of the correspondence to the editor of the *Echo*, he discharged, on November 18th, a broadside which reveals him as a useful hand at the more vigorous type of invective.

Gentlemen,—The grave error that I have committed is the error of assuming you to be more just and more enlightened men than you are. Your answer to my letter tells me what I was previously unwilling to believe—that you have persisted so long in publishing books by authors of all nations, without paying for them, that any protest against that proceeding on my part, which appeals to your sense of a moral distinction between right and wrong, appeals to something that no longer exists.

What am I to say to men who acknowledge that they, and the people whom they employ, all derive profit from publishing my book; and who, owning this, not only repudiate the bare idea of being under any pecuniary obligations towards me as the writer of the book, but shamelessly assert their own act of spoliation as a right—because no law happens to exist which prohibits that act as wrong? There is nothing to be said to persons who are willing to occupy such a position as this. What is to prevent men who trade on such principles as these from picking my pocket, if they see their way to making a profit out of my handkerchief? There is absolutely nothing to prevent their picking my pocket; and, what is more, indignantly informing me that it is their right—unless by some lucky chance, English handkerchiefs are better cared for than English literature, and are protected in Holland by law.

Suppose international copyright to be, one of these days, established between England and Holland. What would become of you and your right then? You would have no alternative left but to curse the cruel fate that made you Dutchmen, and retire from business.

Returning, before I close these lines, to your answer to my letter, I have to add that I have not in the least mistaken the nature of your application to me on the subject of the illustrations. It is the most indecent application I ever heard of in my life. You ask me to help you to pay honestly for obtaining the illustrations to my story—telling me, in the same breath, that you claim a right to take the story itself without paying for it. Do you expect me to notice such an application as that? It would be accepting an insult to notice it.

For the rest—whether you do, or do not, take my book from me—I persist, in the interests of public morality, in asserting my right to regard as my own property the produce of my own brains and my own labour—any accidental neglect in formally protecting the same, in any country, notwithstanding. I declare any publisher who takes my book from me, with a view to selling it in any form for his own benefit—without my permission and without giving me a share in his profits—to be guilty of theft, and to be morally, if not legally, an outlaw and a pest among honest men. And I send the correspondence between us to an English newspaper of wide circulation, by way of openly recording this protest, and openly exposing the principles on which Dutch publishers trade. In this way, my views on the subject of fair-dealing with foreign authors may possibly reach the ears of those other persons of larcenous literary habits, who are ready—as you kindly inform me—to steal my story, without that preliminary notice of their intention, which you yourselves were personally compelled to give me by the honourable conduct, in this affair, of my English publishers.

It was hardly to be expected that such a letter would have any effect beyond inducing a momentary malaise in the piratical conscience. To Wilkie's astonishment, however, it succeeded in penetrating their defences, as his next letter to the *Echo*, which had given editorial support to his campaign, shows:

. . . . I have now to announce a conclusion to this matter which was not anticipated either by you, or by me. My English publishers received a letter yesterday from the Hague, in which Messrs. Belinfaute Bros. concede the point which I endeavoured (good-humouredly) to press upon them in my first letter. Of their own free will (bound by no law whatever) they consent to recognise my moral claim on them, as the author, by giving me a share in the profits produced by my book—if profit is realised by the Dutch translation of *Man and Wife*. Let us never despair of our dear Dutchmen, sir, in any future human emergency; and let us take Belinfaute Brothers to our hearts as brothers in international copyright with ourselves! While I maintain every word I have written as to all publishers who take books from authors without paying for them, I am glad publickly to declare that what I wrote no longer applies to Belinfaute Bros. They publish *Man and Wife* in Holland with my full consent, and with my best wishes for the success of the speculation.

The financial outcome of this concession was hardly spectacular. 'Belinfaute Bros. have made a noble effort,' he wrote some twelve months after publication; 'they have sent me as purchase-money for *Man and Wife* the sum of one hundred guilders—amounting in English money to between £8 and £9! As they have never hitherto paid sixpence to any author (but a Dutchman) in this civilised universe, I feel bound to consider myself as the object of an act of extraordinary munificence.' Sending the draft to Charles Ward at Coutt's Bank he wrote, 'Acknowledge receipt for God's sake— I am afraid of something happening to this precious enclosure. Pay it in to my account—in *red* ink if possible. I never was so excited in my life.' Nevertheless it was a moral victory of some importance. The custom of paying token royalties to foreign authors was adopted by other Dutch publishing firms and continued until full inter-European copyright was secured by the Berne Convention in 1886.

There was trouble across the Atlantic as well. 'I find there is a piracy of *Man and Wife* in Canada, which I can only stop by authorising a publication of the story there, and sending sheets in advance, as I do in America.' Even in those countries which respected the rights of foreign authors, things were often made as complicated as possible. For Germany, he mentions, four copies of each monthly part must be deposited, with the words 'The right of translation is reserved' appearing at the top of each instead of in their usual place at the end. In fact he begins to wonder whether the game is worth the candle. 'For my own part, I am getting so weary of the vexatious and absurd regulations which these foreign laws impose on English literature that I am strongly disposed to let myself be robbed, as the preferable alternative to letting myself be worried . . .' Thus he wrote in 1871. All in all the campaign had been worth waging, and his small triumph marked a stage at least on the road to international copyright.

Man and Wife had pushed up the sales of *Cassell's Magazine* to well over 70,000 by the time it appeared in book-form towards the end of June, 1870. It has the odd distinction of being, so far as one can discover, the only novel issued by F. S. Ellis, the Rossettis' publisher. Towards the end Wilkie had written himself to exhaustion, with Beard in frequent attendance. Both were 'utterly worn out' and took a week-end trip to Antwerp in order to recuperate at sea. Writing to tell the Lehmanns that he has dedicated the novel to them, he adds: 'I am so weak, I can hardly write a note.'

Man and Wife is his first thoroughgoing propaganda novel. The Preface opens with these words: 'The Story here offered to the reader differs in one respect from the stories which have preceded it from the same hand. This time the fiction is founded on facts, and aspires to afford what help it may towards hastening the reform of certain abuses which have been too long suffered to exist among us unchecked.' In March, 1865, the Queen had appointed a Royal Commission to enquire into the Marriage Laws of the United Kingdom. The Commission's Report,† published three years later, expressed strong criticism of certain aspects of the Scottish and Irish laws relating to marriage, and recommended early reform. In Ireland, for instance, the existing law declared null and void a marriage between two Catholics if one of them had been received into the Catholic Church less than twelve months before; any priest celebrating such a marriage was guilty of a felony. More serious in its social consequences was the survival in Scotland of the curious form of matrimony known as the Irregular Marriage, or Marriage by Consent. A contemporary judgment, quoted in *Man and Wife*, underlines the extraordinary state of the law: 'Consent makes marriage. No form of ceremony, civil or religious; no notice before, or publication after; no cohabitation, no writing, no witnesses even, are essential to the constitution of this, the most important contract which two persons can enter into.' Even the exchange of consent could be proved by inference, with the result that persons who did not consider themselves married could be held to be married in law. It is not surprising that a law so unpredictable in its incidence provided a harvest for

† Report of the Royal Commission on the Laws of Marriage. (*H.M.S.O.*, 1868).

lawyers, nor that the Royal Commission should have demanded its abolition.† These were the very real abuses which Wilkie pledged himself to bring before the notice of his extensive public, most of whom would probably be unaware of the existence of the Commission's Report. If the spark which kindled his imagination, in writing *The Moonstone*, was the contemplation of a jewel, here inspiration sprang directly from a Government Blue Book.

So far as we know, Wilkie was not an habitual reader of official publications and it may well have been Reade who drew his attention to this particular Report in the first instance. Certainly Reade's influence is unmistakably evident in *Man and Wife*. Such was Wilkie's indignation at the state of affairs disclosed by the Royal Commission that he did not pause to consider whether his technical equipment was equal to the task of hewing this refractory material into the shape of a novel. In fact the skill with which he constructed his story around the anomalies of the marriage law cannot be denied. It is on other counts that the book falls short of his best work.

For some time there had been growing up among the younger generation of the upper and middle classes a cult of athleticism, particularly at the universities where it was partly responsible for increasing displays of hooliganism. In many quarters, even among older people, this glorification of muscular prowess and excessive devotion to sport was regarded with tolerant approval, and had found expression in several novels of Charles Kingsley. To Wilkie Collins, who saw in it a denial of the intellectual and cultural aspects of education, the idea could only be repellent. Not content with illustrating the case for marriage-law reform, he assumed the further duty of refuting the doctrines of Kingsley and his flock. The acrobatic feat of riding two such horses at once demanded an agility which he did not possess. His attempt was ambitious

---

† An actual case, upon which the novel was partly founded, had been in the courts some ten years earlier. A Scottish marriage contracted by a Mr. Yelverton was pronounced valid in a Scottish court. By a majority decision the Court of Appeal pronounced it null and void. The House of Lords was equally divided with two Law Lords for, and two against the Appeal; the fifth, Lord Brougham, was unable to come to the House to record his judgment which was said to be in favour of the first decision in the Scottish Court. The Court of Appeal decision therefore stood, by the narrowest of margins.

but unwise, even allowing for his brave determination to write 'an unpopular novel.' The instrument of his attack on athleticism —and on the manners of the younger generation—is the character of the seducer Geoffrey Delamayn. A long-distance runner of superb physique, Geoffrey is both brutish and brainless. The author might have held up such a figure to constant ridicule, impaled him with satire; instead, allowing his spleen full play, Wilkie represents him as something of a monster. So obvious a blackguard would not have deceived the most guileless of heroines.

The other main weakness of *Man and Wife* springs from a different source. It was first conceived not as a novel but as a play; in fact we have the evidence of Bancroft, who later produced the drama, that the first act was completed before a line of the novel was on paper. At first glance it seems improbable that this vast novel—the longest of all his books save *Armadale*—packed with incident, complicated in construction, could have grown out of a stage-play, yet that is undoubtedly what happened. Had he recast the story more thoroughly in expanding it into a three-volume novel the result might have been more successful; as it is, too many vestiges of its dramatic origin remain. He failed to appreciate, in retaining the countless exits and entrances, overheard conversations and coincidences of the play, that devices which are legitimate and often necessary in overcoming the limitations of space and time in the theatre, may be unacceptable in a novel.

Man and Wife is a bitter, angry book. It is one of the least typical of all Wilkie Collins' novels; its deeply-felt sincerity recalls the early *Basil*. Despite a certain theatricality, and a tendency towards strident overstatement, *Man and Wife* remains a powerful story which seldom relaxes its grip.

In the person of Sir Patrick Lundie, Wilkie gives us not only one of his most engaging characters but also an ideal portrait of himself. Sir Patrick's urbanity, his dry humour, his broadminded wisdom and hatred of cruelty are all characteristics with which the author himself was in some degree endowed; even his club-foot may have represented Wilkie's increasing lameness. It is Sir Patrick Lundie who expresses the author's views on the new athleticism and on the tragic farce of Irregular Marriages.

In his Essay on Wilkie Collins, Swinburne adapted a well-known couplet:

What brought good Wilkie's genius nigh perdition?
Some demon whispered—'Wilkie! have a mission.'

Whilst one can agree that his missionary zeal did considerable harm to his natural gifts, it is misleading to advance this, as many besides Swinburne have done, as the sole explanation of the steady decline in Collins' work which began with *Man and Wife*. Of his total output not more than half a dozen books can properly be classified as 'purpose-novels.' In a sense *No Name* is a purpose-novel no less than *Man and Wife*, but one in which the story comes first and the problem is more implied than stated. With *Man and Wife* comes a shift of emphasis. Not only is the purpose clearly stated, but reiterated on every other page. The reformer has here won the upper hand over the novelist. Nevertheless, if there is in *Man and Wife* a foreshadowing of the inferior work that was to come, equally there are echoes of the best that had gone before.

In several respects the year 1870 marked a turning-point in Wilkie Collins' life. Although he was to live another twenty years, all his work of significance was already behind him. He had made his contribution to the fiction of his time; none of the dozen or so novels still to come would earn for him more than the passing attention of a devoted public. At the age of 46 he was already in appearance and outlook an old man, largely as a result of ill-health. The intervals during which he could enjoy even reasonably good health were becoming briefer and less frequent; he must have known that all hope of eradicating his rheumatic trouble had gone; that sooner or later he would become, at best, a semi-invalid. His dependence upon opium, hitherto intermittent, was now virtually complete. He had come to need the drug not only to alleviate pain, but often to induce sleep. Similarly, in his private life, one phase had ended with Caroline's marriage, another was beginning. His liaison with Martha Rudd, despite the fact that she had borne him one daughter and was soon to bear another, can hardly have provided a substitute for his comparatively settled domestic life with Caroline. Nor is it certain, in the circumstances, that Caroline's return a year or so later fully re-established their earlier relationship.

This was about the time when Julian Hawthorne, son of the

author of *The Scarlet Letter*, first met Wilkie during a visit to England. Writing more than fifty years after the event†—a fact which inclines one to make certain reservations—he describes Wilkie, whom he found in 'his plethoric, disordered writing-room,' in terms which almost suggest a man in his dotage.

He was soft, plump, and pale, suffered from various ailments, his liver was wrong, his heart weak, his lungs faint, his stomach incompetent, he ate too much and the wrong things. He had a big head, a dingy complexion, was somewhat bald, and his full beard was of a light brown colour. His air was of mild discomfort and fractiousness; he had a queer way of holding his hand, which was small, plump, and unclean, hanging up by the wrist, like a rabbit on its hind legs. He had strong opinions and prejudices, but his nature was obviously kind and lovable, and a humorous vein would occasionally be manifest. One felt he was unfortunate and needed succour.

Poor Wilkie ventured to express his admiration of *The Scarlet Letter*, which he described as 'one of the great novels.' 'Even the second volume, where most novelists weaken, is fine," he continued graciously, 'and the third fulfils the splendid promise of the first.' Julian Hawthorne protested, not very tactfully, that *The Scarlet Letter* was in one volume. 'Pardon me! Three volumes, and large ones!' replied his host and went to the bookshelf to prove his point. Taking down the single volume he looked perplexed. 'You are right. One volume and not over seventy thousand words in all! It is incomprehensible! Such a powerful impression in so small a space!'

Though it is largely in retrospect that the year 1870 stands out in Wilkie's life as one of transition, it contained one event which marked, not only for him but for the people of England, the end of an age. On June 9th, Dickens died. It is probably true to say that they had met less often during the last five years of Dickens' life than during the previous fifteen years. Only a single letter written by Dickens to Wilkie in the last year of his life has survived. It is dated January 27th, 1870, and enclosed a formal letter giving Wilkie the right of disposing of material which had

† *Shapes that Pass.* Julian Hawthorne. (*Murray*, 1928).

originally appeared in Dickens' periodicals. There is a melancholy note about the last few sentences he wrote to his old friend: 'I have been truly concerned to hear of your bad attack. Well, I have two hopes of it—first, that it will not last long; second, that it will leave you in a really recovered state of good health. I don't come to see you because I don't want to bother you. Perhaps you may be glad to see me by-and-by. Who knows?' If these words suggest that they had to some extent drifted apart, it would be wrong to assume that they had ceased altogether to see each other. We know that Wilkie had been staying at Gad's Hill some three months before the date of the letter, and he told a friend that he was engaged to go down there on the very day of Dickens' death.

During the evening of June 8th Dickens had a seizure after which he never recovered consciousness. The last provincial Reading Tour had been prematurely concluded some weeks earlier. Against his friends' advice he had persisted with the readings through various stages of exhaustion, as if some obscure force were driving him to his death. Wilkie had consistently encouraged Dickens to undertake these Reading Tours, which most of his friends condemned as undignified. He knew that the excitement, the histrionics and the applause had become essential as a drug to Dickens. At the same time he realised how much the performance cost him in mental and physical strain, and once told Wybert Reeve that the Reading of the scene between Bill Sykes and Nancy 'did more to kill Dickens than all his other work put together.'

In accordance with the dead man's wishes, no public announcement of the funeral was made, and only three mourning-coaches followed the hearse along Whitehall to Westminster Abbey. In the third coach, with his brother Charles and Frank Beard, rode the man who for most of twenty years had been Dickens' closest friend.

This intimate friendship, thus broken after twenty years, had been a thing of value to both writers. The benefits that Wilkie gained are all too obvious, but the contribution he was able to make in his turn is usually overlooked by Dickens' biographers. From the beginning of their acquaintance he had been a congenial companion, able to adapt himself to Dickens' somewhat mercurial temperament and frequent changes of mood. Unlike Forster he made few demands. He was neither priggish, nor bad-tempered, nor possessive, nor pompous. He was in fact the antithesis of Forster in character and temper, and thereby succeeded, quite unintentionally, in supplanting Forster in Dickens' regard. Uninhibited, scornful of convention, epicurean, Wilkie had, until ill-health overtook him, a remarkable capacity for enjoying the very staff of life. These were the qualities which at first appealed to Dickens, whose febrile determination to extract the last ounce from life contrasted sharply with Wilkie's easy acceptance of its pleasures. He seemed to find in Wilkie's company both a stimulant and a sedative. It was in part due to the intense seriousness with which they both regarded the writer's craft, and to their common devotion to their calling, that an association so begun grew into one of the more enduring literary friendships.

It has been hinted that one of the chief bonds between Collins and Dickens was that they shared a taste for licentious orgies and loose women. Apparently this view is based upon a literal interpretation of certain passages in their letters to each other. Such an interpretation ignores the hyperbole that they were accustomed to employ in their correspondence, and at the same time measures respectability by the standards of the society of their own day. It is probably safe to assume that their experience of women was more extensive than that society would have countenanced, but it is going far beyond the available evidence to deduce that sexual promiscuity was their habit. Certainly, references to 'sybarite Rome in the days of its culminating voluptuousness' and 'furtive and Don Giovanni purposes' are not of themselves evidence of gross immorality. Furthermore, there is no indication that such adventures as they may have shared in the company of women were more than a casual aspect of their relationship, which was based upon far more solid foundations.

For Wilkie the advantages of constant association, during his formative years as a novelist, with so prolific a genius as Dickens were immeasurable. His talents, though of a very different order from those of his friend, developed all the sooner and shone the more brightly for the careful nursing they received at Dickens' hands. By his thoughtful and constructive criticism, offered only when it was invited, and by his generous encouragement, he helped the less experienced novelist to find himself within a very few years. As not only 'one of Mr. Dickens' young men,' but as the chosen one of that select band, Wilkie quickly made his mark in the world of letters. The close association between them developed Wilkie's eye for character and his sense of the dramatic just as surely as it belatedly awakened Dickens to the advantages of a well-constructed plot. Each benefited in his own way and no harm came to either. It seems appropriate to quote here the view of G. K. Chesterton, who wrote, in a typical passage:

In his capacity as editor [Dickens] made one valuable discovery. He discovered Wilkie Collins. Wilkie Collins is the one man of unmistakable genius who has a certain affinity with Dickens; an affinity in this respect, that they both combine a modern and Cockney and even commonplace opinion about things with a huge elemental sympathy with strange oracles and spirits and old night. There were no two men in mid-Victorian England, with their top-hats and umbrellas, more typical of its rationality and dull reform; and there were no two men who could touch them as a ghost-story. No two men would have more contempt for superstitions; and no two men could so create the superstitious thrill.

It is strangely appropriate that, during the last year of his life, Dickens had been at work on a novel of the kind that had made Wilkie Collins' reputation, while at the same time Wilkie himself was turning his back upon pure sensationalism in favour of the propaganda-novel. *The Mystery of Edwin Drood* appears to be a deliberate challenge to Wilkie on his own territory, an attempt to eclipse the acknowledged 'master of sensation.' At the same time it provides the clearest example of Wilkie's influence upon his friend's work. It is therefore small wonder that, when Dickens died with *Edwin Drood* unfinished, many people believed that Wilkie would know all the details of the plot and would complete the story. The rumours that he was about to do so became so prevalent that both he and Chapman and Hall had to issue public statements denying any such intention. These disclaimers did not, however, deter a New York journalist named Henry Morford from writing 'a sequel to *The Mystery of Edwin Drood*,' entitled *John Jasper's Secret* and attributing the authorship to Wilkie Collins and Charles Dickens Jnr. In a letter dated 1878 Wilkie wrote: 'I was asked to finish the story and positively refused.'

In the year following Dickens' death, Wilkie was involved in a trivial but illuminating episode with Forster. George Bentley, son of Richard Bentley, perhaps the most famous of Victorian publishers, was anxious to collect for biographical purposes as many of his father's letters as possible. He probably thought that it would be tactful to use Wilkie as a channel of approach to Forster, who was Dickens' literary executor, in applying for the return of Richard Bentley's letters to Dickens. Wilkie, never quite appreciating the intensity of Forster's dislike, or perhaps hoping that he might respond to new overtures now that the cause of jealousy was removed, accepted without hesitation. But the Bear, as he was called by many of his acquaintances, was not disposed to co-operate. Announcing his failure to George Bentley, Wilkie wrote: 'Mr. Forster's answer to my letter makes it, I am sorry to say, impossible for me to represent your views any further. There is some soreness in his mind on the subject, which I do not in the least understand. He has not answered my second letter.' Even this rebuff did not prevent Wilkie from warmly congratulating Forster upon the first volume of his *Life of Dickens* when it appeared a year or so later.

It was the firm of Bentley which published Wilkie's next novel, *Poor Miss Finch*, then being serialised, like its immediate predecessor, in *Cassell's Magazine*. Michael Sadleir tells an interesting story† relating to its publication in the usual three volumes at half-a-guinea per volume. When Bentley's travellers offered the book to the larger libraries, Mudie's and W. H. Smith's, upon whose purchases depended to some extent the success or failure of a three-decker, they received a negligible order. The libraries had learned by their experience of *Man and Wife* that a bound volume of *Cassell's Magazine* containing the whole of *Poor Miss Finch* would shortly be available at a much lower price. Since there was collusion between the two biggest libraries, it mattered little that their subscribers were forced to wait a few weeks or months. Bentley was faced with a considerable loss on the book, of which he had printed 2,000 copies. Wilkie, whose hard bargaining with publishers did not mean that he was incapable of generosity in special circumstances, immediately offered to return half the sum

† 'The Camel's Back' from *Nineteenth Century Essays.* (Oxford University Press, 1948).

he had already been paid, and launched a fierce campaign against the 'Library Despots.'

Poor Miss Finch was summed up by the *Athenaeum*, a little unkindly, as a 'sensation-novel for Sunday reading.' The plot, in which crime plays a negligible part, is an ingenious piece of carpentry for all its fantastic material. A bald account of the main situation will be sufficient to convey some idea of the extraordinary nature of the story. Lucilla, an attractive girl who has been blind from childhood, falls in love with a young man, one of twins, who becomes subject to epilepsy. In his desperate search for a cure he has recourse to silver nitrate treatment, an incidental effect of which is to turn the patient's skin blue in colour. It is only when the other twin brother has secretly fallen in love with her that Lucilla regains her sight after a brilliant operation. Although Wilkie executes some intricate variations on the old theme of mistaken identity he cannot disguise the fact that the whole situation is somewhat preposterous. All ends more or less happily with Lucilla going blind again.

The book's virtues lie primarily in the characters of Lucilla and Madame Pratolungo, the narrator of the story and Lucilla's companion. Cheerful, sensible—'I am not rich enough to care about money'—as garrulous as her name suggests, she is the French-born widow of a South American patriot, and a staunch believer in her late husband's Socialist theories and prophecies of revolution. Her exotic presence in the midst of the Sussex Downs somehow gives an air of reality to the improbable happenings she has to relate. Lucilla herself is a thoroughly charming person, slightly reminiscent of Madonna in *Hide and Seek*, living a happy and useful life despite her blindness. She illustrates once more Wilkie's belief that, in the words of his Preface, 'the conditions of human happiness are independent of bodily affliction, and that it is even possible for bodily affliction itself to take its place among the ingredients of happiness.' Herr Grosse, the eminent German specialist who restores Lucilla's sight, is no more than a caricature of a type of German once popular on the stage. He was, however, a great favourite with readers of Wilkie's day, many of whom, assuming him to be drawn from life, wrote to the author begging him to disclose Herr Grosse's real name and address in order that their blind friends or relatives might consult him. After replying to many such letters, Wilkie

P

had to insert a note in the second edition assuring his readers that 'Herr Grosse has no (individual) living prototype.' He bore in fact a close resemblance to Wilkie's doctor at Aix-la-Chapelle, who was not, however, an oculist. The other remarkable character is the little girl, Jicks. It is interesting to note that what is in effect Wilkie's first portrait of a small child should appear at a time when his own first-born, Marian, was in her third year. Jicks is natural and delightful; she behaves like a real child, in contrast to the sentimentalised children so dear to the Victorian novelist.

With all its faults, *Poor Miss Finch* is a story told, if not in his most beguiling manner, at least skilfully enough to capture and hold the reader's attention. Whilst admiring the assurance with which the author tackles his self-imposed obstacles, one cannot wholly disagree with *The Spectator's* description of *Poor Miss Finch* as 'that repertory of wasted cleverness.' On the other hand it is difficult to see why this innocuous work should have been specific-ally included by Ruskin in what he called 'the loathsome mass of modern fiction.' At least it is unencumbered with any mission and has the advantage over both its forerunner and its successor in having been conceived as a novel, without even half an eye upon the stage. In fact Wilkie wrote to a friend: 'My *Poor Miss Finch* has been dramatised (without asking my permission) by some obscure idiot in the country. I have been asked to dramatise it but have refused because my experience tells me that the book is eminently *unfit* for stage purposes.'

14

American Journey

ONE of Wilkie's closest friends, now that Dickens was dead, was his doctor and near neighbour, Francis Carr Beard. We do not know a great deal about Frank Beard himself, except that he was ten years older than Wilkie and greatly attached to him, but his son, Nathaniel, had left an intimate sketch of the novelist in the course of some reminiscences.† Wilkie was a frequent visitor at their house and used to turn up in 'a strange variety of costumes.' He would be as likely to sit down to dinner in a light camel-hair or tweed suit, worn with a shirt of broad blue or pink stripes, and perhaps a bright red tie, as in a dark suit or evening dress. Whenever he was feeling well the family looked forward to his entertaining conversation and amusing stories, but they always knew when an attack of gout was imminent by the nervous depression which overcame him, and by 'the horrible shaking of the room produced by his fidgetting with one foot upon the floor.'

There were times when the ocular gout would compel him to keep his eyes bandaged for days, and sometimes weeks, at a stretch, and on many such occasions Frank Beard would write down page after page of his book as he dictated. Wilkie invariably consulted him on the medical details that were so liberally sprinkled about his novels—silver nitrate treatment for epilepsy, for instance, or ophthalmic surgery, or the effects of various poisons. Frank was even called upon to conduct him to a professional running-track in order that the scene of the 'foot-race' in *Man and Wife* might be authentic in atmosphere and detail.

Nathaniel Beard found him strangely uninformed about topics of current interest, and accustomed to ask naïve questions about

† 'Some Recollections of Yesterday.' Nathaniel Beard. (*Temple Bar Magazine*, Vol. cii).

matters which, although possibly of no great moment, were
common knowledge at the time. This he largely attributed to the
fact that Wilkie seldom read newspapers and would normally,
when discussing a particular subject, use the phrase 'I hear' or 'I
am told' where other people would say 'I read' or 'I see.' This view
conflicts with that of an American journalist who wrote in an
article on Wilkie Collins: 'He is an excellent representative and
type of a modern class of English literary men, who mingle freely
and happily with the world and are of it; who take a keen interest
in the events of the world and keep well apace with their times . . .
He thinks positively on all subjects, and in politics he stands fairly
on the liberal and progressive side.'†

Beard was not the only one to discover that Wilkie was a man
of strong prejudices, and in particular, an unabashed Francophile.
Almost everything, he considered, was better done on the Continent, especially cookery. He kept a French cook and had himself
studied French cuisine. When he was in France he made friends,
in his favourite role of gourmet, with every good chef he came
across. In the same spirit he had written to the Padrona: 'I wish
I knew of another cook to recommend—but unless you will take
me, I know of nobody. And I am conscious of one serious objection
to myself. My style is expensive. I look on meat simply as a
material for sauces.' At dinner he used to discourse lyrically on
the subject of French dishes and succeeded in infecting Frank
Beard with his enthusiasm. Inevitably Beard learned to share his
friend's passion for garlic-flavoured food. To his family's horror
he persuaded their plain English cook to experiment with garlic, a
task she undertook with such zeal that soon it was introduced
into every dish—in grossly excessive quantities. The end of the
sad story can best be told in Nathaniel Beard's own words:

> One evening Wilkie and my father had talked themselves into
> quite a culinary frenzy over a certain 'Don Pedro pie' which
> Wilkie had recently tasted during his travels. At last they
> arranged that the thing should be put to tangible proof. The
> next day, the materials having been procured for this delicacy,
> Wilkie came round and he and my father went solemnly into
> the kitchen together, each adorned with an apron which had

† 'Wilkie Collins.' George M. Towle. (*Appleton's Journal*, New York, 3rd
Sept., 1870).

been borrowed from the cook, and instructing, pointing out, and occasionally joining with the cook in the practical details of the manufacture of the much-praised dish . . . It was a glorious success, but there was just one little drawback. The garlic had predominated so strongly that no one save the two chefs themselves could venture upon tasting it. The upshot of it all was that Wilkie went home and took to his bed, while my father remained at home and took to his. They were both very ill for several days with a horrible gastric attack, and garlic was nevermore mentioned in the house.

Another of Wilkie's peculiarities in the matter of flavours was his intense liking for black pepper. 'It is seldom provided at dinner-tables to which I repair,' he said on one occasion, 'and therefore I take care to provide it myself.' He used to produce his private pepper-mill with great flourish and mock ceremony.

The Beard family had a strong affection for him which offset any faint disapproval they may have felt towards his unconventional way of living—'a rather "rapid" mode of existence,' as Nathaniel primly describes it. He always took the greatest interest in the three children—'ill-behaved young people' according to the eldest of them—and they loved him dearly. Then there was Frank's elder sister who, whilst liking Wilkie as a person, took strong exception to his books and opinions, and frequently crossed swords with him at dinner-table conversation. She was very indignant at his description of Jenny Lind as a superb singer but in other respects a charlatan, and declared that he was incapable of appreciating the absolute truth and purity of Jenny Lind's life. He retaliated by telling the story of her watching from a window the crowds streaming into Her Majesty's Theatre, and saying, 'What a pity to think of all these people wasting their time in going to hear me sing, when they might be doing so much good with it.' For Wilkie no further evidence of her insincerity was needed.

During the early eighteen-seventies, although his output of fiction was maintained, he was far more interested in the theatre. In a period of about eighteen months no fewer than three Wilkie Collins plays were produced in the West End of London; two of them ran for a time concurrently. They were his three greatest stage successes. An incidental outcome of their production was that each brought him at least one enduring friendship in the theatrical world.

First came the dramatic version of *The Woman in White* upon which he had lavished exceptional pains. It had proved an intractable book to dramatise, and he was never entirely satisfied with the stage version. There had been a preliminary try-out in August, 1870, at the Theatre Royal, Leicester, with Wilson Barrett as Fosco, but for some reason London did not see the play until more than a year later. The popularity of the book ensured plenty of advance interest in the play which was further stimulated by the appearance on the hoardings of a strikingly original poster. Frederick Walker's design for *The Woman in White* can almost be said to mark the birth of modern English poster art. Walker, an Academician who died young, dashed off the original sketch at Charles Collins' house in Thurloe Place, Kensington. Wilkie was delighted when he saw the design, a woodcut of a woman in a white dress gliding through a French window against a background of starlit night; it caught exactly the atmosphere of mystery and romance that he wanted. This was apparently the first time an artist of repute had been commissioned to design a poster for the theatre. The original was twice exhibited during the 'seventies, and is now in the possession of the Tate Gallery.

The play was presented at the Olympic Theatre on October 9th, 1871, with a cast which included Ada Dyas in the dual role of Anne Catherick and Laura Fairlie, Mrs. Charles Viner as Marian Halcombe, George Vining as Fosco, and a little known actor named Wybert Reeve as Walter Hartright. The friendship which sprang up between Reeve and the author dates from the play's second rehearsal. Wilkie attended many rehearsals, in the course of which endless arguments arose among the cast and tempers became frayed. The author, Reeve tells us, 'looked through it all perplexed in the extreme, but he was gentlemanly, patient and good-tempered, always ready with a smile if a chance offered itself, or a peaceful word kindly suggesting when a point was to be gained.' He also mentions Wilkie's 'full, massive, very clever head and forehead, and bright, intellectual eyes looking out of strong glasses mounted in gold.' His beard was already flecked with white.

The Woman in White was well received on the first night and achieved a run of twenty weeks at the Olympic. The provincial tour which followed lasted for several years. In the provinces Wybert Reeve took over the more important part of Count Fosco, in which he made his reputation. He played it more than 1,500 times on both sides of the Atlantic.

His next play, *Man and Wife*, was accepted by the Bancrofts for inclusion in their highly successful season at the Prince of Wales Theatre, now the Scala. In selecting a melodrama such as this to succeed the light comedies of T. W. Robertson which had put the theatre on the map, the Bancrofts made a surprising decision, but had no reason to regret the choice. Negotiations began eighteen months before the play was produced, for on August 1st, 1871, Wilkie wrote to Bancroft:

> Let me assure you that I feel the sincerest gratification that *Man and Wife* has been accepted for the Prince of Wales Theatre. Every advantage that I could possibly wish for is, I know beforehand, already obtained for my work, now that it has secured the good fortune of addressing itself to the public with Mrs. Bancroft's introduction.

In their reminiscences, *On and Off the Stage*, the Bancrofts commented: 'So commenced a friendship, which it has been our privilege to enjoy ever since, with one whose masterly romances had lightened many an hour and given us infinite delight.'

After various postponements *Man and Wife* was billed to follow Lord Lytton's *Money*. Towards the end of 1872 Wilkie was invited to read the play to the company. 'This he did,' wrote Bancroft, 'with great effect and nervous force, giving all concerned a clear insight into his view of the characters.' He too bears witness to the author's valuable suggestions and accommodating attitude at rehearsals, and his readiness to make alterations for the improvement of the play. The chief parts were to be filled by John Hare as Sir Patrick Lundie, Lydia Foote as Anne Sylvester and Coghlan as Geoffrey Delamayn, the Bancrofts being content with comparatively minor roles.

It was an especially brilliant first night, and seats were at premium, ticket speculators extracting as much as five guineas for a stall. Of the audience the Bancrofts wrote: 'Literary and artistic London was present in unusual force, and an audience more representative of the intellect of the time has seldom been gathered within the walls of a theatre.' All this served to reduce poor Wilkie's nerves to an even more shattered state than usual. He remained in Bancroft's dressing-room throughout the performance 'in a state of nervous terror painful to see,' and the frequent loud bursts of applause coming from the auditorium provided only momentary relief for his sufferings. He had his sole view of the stage that night when the audience called enthusiastically for the author after the final curtain. He devoted the few sentences he could stammer out to unstinted praise for the acting, which he had not of course seen. The following day he wrote to a friend, 'It was certainly an extraordinary success. The pit got on its legs and cheered with all its might the moment I showed myself in front of the curtain. I counted that I had only thirty friends in the house to match against a picked band of the "lower orders" of literature and the drama assembled at the back of the dress circle to hiss and laugh at the first chance. The services of my friends were not required. The public never gave the "opposition" a chance all through the evening. The acting, I hear all round, was superb.'

Dutton Cook wrote of the first performance on February 22nd, 1873: 'Mr. Collins has successfully accomplished the end he had in view, and has proved himself to be a dramatist of unusual ability. His play is . . . a complete and coherent work, endowed with an independent vitality of its own.' A technical innovation in *Man and Wife* was the first use on the stage of electric lightning during the storm scene. Towards the end of the run of 136 nights, Wilkie wrote to Bancroft:

> I should be the most ungrateful man living if the result of *Man and Wife* did not far more than merely "satisfy" me. My play has been magnificently acted, everybody concerned with it has treated me with the greatest kindness, and you and Mrs. Bancroft have laid me under obligations to your sympathy and friendship for which I cannot sufficiently thank you. The least I can do, if all goes well, is to write for the Prince of Wales Theatre again, and next time to give you and Mrs. Bancroft parts that will be a little more worthy of you.

An unauthorised version of *Man and Wife* had been given on the New York stage more than two years before. The adaptation had been made by that most industrious of dramatic 'pirates,'

Augustin Daly. Not until a week after the first night on September 13th, 1870, had Wilkie got wind of the venture, and he hastily wrote off to New York to try and put a stop to it. Needless to say he failed, and the piece was highly successful.

It was during the run of *Man and Wife* at the Prince of Wales that Charles Collins fell desperately ill. Never very robust, his health had been gradually worsening for many years. For a time he and Katey had lived in the warm Mediterranean climate, but he seemed to get no better. Although his final illness was caused by gastric ulcers, it was assumed by many of his friends that he was consumptive, and this may well have been so. Dickens, as long ago as 1864, had feared that he would never recover and that Katey would be left a young widow. On April 9th, 1873, Wilkie had arranged to accompany Wybert Reeve to the theatre in order to see how his play was progressing. Reeve found him very depressed at the grave news he had just received of his brother's condition; Charley was lying unconscious in his home in Kensington. Reeve went alone to the play, promising to come back to supper and report on the performance. When he reached Gloucester Place late at night, he found Wilkie just returned from his brother's bedside, to which he had been hastily summoned to witness the end. He was so utterly broken down with grief that he even talked to Reeve of a possible 'future state of existence,' about which, as an avowed materialist, he was normally sceptical. It was his firm belief that death meant 'a sleep of eternity,' and ended everything.

From childhood there had always been a strong attachment between the two brothers and, though dissimilar in temperament, they had remained close friends in adult life. Charley, whose own comparative failure was inherent in his character, had never been in the least jealous of his elder brother's success. Wilkie performed the last service to his brother's memory in writing the brief article on Charles Allston Collins in the *Dictionary of National Biography*. In it he said: 'His ideal was a high one; and he never succeeded in satisfying his own aspirations.' The entry concludes with these words, which could apply with equal truth to the writer's own last years: 'The last years of his life were years of broken health and acute suffering, borne with a patience and courage known only to those nearest and dearest to him.' Wilkie Collins might have been writing his own epitaph.

Work was always an anodyne for his mental and bodily suffering, and it was fortunate that at this time of bereavement preparations were in full swing for the publication of his latest novel, *The New Magdalen*, and for the production of the stage version. He had been kept busy with both during most of the previous year, in the course of which the novel had been appearing serially in the *Temple Bar Magazine*. He mentioned it in a letter to Forster, dated November 16th, 1872, which is remarkable on two counts; first, for the friendly, almost deferential tone he adopts towards the man who had so recently snubbed him over the Bentley-Dickens letters; secondly, because it contains his only favourable criticism on record of Forster's *Life of Dickens*:

> 90, Gloucester Place,
> Portman Square.

My dear Forster,—For three days past I have been trying—and vainly trying—to get to Palace Gate House, and to thank you heartily (as I thank you now) for the new volume of the Life. I am devouring you at night (the only time when I have any 'leisure hours' at my disposal) and I am more interested than any words of mine can tell in your admirable narrative—to my mind, the most masterly biographical story you have ever told. More of this when I do contrive to see you. In the meantime, I congratulate you with all my heart.

Ramsgate cured me. I was there five weeks—and felt better and better every day.

How are you? I have heard a report (which I hope and trust is as false as most reports) that you are suffering again. Pray send me a line to say what the truth is, and whether you are settled in London for the present.

I know you will be glad to hear that my story (*The New Magdalen*) is, so far, a great success. Will you wait till it is done? or shall I send you the proofs, when the number I am now writing is in type—say in a week's time?

Pray give my kindest regards to Mrs. Forster and believe me,
> Ever affectionately yours,
>> Wilkie Collins.

The fulsome tribute to Forster's book may be explained by the fact that he had not yet had the opportunity of reading the

third volume, which appeared later. It was this concluding volume, dealing with the period of Dickens' life so well known to Wilkie, which aroused his anger. His own copy of the book was freely annotated with marginalia, usually critical of Forster. Some of these notes are described in an article which appeared in the *Pall Mall Gazette* a day or two before the sale of Wilkie's library in 1890.†
They are of special interest as containing his only recorded opinions of Dickens' works. On the first page, where Dickens is described as 'the most popular novelist of the century,' Wilkie adds the words 'after Walter Scott.' Forster's opinion that *Oliver Twist* was a well-constructed story is dismissed as nonsense:

The one defect in that wonderful book is the helplessly bad construction of the story. The character of Nancy is the finest thing he ever did. He never afterwards saw all sides of a woman's character—saw all round her. That the same man who could create Nancy created the second Mrs. Dombey is the most incomprehensible anomaly that I know of in literature.

Another note concerns the plot of *Barnaby Rudge*. Dickens had a notion of introducing three men who should become the natural leaders of the crowd in the Gordon Riots, and later turn out to have escaped from Bedlam. Forster thought the idea unsound and records that he dissuaded Dickens from adopting it. Wilkie comments in the margin, 'Where is the unsoundness of it? I call it a fine idea. New, powerful, highly dramatic, and well within the limits of truth to nature. It would have greatly improved the weakest book that Dickens ever wrote.' In a note in the second volume he describes *Martin Chuzzlewit* as in some respects Dickens' finest novel, but severely criticises its successor:

The latter half of *Dombey* no intelligent person can have read without astonishment at the badness of it, and the disappointment that followed lowered the sale of the next book *Copperfield*, incomparably superior to *Dombey* as it certainly is:

Forster's assertion that there is scarcely a page of Dickens which could not be placed in the hand of a child provokes the explosion we might expect:

† I am indebted to Mr. K. J. Fielding for tracing this article.

It is impossible to read such stuff as this without a word of protest. If it is true, which it is not, it would imply the condemnation of Dickens' books as works of art, it would declare him to be guilty of deliberately presenting to his readers a false reflection of human life. If this wretched English claptrap means anything it means that the novelist is forbidden to touch on the sexual relations which literally swarm about him, and influence the lives of millions of his fellow creatures [except] those relations are licensed by the ceremony called marriage. One expects this essentially immoral view of the functions of the novelist from a professor of claptrap like the late Bishop of Manchester. But that Forster should quote it with approval is a sad discovery indeed.

Elsewhere he takes Forster to task for comparing a descriptive passage in *Edwin Drood* unfavourably with a page of dialogue from *Oliver Twist*, observing that 'a novelist knows what Forster did not know—that dialogue is more easily written than description.' He adds, however, 'To my mind it was cruel to compare Dickens in the radiant prime of his genius with Dickens' last laboured effort, the melancholy work of a worn out brain.'

When Forster writes in his final chapter of his thirty-three years' friendship with Dickens, marked by 'unbroken continuity of kindly impulse,' Wilkie comments:

The "kindly impulse" did unquestionably exist, but not in "unbroken continuity". More than once there were fierce quarrels between Dickens and Forster (sometimes at Forster's own table), which took place in my presence. Dickens' sense of what he owed to Forster's devotion—right and properly a strong sense—was often subjected to severe trial by Forster himself. The assertion (quite sincerely made) that no letters addressed by Dickens to other old friends revealed his character so frankly and completely as his letters to Forster, it is not necessary to contradict. Dickens' letters published by his sister-in-law and his eldest daughter may be left to settle the question.

It is said that he used to refer to the book as 'The Life of John Forster with occasional anecdotes of Charles Dickens.' If this cynical description does scant justice to a great biography, Wilkie would have been more than human had he accepted in silence his virtual elimination from the story of Dickens' life. Whether or not Forster liked or approved of him, it is a fact that for twenty years he was as close to Dickens as any man. To gloss over such an association in a few sentences is to sacrifice biographical truth on the altar of personal jealousy. The letter quoted above marks the end of those friendly overtures Wilkie was prone to make towards 'the Bear' from time to time, and during the few years that remained of Forster's life there is no record of any further communication between them.

There can be no doubt that *The New Magdalen* was first conceived as a stage-play. The novel betrays, and suffers from, its dramatic origins even more obviously than *Man and Wife*. Dialogue was never his *forte*, and the book consists in the main of long stretches of dialogue, more stilted and theatrical than usual, connected by narrative passages which are little more than amplified stage directions. The theme is the age-old one of society's intolerance of the fallen woman. The story tells of a young woman forced by poverty to earn her living on the streets, who seizes a desperate chance to rehabilitate herself in the eyes of society, and of her eventual reformation at the hands of the clergyman of noble mien and still nobler character. It is a theme which, if it fails to evoke tragedy, can hardly avoid sentimentality, and Wilkie Collins had not the powers to carry through the task he set himself. He had, here and there in his best work, touched upon genuine tragedy, in the stories of Rosanna Spearman and Anne Catherick, for example and perhaps of Ezra Jennings or Magdalen Vanstone, but to sustain tragedy, to keep an entire novel on the tragic plane, was now beyond his capabilities. He was more interested in the propaganda aspect of his story, in upbraiding society for its hypocrisy and inhumanity, and in preaching tolerance toward human frailty. Unfortunately, he insisted on weighing the scales so heavily in favour of the reformed prostitute as to destroy any illusion of impartiality, and his plea thus loses much if its effectiveness. The crude melodrama and sentimentality of the book were perhaps more acceptable on the stage, but *The New Magdalen* must be numbered among his least satisfactory novels. This was not however the view of Matthew Arnold, who said it was his favourite sensation-novel.

It was of course a daring theme in its day, which may account for the remarkable success of both novel and play. The first production took place at the Olympic Theatre on May 19th, 1873, two days after publication of the book, under the management of Ada Cavendish, who also played the leading role of Mercy Merrick; the Reverend Julian Gray was played by Frank Archer. Both became life-long friends of the author. *The New Magdalen* was rapturously received by the public, although the ethics of the play were condemned by the Press. *The Times* ventured the opinion that 'in the time of our fathers the conclusion of the New Magdalen's history would not have been tolerated.' After a run of 19 weeks Ada Cavendish took the production on an extended provincial tour; she subsequently revived it twice in London, and altogether made a good deal of money out of the play. Early in the run Wilkie wrote to Wybert Reeve:

'The reception of my *New Magdalen* was prodigious. I was forced to appear half-way through the piece, as well as at the end. The acting took everyone by surprise, and the second night's enthusiasm quite equalled the first. We have really hit the mark. Ferrari translates it for Italy, Regnier has two theatres ready for me in Paris, and Lambe of Vienna has accepted it for his theatre.' Nor was this catalogue complete, for within a year or so one could have seen "Die Neue Magdalena" in Berlin, "De Newe Magdalen" in The Hague, and "Novaia Magdalena" in Moscow.

Some months earlier he had received an invitation from America to undertake a Reading Tour in the autumn and winter of 1873. The project was a formidable one for a man in his state of health but it held at the same time many attractions. He wrote to Wybert Reeve: 'I have had a great offer to go to America this autumn and "read." It would be very pleasant and I should like it if we could go together. I am really thinking of the trip.' He doubtless recalled the prodigious sums which Dickens had been able to earn during his last Reading Tour of the U.S.A., and if he could hardly expect similar rewards, his reputation across the Atlantic stood high, perhaps higher than at home, and the financial return would not be negligible. His books had made him many friends in the States, and as for his relations with Harpers, seldom can an author have been on better terms with his publisher. Bouquets from the one to the other had become almost monotonous. Only the previous year Harpers had written: 'You know that we are always glad of your stories, and we know that there is no author more prompt and thoughtful of the interest and convenience of publishers than you. Your careful and regular transmission of copy . . . has frequently elicited the grateful admiration which is naturally felt by us as practical printers for authors who are never behindhand.' Finally, America interested him, and he had often expressed a wish to see that country. All things considered, it was worth taking the chance, and hoping for the type of weather which best suited his ailments, he chose the season when the climate of the Eastern States would be mainly cold and dry.

Having had no experience of reading in public he thought it desirable to give a 'try-out' performance in London. The opportunity came when a special charity matinée was arranged at the Olympic Theatre, during the run of *The New Magdalen*, for the benefit of a M. Waldec, a baritone. The programme lacked nothing in variety. Mme. Aimée Desclée, the great French actress—to die soon afterwards at a very early age—recited Victor Hugo's 'Le Revenant' and was billed to give an organ solo when it was discovered that no organ was available. Gounod played several pieces including his 'Funeral March of a Marionette,' upon which the pianist Ferdinand Hiller subsequently improvised. Ada Cavendish recited 'The Charge of the Light Brigade.' In the midst of this rich feast Wilkie read his early short story 'A Terriby Strange Bed.' There seem to have been conflicting views as to his reception. Percy Fitzgerald was present and, some forty years later, described the occasion with at least a touch of malice.† The reader, he said, had little or no voice and scarcely attempted to raise it; he seemed to think that the word 'bedstead' was full of tragic significance and repeated it until it became almost comic. It was 'a most singularly inefficient performance,' and he was reminded of 'an elderly gentleman at his club boring his neighbour with a long story of something he had read in the papers.' Fitzgerald hastened away to share his glee with Forster, who 'laughed his rhinocerous laugh,' as one might have expected. Frank Archer, prejudiced in the other direction, listened to the reading and thought it 'earnest and impressive.' The press was also in two minds. The *Pall Mall Gazette* reported: 'Mr. Wilkie Collins, appearing for the first time in the character of a reader,

† *Memoirs of Charles Dickens*. Percy Fitzgerald. (*Arrowsmith*, 1914).

may be congratulated on the favourable reception accorded to him as a novelist.' It described the reading as a failure largely because he attempted unsuccessfully to 'act' the story, an opinion which hardly squares with Fitzgerald's. Quick to Wilkie's rescue came the *Illustrated Review*. Having quoted the *Gazette's* verdict that the reading was a failure, the article continues:

That it was nothing whatever of the kind, we can attest from our own careful and certainly dispassionate observation . . . The novelist was cordially welcomed, was attentively (at moments breathlessly) listened to throughout, was rewarded every now and then with sudden bursts of laughter, and at the end with distinct rounds of applause of the heartiest possible description. If that constitutes a failure, he certainly had one to his heart's content. What better reception any new entertainer could possibly be expected to elicit we cannot for the life of us conjecture.

Wilkie himself was sufficiently encouraged by his reception to press on with arrangements for the American tour. Since Wybert Reeve was unable to get away until later, he sailed alone in early September in the Cunard steamship *Algeria*, arriving at New York on the 25th. The first person he recognised on disembarking was his old friend Fechter who had come to the wharf to meet him. They went along together to his hotel, the Westminster, where Dickens had stayed five years earlier. He was given the same suite that Dickens had occupied and when he saw the desk at which his friend had worked, he appeared deeply moved. Fechter took him out to dinner that evening and Wilkie recalled his saying when they parted for the night, 'You will find friends here wherever you go. Don't forget that I was the friend who introduced you to Soft Shell Crab.'

Within a few days of his arrival Wilkie received an invitation from his New York publishers to dine with them in Twenty-second Street. In accepting he mentioned that he only drank dry champagne, a remark that sent Harpers scurrying around New York to find the wine he required. It was procured with the greatest difficulty since Americans at that time drank only the sweet variety. Shortly afterwards Harpers wrote to Reade:† 'Mr. Wilkie Collins,

† *The House of Harper*. J. Henry Harper. (*Harper Bros*. 1912,).

whom we have seen repeatedly since his arrival in New York, seems to be enjoying his American sights and sensations.' To celebrate Wilkie's visit they issued a library edition of his works. This incidentally included the first U.S. publication of *The Dead Secret*, which had appeared in 1857 as an anonymous serial in the first volume of *Harper's Weekly*.

For the first two or three weeks after landing he was constantly beset by newspaper reporters, whose methods, then as now, were more ruthless than those of their English counterparts. In particular he suffered at the hands of that formidable species, the female reporter, already common in the United States. One of these ladies burst into a dinner-party at which he was being entertained and begged for a few minutes private conversation with the guest of honour. He was in the midst of apologising to his hostess when he realised that she saw nothing unusual in the intrusion, and was in fact pleading with him not to disappoint the enterprising reporter. On another occasion he found himself surrounded in his hotel by a grim circle of a dozen female magazine-editors, of which 'the oldest and ugliest stood forth and solemnly observing: "Let me embrace you for the company," offered me a chaste salute.' His lukewarm reception of the embrace, 'however much I might have appreciated the same from a youthful beauty,' was such as to summon forth 'very moderate praises' of his personal charms in the pages of the magazine concerned.

The other plague with which he had to contend was the autograph-hunters. They pursued him everywhere. In Boston he went so far as to change his hotel for the sole purpose of avoiding them. One experience he described in a charming letter written some years later to young Nathaniel Beard, in response to a request for his autograph:

Once upon a time, while I was on my way to a grand breakfast in the City of New York, I was stopped in one of the squares by a very well-bred young gentleman, who said he recognised me by my photographic portraits, and who asked me if I would give him an autograph. I said, 'Yes, but where am I to send it?' He said, 'Quite unnecessary, sir. If you don't mind you can give it to me now.' With that he pulled an autograph book out of one pocket, a pen out of another, and an ancient 'inkhorn' out of a third. 'How am I to write it?' I asked. He answered, 'You

Q

can write it on my back.' He turned round and 'gave me a back' as
if he were playing at leap-frog. I wrote him his autograph (greatly
to the amusement of the public in the square), and we shook
hands and parted. I quote this young gentleman's example as
giving you a useful hint in the pursuit of autographs. If he had
not stuck to me while he had me, I might have forgotten him—
just as inexcusably as I forgot *you*.
And now here is my autograph *at last*!

Greatly to his surprise he acquired an immediate reputation for
being well-dressed. There are two versions of the story. According
to Mrs. Walford,† whom he saw shortly after his return to
England, he told her that on the trip across to America rats gnawed
into his luggage and ruined the best suit which he was carefully
keeping for his first press interviews. On arrival in New York he
had therefore to visit the tailor and buy a ready-made suit which
he described as 'atrocious.' Thus attired he met the Press. Next day
he was astonished to read 'Mr. Collins is a small man, but well
made and very well dressed,' and could only assume that the cut
he had objected to was in fact the accepted 'Yankee cut.' The other
version, recounted by Wybert Reeve, insists that the suit in
question was purchased, not in New York, but in the East End
of London, as a rough travelling-suit. Whatever its origin, its
success seems to have been complete.

The first important function to which he was invited was a
reception and dinner at New York's famous Lotos Club, where the
guests included Bret Harte and Charles Bradlaugh, also on his first
visit to the States. Whitelaw Reid, the United States Ambassador
to Britain, presided and paid a gracious tribute to the guest of
honour. Replying, as an author of 'that order of books for which
heavy people have invented the name of light literature,' Wilkie
recalled his first experience of American kindness and hospitality,
at Sorrento thirty years before. He continued: 'I venture to say
that I see in this reception something more than a recognition
of my humble labours only. I think I see a recognition of English
literature, liberal, spontaneous and sincere, which, I think, is an
honour to you, as well as an honour to me . . . On my own behalf,
I beg to assure you that I shall not soon forget the encouragement
you have offered to me at the outset of my career in America.

† *Memories of Victorian London*. L. B. Walford. (*Arnold*, 1912.)

Permit me to remind you that I am now speaking the language of sincere gratitude, and that it is essentially a language of very few words.'† He told Reeve that it was a delightful evening, which ended only as dawn was breaking.

After spending a few days with Fechter at the beginning of October on his small Pennsylvania farm, he opened his tour with Readings in a number of towns in New York State, including Troy, Syracuse, Albany and Rochester. The first large city he tackled, Philadelphia, was also the scene of his first unfavourable reception. He had chosen for his reading a revised version of *The Dream Woman*. The story proved too strong meat for Philadelphia, whose *Press* thought it was 'not fit for intelligent and cultured people,' and that 'the moral was just as bad as bad could be.' 'It was not pleasant,' the newspaper went on, 'to hear a famous Englishman describing, before several hundred pure girls, how one wretched, fallen woman, after mysteriously killing her man, had captivated two more, and stabbed another to death in a drunken frenzy.' The audience found his voice too low and monotonous, and showed some disappointment after a hearty initial welcome. Nowhere in America was there criticism that his style was histrionic, which had been the complaint of the *Pall Mall Gazette*. His introductory remarks made it clear that his intention was precisely the reverse. After explaining that the story was 'a re-written, enlarged, and I hope greatly improved version of one of my shorter stories,' divided into two parts between which there would be 'an interval of ten minutes for the repose of the audience and the reader,' he continued: 'I have never, in presenting myself to your notice, had the object in view of acting, or even attempting to act, as in my opinion the duties of the reader and the duties of the actor are widely at difference. My position as a reader is, as I understand it, this: I am in a very large parlour surrounded, I hope I may say, by friends, and it is my duty to keep myself in the background and to let my story find its way to your favour with whatever merits of its own it may be so fortunate as to possess.' The *New York Herald* commented on this last sentence with tart brevity: 'Since Mr. Collins' enterprise is commercial, appeals to friendship are humbug.'

† The speech was reprinted in full in *Speeches to the Lotos Club* (printed for private circulation, New York).

With the commercial motive well in mind, Wilkie made no attempt to appease the moralists by substituting a more innocuous story. He knew the value of a '*succès de scandale*' and perhaps recalled that Dickens' greatest successes had been made with his more gruesome Readings. After a brief visit to New York where he was entertained to breakfast at the Union Club, he travelled to Boston on October 29th. The following day he read to a very large audience at the Music Hall, Boston, where he might have expected another outburst of moral indignation, liked him. The papers were friendly, commenting on his 'handsome long beard' and 'fine robust countenance.' The *Boston Advertiser* said that he held the audience's attention despite 'the London intonation which was apparent on the flattening of his vowels.' Wilkie was particularly delighted when he heard that a Western newspaper, copying this report, had written: 'Mr. Collins is decidedly a Londoner which is apparent in the flattening of his bowels.'

Rehearsals for *The New Magdalen* were in progress at Daly's Broadway Theatre, and Wilkie returned to New York early in November to lend what assistance he could. The play opened on November 10th to an enthusiastic reception. He had to appear on the stage at the end of the second Act with Carlotta Leclercq, who played the lead, and took several bows and thanked the audience. The critics were on the whole favourable, although the *Daily Tribune* advanced the type of argument that was to be used against Ibsen's plays on the London stage twenty years later:

> Its subject is one that ladies and gentlemen cannot discuss . . . The theatre is not a dissecting room, nor a place for the examination of social problems.

The review concluded:

> But if [the author] means to say that society, organised on virtuous principles, ought to accept reformed courtesans as wives and mothers, and place them on the same footing with women of unblemished purity, he announces a doctrine that is false in itself and that may prove pernicious in its results.

One correspondent went so far as to assent: 'A play so utterly vicious . . . has never before been produced in a New York theatre.

The day following the 'Magdalen' first night he gave his first reading in the city of New York, at Association Hall, where he scored a great success. The *New York Times* referred to his 'pleasant clear voice and agreeable manner,' and reported that the audience had listened attentively and applauded heartily. The *Herald* condemned the story as 'a mixture of voluptuousness, cruelty and horror' and claimed that some of the audience went to sleep and others left before the end. He was on tour again during the latter half of November, and appeared at Washington on the 28th. Soon afterwards he was back in New York to supervise the production of *The Woman in White*, which succeeded *The New Magdalen* on December 15th. Wybert Reeve, who had followed Wilkie across the Atlantic, played his familiar part of Count Fosco.

Towards the end of the month he set off on a short Canadian tour, spending Christmas in Toronto and reading there on Boxing Day. By January 2nd, 1874, he was back in the United States and from Buffalo, N.Y., he sent Frederick Lehmann an account of his impressions of the country, and of his tour to date.

I hear you have called like a good fellow at Gloucester Place, and have heard something of me there from time to time. No matter where I go, my reception in America is always the same. The prominent people in each place visit me, drive me out, dine me, and do all that they can to make me feel myself among friends. The enthusiasm and the kindness are really and truly beyond description. I should be the most ungrateful man living if I had any other than the highest opinion of the American people. I find them to be the most enthusiastic, the most cordial, and the most sincere people I have ever met with in my life. When an American says, 'Come and see me,' he *means* it. This is wonderful to an Englishman.

Before I had been a week in this country I noted three national peculiarities which had never been mentioned to me by visitors to the States.

I. No American hums or whistles a tune either at home or in the street.

II. Not one American in 500 has a dog.

III. Not one American in 1,000 carries a walking-stick.

I who hum perpetually, who love dogs, who cannot live without a walking-stick, am greatly distressed at finding my dear Americans deficient in the three social virtues just enumerated.

My readings have succeeded by surprising the audiences. The story surprises them in the first place, being something the like of which they have not heard before. And my way of reading surprises them in the second place, because I don't flourish a paper-knife and stamp about the platform, and thump the reading desk. I persist in keeping myself in the background and the story in front. The audience begins at each reading with silent astonishment, and ends with a great burst of applause.

As to the money, if I could read often enough I should bring back a little fortune in spite of the panic. The hard times have been against me of course, but while others have suffered badly I have always drawn audiences. Here, for example, they give me a fee for a reading on Tuesday evening next—it amounts to between £70 and £80 (English). If I could read five times a week at this rate (which is my customary rate), here is £350 a week, which is not bad pay for an hour and three-quarters reading each night. But I cannot read five times a week without knocking myself up, and this I won't do. And then I have been mismanaged and cheated by my agents—have had to change them and start afresh with a new man. The result has been loss of time and loss of money. But I am *investing* in spite of it, and (barring accidents) I am in a fair way to make far more than I have made yet before the last fortnight in March, when I propose to sail for home. I am going 'Out West' from this, and I *may* get as far as the Mormons.

The nigger waiters (I like them better than the American waiters) are ringing the dinner bell. I must go and feed off a variety of badly cooked meats and vegetables ranged round me in (say) forty soap dishes. Otherwise I am comfortable here; I have got the Russian Grand Duke's bedroom, and a parlour in which I can shake hands with my visitors and a box at the theatre, and the freedom of the club.'

The reference at the beginning to Frederick's calling at Gloucester Place would seem to indicate that Caroline Graves was installed there once more, and was in regular receipt of letters from Wilkie. Although he moved west from Buffalo, giving readings at Cleveland and Chicago on January 8th and 16th the projected tour 'as far as the Mormons' fell through, perhaps because he felt unequal to the strain of travelling further long distances by train. Instead, he toured a number of towns in New England. In a postscript he mentioned that 'Providence (the city, not the Diety) paid me 400 dollars in spite of the panic.'

At home there was talk of reviving *The New Magdalen* and Wilkie was kept informed of developments by his friend Frank Archer. A certain Stefan Polès, of doubtful nationality and repute, whom Archer describes as 'a skilful linguist of persuasive, insinuating manners,' had been given some vague commission to look after Wilkie's interests in connection with the play. He seems to have been in the first instance an acquaintance of Reade, who had employed him in some capacity before introducing him to Wilkie's notice. Polès, of slight build with small searching eyes, bore, it is said, a marked resemblance to a well-known Russian spy. During Wilkie's absence in the States, Polès had been trying to negotiate a revival of *The New Magdalen* at the tiny Charing Cross Theatre where there had been for some time an unbroken run of failures. Against his better judgment Wilkie gave his consent upon learning from Ada Cavendish that she had taken the theatre on her own responsibility. Writing to Archer on January 8th, he hoped he would be able to play Julian Gray again, and asked him for news of 'how this venturesome Charing Cross experiment promises to turn out.'

Some three weeks later he learned that the revival plan had fallen through and that someone, presumably Polès, had entered into negotiations on his behalf to present the play at the Holborn Amphitheatre, a totally unsuitable home for it. His next letter to Archer is dated January 27th, 1874, from St. James' Hotel, Boston:

A thousand thanks for your kind attention to my interests. *Nobody* has any right to sanction any performance of the 'Magdalen' in London but myself. Nobody has any authority to sign an agreement for me. They must be mad—I can account for the selection of the Holborn Amphitheatre and the utter setting aside of my rights in the matter in no other way.
I write by this mail to caution Miss Cavendish—without mentioning to whom I am indebted for my knowledge of the state of affairs. I also write to my lawyer (this is between ourselves) to tell him to interfere at once if any new absurdity is perpetrated in my absence. You will be adding to the service which I already

owe to your friendly kindness, if you will inform him of any
new attempt to produce the piece without my authority.

Henceforth Polès disappears from the story, and all we know is
that he died in Middlesex Hospital where his body was unclaimed.
The play was in fact revived a year later at the theatre first
selected, the Charing Cross.

At the St. James' Hotel, Boston, a reception was given in Wilkie's
honour to which were invited Longfellow, Mark Twain, Whittier
and Oliver Wendell Holmes. Whittier and Mark Twain made
speeches and Holmes read a tribute in verse. We learn, on the
authority of the *Boston Evening Transcript*, that 'each gentleman
was presented with a bon-bon box, in shape and size like the
cabinet edition of Mr. Collins' work, covered in Turkey morocco,
and containing the author's photograph and autograph, the number
of his important works corresponding with the number present at
the reception.' The same newspaper provided a voice for the
Pecksniffs who had been gathering their forces in and around
Boston since his first visit. 'It is surprising,' wrote the editor, 'that
an Englishman with the reputation and favour enjoyed by Wilkie
Collins, should be willing to create such an impression as the
reading of *The Dream Woman* creates, and having created it,
knowingly to spread it all over New England by nightly repetitions.
Great names are not achieved by such work, nor can they long
survive such.' For his Farewell Reading at Boston he decided to
try a different story, and dug out of his trunk the old play, *The
Frozen Deep*. Having refurbished it in narrative form he read it to
an appreciative audience at Parker's Hall on February 27th.

It was now nearly six months since he had sailed from England
and he was due to return home. After a farewell dinner in New
York with Fechter, whom he never saw again, he sailed on March
7th from Boston on the s.s. *Parthia*. To Oliver Wendell Holmes he
wrote:

I must say (most imperfectly) in writing that I am indeed grate-
fully sensible of all that I owe to your cordial welcome, and
that I shall prize as long as I live the charming little poem which
speaks to me of your genius and your kindness whenever I look
at it. Farewell, dear Doctor Holmes, *for the present*. I have few
dearer hopes than the hope of my return to America.

Whilst at sea he wrote to another American friend, Cyrus T. Field:. 'I leave America with feelings of sincere gratitude and sincere respect. If all goes well with me, my first visit to my kind friends in the United States shall not be my last.' It is doubtful if he really expected to cross the Atlantic again.

Wilkie must have earned something like £2,500 in the course of his American tour. Any disappointment he may have felt that the Readings had been less successful or less profitable than he hoped at the outset, was mitigated by his real enjoyment of the tour. He returned home with the sincerest admiration for the American people and with a deep appreciation of their hospitality, their good humour and their fresh outlook on life. Unlike Dickens he made no violent criticisms of his hosts and in consequence left no enemies behind. If he missed the kind of triumph that Dickens had enjoyed on his last tour of the States, at least there can be no doubt of the genuine welcome accorded to him as a novelist by the American public. The dry winter climate of the Eastern States he could not praise too highly. A few days after his return he said to Lucy Walford, 'I was never better in my life. I did not have an ache or a pain all the time. As for gout, it left me entirely for the time being. I shall certainly crack up America as *the* place for sufferers from rheumatic gout. And whatever else I can say in its favour I will, for a kinder, warmer-hearted set of people surely does not exist—only their ways *are* queer.'

His two Readings, the narrative versions of *The Dream Woman* and *The Frozen Deep*, were published by Bentley in November, 1874, together with a story *John Jago's Ghost, or The Dead Alive*, written during his stay in America and based upon a murder trial at Manchester, Vermont, which had in its day caused a great sensation. The two volumes were entitled *The Frozen Deep and Other Tales: Readings and Writings in America*. The English edition was dedicated to Oliver Wendell Holmes 'in sincere admiration of his genius and in cordial remembrance of our intercourse during my visit to America.'

15

Downhill

WILLIAM FRITH, the painter, had long been a friend
of Wilkie Collins. The only correspondence between
them that the present writer has seen is a brief note
thanking Frith for obtaining tickets for the Academy soirée, but
Frith in his autobiography describes Wilkie as 'delightful in his
private, as in his public life.' He also tells the story of a guest at
his dinner-table who somewhat offensively charged Wilkie to his
face with writing books which were read in every back-kitchen.
Frith reports that Wilkie was quite unperturbed, well knowing
that his books were also to be found in every library and drawing-
room. At the same time the incident may have stimulated a notion
that had long been germinating in the novelist's mind, the possibility of issuing really cheap editions of his books. He had the
idea that an edition costing as little as a shilling or two would sell
in enormous quantities and easily recoup the publisher for his
outlay. At present there was, he believed, a considerable public for
his books still to be tapped, people who were outside the scope
of the libraries and also of the existing 'cheap' editions.

He first discussed the matter with George Smith, of Smith, Elder,
who showed little enthusiasm for the proposal and would have no
part in it. He thought such an enterprise would only bring disappointment to Wilkie who was, at existing prices, 'selling very
fairly.' Smith later admitted in his memoirs that his judgment
might have been at fault. Some time later Wilkie approached
Harper Brothers on similar lines, saying that the idea had come to
him 'while tasting wine at the London Docks.' Harpers pointed
out, quite legitimately, that so far as the American market was
concerned such cheap editions would be much more easily produced by pirates than by respectable publishers who paid their

authors a royalty. In fact Wilkie's novels, for which Harpers had
paid large sums, were pirated in the *Seaside and Lakeside
Libraries* at 10 and 20 cents each, roughly the prices he had in
mind.

In London the first publisher who listened favourably to the idea
was Andrew Chatto, of the newly-established firm of Chatto and
Windus. The result was that early in 1875 the copyright of all
Wilkie's published work was transferred to Chatto and Windus,
who became his main publishers for the remainder of his life.
Within a year or two of the transfer all his books were available
at two shillings each, and ultimately certain titles were issued in
a sixpenny edition. Thus Wilkie became to some extent the pioneer
of the modern very cheap edition, and there is every reason to
believe that the experiment was profitable to both publisher and
author.

The first two novels published for him by Chatto and Windus
were *The Law and the Lady* and *The Two Destinies*. Neither
measures up in any way to his own earlier standards. Deficient in
those qualities of inventiveness and ingenuity which distinguished
his novels of the sixties, both books display that dull mechanical
competence which we find all to often in his later work. Even the
narrative power which used to flow like the ink from his pen
has lost most of its spontaneity. His faithful public continued to
read them, however, and there were few signs of any falling-off in
his popularity.

The Law and the Lady, published in February, 1875, is first a
story of crime, and secondly a purpose-novel in that it seeks to
attack the Scottish verdict of 'Not Proven.' The plot concerns an
innocent man who has been charged in a Scottish court with
poisoning his first wife, without being either convicted or acquitted
of the charge. The 'Lady' of the title is his second wife who sets
herself the task of clearing his name by discovering new facts
which were not revealed at the trial. The detective work required
to bring about the happy ending is negligible, the merest child's
play for the author of *The Moonstone*. In stating the case against
the Scottish verdict, Wilkie fails to convey the essential tragedy
of an innocent man suffering under the stigma of public suspicion;
the hero protests at his unlucky fate, but we are left unmoved.
Perhaps the most remarkable feature of *The Law and the Lady* is

the character of Miserrimus Dexter. In his portrait of this legless megolomaniac, Wilkie's preoccupation with physical deformity, and indeed with mental abnormality, finds its fullest expression. Nothing is spared us. We are shown this half-human monster, dressed like a dandy, playfully torturing the strange young woman who attends with dog-like devotion to his needs; we see him hopping madly about his room like some fantastic bird; we hear him declaim, in the belief that it is great poetry, some crazy ditty of his own composing. Preposterous though he is in many respects, Miserrimus Dexter provides a striking study in the macabre.

The Two Destinies, published 18 months later, after being serialised in *Temple Bar*, is even less successful. Both story and treatment are conventional to a degree. This time there is virtually neither mystery nor surprise to attract the interest. A man and woman, bound together by an emotional attachment formed during childhood, find themselves in adult life endowed with powers of telepathic communication, by means of which their widely divergent paths are made to cross from time to time. The author follows his couple through various commonplace vicissitudes without evoking either the reader's sympathy or his credulity. When they become at last man and wife they are shunned by 'respectable' society because the woman has been the innocent victim of a bigamous marriage.

Charles Reade, to whom the *The Two Destinies* was dedicated, wrote to him on March 19th, 1876:

I am truly sorry to hear that you are suffering from gout in the eye again. This is the cause of all your troubles being so painful and so hard on you in your art. I do hope you will soon recover and resume these labours, which to my mind were never more successful.
In this story [*The Two Destinies*], as far as I have read it, there is a pace of language, and a vein of sweet tenderness running through the whole, which reveals maturing genius.
It is deplorable that such an artist as you now reaching your zenith should carry such heavy weight in every race you run with your contemporaries.
You can distance them all the same: but I who know and value you in private as well as in public, do deeply deplore the distress

and pain in which you have to write these works that afford
unmixed pleasure to others.

The friendship between the two novelists had become closer
since the day of Dickens' funeral, when Reade had laid his head
on Wilkie's shoulder and wept. Reade had a high opinion of his
friend's work, and greatly exaggerated the worth of his later books.
Shortly before his death he said to James Payn: 'I can imagine
that Wilkie's work fails to appeal to some people otherwise good
judges, but he is a great artist.' In the Memoir of Reade by two
members of his family,† it is stated that he ranked 'his very dear
friend Mr. Wilkie Collins' next to Dickens, and that he extended
to him 'that sort of genuine admiration which an author offers his
brother in art when he esteems him greater than himself.' As early
as 1870, Reade, encountering difficulties with his Cornhill serial,
Put Yourself in his Place, had appealed to Wilkie for criticism and
advice. Wilkie took a good deal of trouble and replied at length
in a letter headed 'Considerations for R.,' in which he set down
detailed and constructive suggestions for the coming instalments.
Many of these Reade adopted, making a note at the foot of the
letter, 'I was so fortunate as to please him at last.' He in his turn
had a considerable influence over Wilkie, and it is perhaps to be
regretted that he was content to admire where he might have
criticised to advantage.

Each was welcome at the other's house, and on one occasion
Reade, learning while away from London that Wilkie was ill, wrote
peremptorily to his friend Mrs. Seymour: 'Go at once and see
him, in bed or out of bed.' Wybert Reeve described a visit to Reade
in company with Wilkie and 'a lady friend'—most probably
Caroline Graves. She insisted upon having a joke at the expense of
Reade's well-known personal vanity and, fixing her eyes upon him,
said: 'Oh! Mr. Reade, pardon me, do forgive me, I like looking at
you. There is something in your face so good and so manly.' 'My
dear Mrs.—,' he replied, 'you flatter me. Upon my life I should
be angry if I did not know you were a woman of judgment,' and
thereupon turned automatically to the mirror. Although Reade
announced his intention of preserving Wilkie's letters as heirlooms

† Memoirs of Charles Reade. C. L. Reade and Rev. C. Reade (Chapman &
Hall, 1887).

for his family, no such collection appears to have survived. Indeed little evidence remains of this significant friendship between two of the most popular writers of their time.

Wilkie's health was steadily deteriorating; to the gout which attacked his eyes and limbs with increasing frequency were now added bronchial troubles. In April, 1876, he wrote to Frederick Lehmann:

> I am slowly mending—able to use my good eye, and still obliged to take care of the other ... I am still forbidden dinners, theatres, and all assemblies in which part of the pleasure consists in breathing vitiated air and swallowing superfluous particles of flesh given off by our fellow creatures and ourselves in the act of respiration. Work, walk, visit to my morganatic family—such is life.

The morganatic family by now numbered three children, Marian aged seven, Harriet Constance aged five, and his son William Charles born eighteen months before at 10, Taunton Place, Marylebone, where Martha Rudd now lived under the name of Mrs. Dawson. Three months later he was 'wandering about the south coast' and wrote to Archer just after finishing *The Two Destinies*: 'I am feeling too much fagged to do any more work for some little time to come ... I must for my health's sake let my brains rest. Plans for the autumn were 'to go abroad and get new ideas among new scenes.'

He was now taking laudanum more or less regularly and his reliance upon the drug was absolute. Curiously enough he seems never to have become a 'slave to opium' in the popularly accepted sense. It can only have been his strength of character which preserved him from sinking into the degradation of the typical opium addict, and to the end of his life he persisted in regarding the drug as no more than an essential medicine. He seemed to experience no sense of guilt and talked of his addiction among friends with the utmost frankness. Included in their number was an American, William Winter, whom he used to see on his periodic visits to London. To him Wilkie described an incident of his childhood which may have been of deep significance as regards the moral issues. Coleridge, a frequent visitor at William Collins' house, arrived one day in a state of acute distress. Despite a supreme effort to conquer the opium habit, he had discovered that his craving for the drug remained irresistible. Unburdening his mind to Collins he even burst into tears. Finally Mrs. Collins said to him, 'Mr. Coleridge, do not cry. If the opium really does you any good, and you must have it, why do you not go and get it?' At this Coleridge recovered his composure and, turning to Collins, said, 'Your wife is an exceedingly sensible woman!' Wilkie commented to Winter, after telling him the story: 'I suppose that he did not long delay to act upon the mother's suggestion. I was a boy at the time but the incident made a strong impression on my mind, and I could not forget it.' He also mentioned the account, in Lockhart's biography, of Sir Walter Scott having recourse to laudanum while writing *The Bride of Lammermoor*, and on another occasion, he said to Winter, 'Opium sometimes hurts, but also sometimes, it helps. In general people know nothing about it.'†

Many tales are told of the quantity of laudanum which he required for an effective dose during his latter years. Frederick Lehmann's brother Rudolf, the portrait painter, put the amount at a tablespoonful before retiring at night. In his Memoirs‡ Rudolf tells of an occasion in 1868 when Wilkie and Frederick were travelling together in Switzerland and supplies of the drug were running low. Wilkie was in great pain and Frederick went out to replenish the stock, only to find that Swiss chemists were strictly limited by law in the quantity they could sell to one customer. It required visits to four separate chemists before an adequate dose could be mustered.

Hall Caine actually saw him, a year or two before his death, drink a wineglassful of laudanum. They had been discussing a knotty problem arising from a dispute between Hall Caine and a literary collaborator, in which Wilkie had been asked to adjudicate. Suddenly Wilkie said: 'My brain is not very clear,' and walking over to a cabinet took out a wineglass and a bottle of liquid resembling port wine. Pouring himself out a full glass, he said: 'I'm going to show you one of the secrets of my prison-house. Do you see that? It's laudanum.' And to Hall Caine's great alarm he drank it off at a single gulp. Asked how long he had been taking

† *Old Friends.* William Winter. (New York, 1909).
‡ *An Artist's Recollections.* Rudolf Lehmann. (*Smith, Elder,* 1894).

the drug Wilkie replied, 'Twenty years' (which was an under-estimate). 'More than once a day?' persisted Hall Caine, somewhat horrified. 'Oh, yes, much more,' replied Wilkie and reminded him that de Quincey used to drink the stuff out of a jug. He then told his visitor a long and gruesome story of a man-servant of his who had killed himself through taking less than half one of Wilkie's normal doses.

'Why do you take it?' asked Hall Caine finally.

'To stimulate the brain and steady the nerves,' he replied.

'And you think it does that?'

'Undoubtedly.'

'Has it the same effect on other people?'

'It had on Bulwer-Lytton, he told me so himself.'

'Well then, my dear Wilkie, you know how much I suffer from nervous exhaustion. Do you advise me to use the drug?'

Wilkie paused, and then said, quietly and emphatically, 'No.'†

Further evidence is furnished by Sir Squire Bancroft who tells in his reminiscences‡ of a dinner-party at which his guests included Wilkie Collins and a famous surgeon, Sir William Fergusson. Conversation between Wilkie and his neighbour turned to drugs and with his customary candour Wilkie mentioned the quantity he took before going to bed. The incredulous neighbour exclaimed that such an amount would prevent any ordinary person from ever waking. An appeal was made to the doctor who not only agreed but asserted that Wilkie's normal dose was sufficient to kill every man seated at the table.

Wybert Reeve also mentions Wilkie's opium habit, and adds the information that he had frequent injections of morphia latterly in order to relieve his neuralgic pains. In view of the tolerance he had acquired for opium in its various forms it would be misleading to suggest that he was continuously under its influence. One cannot, however, avoid attributing the decline in the quality of his writing, at least in some measure, to the effects of the drug.

Public opinion in the nineteenth century did not of course condemn excessive drug-taking in quite the uncompromising terms of today, nor was the law as stringent then as now. None the less

† *My Story*. Hall Caine. (*Heinemann*, 1908).
‡ *Empty Chairs*. Squire Bancroft. (*Murray*, 1925).

it is an illuminating comment on the moral standards of their time that, while so many of his friends did not hesitate to publish his addiction to opium, Kate Perugini alone could bring herself to mention the equally important and no more scandalous fact of his association with Caroline Graves.

During the years 1875 to 1877, although he continued to occupy himself with writing novels, Wilkie's focus of attention shifted once more to the theatre. In January, 1875, the much-postponed revival of *The New Magdalen* took place at last at the tiny Charing Cross Theatre, with Ada Cavendish again in the principal role. The author, who had been confined to bed with a bad cold, did not see the play until the third week when he reported to Frank Archer: 'Financially we are playing the piece at a profit. The first week's returns are decidedly encouraging—£93 in the house on the first Saturday . . . My week's fees were at least ten pounds higher than my calculations anticipated.' Archer had been prevented by another engagement from playing Julian Gray.

For Ada Cavendish Wilkie had a great regard, personally as well as in her professional capacity. Their association, dating from the original production of *The New Magdalen*, ended only with his death. On the occasion of her United States tour in 1878 during which she played Mercy Merrick and Lydia Gwilt, he wrote to his friend Winter in New York: 'She has, I think, more of the divine fire in her than any other living English actress—and she has the two excellent qualities of being always eager to improve and always ready to take advice in her art. I am really interested in her well-doing . . .' *The New Magdalen* continued to be a profitable venture for both of them. In March, 1877, he wrote to Archer: 'Your old friend Julian Gray still strolls through the country theatres with Miss Cavendish. He has been translated into Italian, and turned into *an austere magistrate*. The Italian public won't have a priest of any sort on the stage! The piece has been a great success at Rome, Florence, and Milan.' The play was again revived in London in January, 1884, with both Ada Cavendish and Frank Archer in their original roles, at the Novelty Theatre in Great Queen Street, of which the author wrote: 'Our chance of success depends entirely, in my opinion, on making the public understand that there is such a theatre, and on telling them where to find it.'

R

In this they partially succeeded, for the play lasted 61 performances.†

It was Ada Cavendish who also played the lead in the long-delayed staging of the dramatic version of *Armadale*. The first dramatisation, written in collaboration with his friend Regnier, had been shelved as unsuitable for the English stage—a view strongly held, it will be recalled, by Dickens. A later version had been done by Wilkie alone and entitled *Miss Gwilt*. It still offered formidable difficulties in performance and for this reason a preliminary tryout was given in December, 1875, at the Alexandra Theatre, Liverpool. Some of the small part actors were the remnants of an Edinburgh repertory company recently disbanded following the destruction of their theatre by fire. Among them was A. W. (later Sir Arthur) Pinero, who played Mr. Darch, an elderly solicitor, the part in which he subsequently made his West End *début*, at the age of 21. Some fifty years later Sir Arthur Pinero wrote: 'In the course of the rehearsals Collins was extremely kind to me . . . I remember his appearances at rehearsal very clearly. He used to sit, his manuscript before him, at a small table near the footlights, and there he made such alterations and additions as Miss Ada Cavendish deemed necessary. He did this with the utmost readiness and amiability, influenced perhaps by her habit of calling him 'Wilkie,' a familiar mode of address which, I recollect, surprised and shocked me not a little . . . His goodness to me, so flattering from an eminent man to a mere youth, was ever in my mind, and to this day I feel grateful to him.'‡

Another anecdote told of this Liverpool tryout reveals Wilkie in a different, and somewhat unusual light. A certain young actor was disappointed with the size of his part, that of Abraham Sage, the gardener, and at one of the last rehearsals decided to amplify his lines with numerous repetitions of the word 'Sir.' When he had finished Wilkie looked sternly at him over his spectacles and said:

† In 1895 *The New Magdalen* was once more revived in the West End, probably for the last time. On this occasion Janet Achurch played Mercy Merrick, and an extended review by George Bernard Shaw of the production is included in Volume I of *Our Theatre in the Nineties* (Constable). Shaw, who probably saw the earlier revival at the Novelty, draws an interesting comparison between the performances of Ada Cavendish and Janet Achurch.
‡ Quoted in a footnote to *The Early Novels of Wilkie Collins* by Walter de la Mare.

'Young man, I have written the word "sir" four times. You have used it thirteen times. Please understand that I want my words spoken as I wrote them.' 'I am very sorry, Mr. Collins,' replied the young actor, 'but, you see, the part is such a poor one, and I wanted to give it character.'

'Thank you,' said Wilkie very quietly, 'I will look into it.'

As soon as the rehearsal was over he turned to the stage-manager and asked for a pencil. 'I think,' he said, 'that if we put our heads together, we may do without Abraham Sage.' As a result every line spoken by Sage was struck out, and the character declared redundant. We know that Wilkie took his work with extreme seriousness and that he could be irritable on occasion, but there is no other recorded instance of these characteristics prompting him to act with even the smallest degree of spite.

A few months later, in April, 1876, *Miss Gwilt* was produced at the Globe Theatre. It created something of a stir, and exception was taken in some quarters to 'the uniform unwholesomeness of the subject and to the excess of physical horror' which marked the closing scenes. This five-act drama seems, however, to have been one of his more successful stage adaptations. Dutton Cook likened it to 'one of those sombre but exciting dramas of the Boulevards in which crime and criminals figure considerably, and success is sought not so much by enlisting sympathy as by shocking sensibility and appealing to a love of the terrible.' For Ada Cavendish's performance he was full of admiration, but his comments upon the stage Allan Armadale serve to show how much more forthright dramatic criticism could be in those days. The character was, he wrote, 'perhaps even more inane in the play than in the novel, the inferiority of his theatrical representative depriving him even of those personal graces of bearing and look with which he was supposed to be highly endowed.'

A dramatic version of his early novel *The Dead Secret*, adapted 'with the author's permission' by E. J. Bramwell, was given in August, 1877, during Miss Bateman's season at the Lyceum. The play seems to have made little impression, and soon sank into an oblivion so complete that it does not even appear in Professor Allardyce Nicoll's exhaustive catalogue of *XIX Century Drama*.

The last of his four major novels reached the stage during the following year. *The Moonstone* was to have opened the Bancroft's autumn season of 1876, with Mr. and Mrs. Kendal as Franklin Blake and Rachel Verinder, Bancroft as Sergeant Cuff and his wife as Miss Clack. After much discussion it was decided by both Wilkie and Bancroft that the play was too melodramatic for the Prince of Wales Theatre, being better suited to the Olympic where in fact it was produced on September 17th, 1877.

The printed versions of those plays which he adapted from his best-sellers are all described on the title-page as having been 'altered' from the novel in question. The use of this word is peculiarly apt in the case of *The Moonstone*, where liberties are taken with the original story which, had they been taken by anyone but the author, would be denounced as literary vandalism. For example, all reference to opium, the very key to the original plot, is omitted and Franklin Blake's somnambulism results, in the play, from an indigestible supper! As with the drug, so with the drug-addict, Ezra Jennings, and the audience was deprived of seeing a character in which almost any competent actor could have scored a triumph. The moonstone itself loses all its historic associations and, thereby, its aura of romance; it might be, as a critic said, 'any other diamond contained in a jeweller's shop.' Finally, and unbelievably, Rosanna Spearman disappears from the stage version. The dramatic *Moonstone* was indeed Hamlet without the Prince of Denmark, and without most of the Court as well. One newspaper actually described it as 'a sort of domestic comedy.'

It is, of course, possible that the whole business of opium may have been eliminated in deference to the requirements of stage censorship, but the same excuse can hardly apply to the many other changes involved in the translation of novel into play. Admittedly there is in the novel a superabundance of material, much of which had to be excluded anyhow. It is the selection of discards which seems curious. Was it necessary for so many important characters and incidents to go by the board when, as a contemporary critic remarked, precious minutes of the play were devoted to proving the phenomena of somnambulism by quotations from 'such works as Combe on *Phrenology* and Elliotson's *Human Physiology* in reference to diseased brains and disordered stomachs?' The fact is that the theatre was not a suitable medium for those analytical qualities which distinguished his novels. He failed to realise that the dramatist has neither the time nor the obligation to prove beyond doubt every point in a complicated plot, and that to attempt it is the negation of drama. His sense of the dramatic, so infallible in his best stories, was seldom more than intermittent when writing for the stage.

The action of *The Moonstone* was telescoped into a period of 24 hours and the scene, the inner hall of the Verinders' house, remained unchanged throughout. The play by all accounts was indifferently performed apart from Bella Pateman as Rachel Verinder, and the comic characters overplayed desperately. It was not many weeks before the Olympic management was looking for a successor.

There is no doubt that Caroline Graves had been permanently re-established at 90, Gloucester Place, for some time. Her daughter Harriet—now that she had reached her twenties she could no longer be called 'little Carrie'—had come to be regarded generally as Wilkie's adopted daughter. On October 30th, 1877, a few weeks after the production of *The Moonstone*, Archer received a letter from Harriet Graves: 'Wilkie and my mother are abroad travelling —he is better for the change. When I last heard, they were at Munich. Thank you for your courteous reminder about the letter. As I have charge of his correspondence during his absence, I have written for it.' The following year, 1878, Harriet married Henry Powell Bartley, of 30, Somerset Place, Portman Square, who was, or subsequently became, Wilkie's solicitor and one of his executors. She was extremely fond of Wilkie and continued, even after her marriage, to act as his amanuensis from time to time.

The Continental tour which Wilkie and Caroline made in the autumn and winter of 1877 may well have been his last trip abroad. They were away for about a couple of months, and by the end of December he was 'recaptured by the great London net' and facing 'the most hateful of all English seasons (to me), the season of Cant and Christmas.' He wrote to Nina Lehmann: 'Good-natured friends tell me that I look twenty years younger after my travels. I am certainly much stronger than I was, and I hope to fight through the winter. The fog and rain met me in Paris, and prepared me for the horrors of London . . . I have returned to heaps of unanswered letters, bills, payments of pensioners, stupid and hideous Christmas cards, visits to pay, and every social nuisance that gets in the way of a rational enjoyment of life.' The Lehmanns were wintering in Cannes, which he remembered as, thirty years earlier, 'a delightfully snug, small, cheap place, with two English people only established in it—Lord Brougham and another Britisher whose name I forget.' The letter concludes with a rather jaundiced view of his French contemporaries: 'As to modern French novels in general, I have read them by dozens on my travels, and my report of them all is briefly this: Dull and Dirty. *The Nabob* by Daudet (of whom I once hoped better things) proved to be such realistic rubbish that I rushed out (it was at Dijon) to get something 'to take the taste out of my mouth,' as the children say. Prosper Mérimée's delicious *Colomba* appeared providentially in a shop window; I instantly secured it, read it for a second time, and recovered my opinion of French literature.' For Wilkie the moral protest is rare, and comes strangely from one who always claimed for himself the greatest latitude of expression and had frequently deplored the narrow fictional conventions of his day.

Apart from Munich, the only place at which we know they stayed during the European holiday is Venice; and Venice provides the setting of his next book, *The Haunted Hotel*. This short novel was published in November, 1878, in two volumes, together with another entitled *My Lady's Money*, and originally written a year earlier for the Christmas Number of the *Illustrated London News*. *The Haunted Hotel* echoes here and there his best work, and hardly merits the description—'a hideous fiction'—which Swinburne bestowed upon it. But if Swinburne overlooked the story's virtues, the judgment of a later poet shows some indulgence towards its defects. T. S. Eliot wrote in an article on 'Wilkie Collins and Dickens' which appeared in 1927 in *The Times Literary Supplement*:

What makes it [*The Haunted Hotel*] better than a mere readable second-rate ghost story is the fact that fatality in this story is no longer merely a will jerking the figures. The principal character, the fatal woman, is herself obsessed by the idea of fatality; her motives are melodramatic; she therefore compels the coincidences to occur, feeling that she is compelled to compel them. In this story, as the chief character is internally melodramatic, the story itself ceases to be merely melodramatic, and partakes of true drama.

This idea of an ineluctable Fate is an echo of *Armadale*. Perhaps the main weakness here, and it is largely a weakness of construction, is that Countess Narona, even more completely than Miss Gwilt in *Armadale*, condemns herself by her own pen. Abjuring detection, Wilkie lamely allows her to explain the mystery of her husband's disappearance in a written narrative which carries little conviction. Up to that point the book is competent melodrama— indeed its opening pages raise hopes of something more than competence—but the Countess's confession is the kind of clumsy device which Wilkie would never have employed ten years earlier. Significant, too, is his recourse to the supernatural. One of his special attributes as a sensation-novelist had been his ability to achieve by rational means effects of atmosphere more arresting than most writers could achieve by calling upon the whole paraphernalia of the supernatural. That he should have to fall back, in *The Haunted Hotel*, upon such an expedient as the apparition of a disembodied head is further evidence that his pen was beginning to falter.

My Lady's Money is a trivial story about a stolen banknote. Most of the characters are taken from stock and the *dénouement* can hardly have caused a flicker of surprise on the countenance of even the most ingenuous reader. Its main interest is in introducing a member of Wilkie's household of whose existence we might otherwise have been unaware, a Scotch terrier named Tommie, who would eat anything from *pâté de foie gras* to potatoes. At the end of the story, having said goodbye to each of the characters in turn, Wilkie writes: 'And last, not least, goodbye to Tommie? No. The writer gave Tommie his dinner not half an hour since, and is too fond of him to say goodbye.' The real Tommie died seven years later. A page torn from a pocket-diary, which happens to have survived, records in Wilkie's handwriting ten anniversaries. In one column are the birthdays of Caroline and her daughter, of Martha Rudd and her three children. The other column shows the dates of his parents' and his brother's deaths, and that of 'our dog Tommy'—August 28th, 1885.'

During 1878 another and longer novel, *The Fallen Leaves*, had been appearing both in *The World* and the *Canadian Monthly*. It was published in July of the following year by Chatto and Windus in three volumes. He intended at the outset to follow it up with a sequel, for the title-page bore the words 'First Series' and a second series was announced in a postscript to the third volume. It was the only novel he dedicated 'To Caroline.' These and other indications suggest that he regarded this as his most important work for some time. Its theme, that of the reformed prostitute, was not dissimilar to *The New Magdalen* which had scored a major success. But *The Fallen Leaves* failed, perhaps more completely than any other book he wrote. The critics disliked it, but that alone would never worry Wilkie Collins. The public was the ultimate court of judgment. This time even the public disappointed him. In the preface to his next book, addressed to the dedicatee, he explained at some length why he had not yet written the promised sequel. *The Fallen Leaves* had by then reached only 'a comparatively limited class of reader in England.' Only when the book was reprinted in its cheapest form would it appeal to 'the great audience of the English people,' and not until then would the sequel, which existed in rough notes, appear. There followed a bitter tirade against 'the nasty posterity of Tartuffe' who had objected to his character of the prostitute, as it had objected to *Basil*, to *Armadale*, and to *The New Magdalen*. He refused to allow limits which no other country but England imposed to be 'wantonly assigned' to his work. 'When my work is undertaken with a pure purpose,' he wrote, 'I claim the same liberty which is accorded to a writer in a newspaper or to a clergyman in a pulpit.' To another correspondent he said he was 'waiting (with some confidence, inspired by previous experience), for the Verdict of the People.' But the People's reaction to the two-shilling edition failed to give him the encouragement he needed to proceed with the Second Series, and the project was abandoned. The published novel ends with the marriage of the young Socialist hero to the girl he has rescued from the streets. Of the proposed sequel Wilkie wrote, in a letter dated June 22nd, 1880: 'The married life—in the second part—will be essentially a happy life, in itself. But the outer influence of the world which surrounds this husband and wife—the world whose unchristian prejudices they have set at defiance—will slowly undermine their happiness and will I fear, make the close of the story a sad one.' Had this Second Series been written he could no doubt have drawn upon his own experiences of the censorious world and its attitude towards those who defy its prejudices.

The most interesting part of this unpleasantly sentimental novel is the account in the first volume of an American community known as the Primitive Christian Socialists, among whom the young hero is brought up. It was thought by S. M. Ellis that Wilkie found time during his American tour to visit a community, supported for some time by Laurence Oliphant, which had settled at Brocton (Salem-on-Erie) calling itself the Brotherhood of the New Life.† Whether or not his account is based upon first-hand knowledge, we know that he possessed a copy of Charles Nordhoff's book *The Communistic Societies of the United States*, published in New York in 1875, from which he could easily have drawn all the material he required. He describes his Utopian community, in which 'all men have a right to be rich—provided they don't make other people poor as part of the process,' with the sympathetic approval that one would expect a genuine Radical to feel towards these fumbling experiments in the direction of Socialism.

One or two scenes stand out on their own merits, notably the suicide of Mrs. Farnaby, described with a gruesome realism which calls to mind the death of Emma Bovary: 'The fell action of the strychnine wrung every muscle in her with the torture of convulsion. Her hands were fast clenched; her head was bent back; her body, rigid as a bar of iron, was arched upwards from the bed, resting on the two extremities of the head and the heels: the staring eyes, the dusky face, the twisted lips, the clenched teeth, were frightful to see.' For the rest, the story seldom emerges from a morass of novelettish mediocrity. *The Fallen Leaves* must stand as the low-water mark of Wilkie's achievement.

Though a visiting American writer had said that Wilkie 'still lingered, not superfluous but not indispensable; like an historic edifice, respected, but unoccupied,' he still had news-value in his own country. About this time Edmund Yates, whom he had known for twenty years, published in his paper *The World* an interview

† The Brotherhood of the New Life was founded in 1861 by Thomas Lake Harris, a successful charlatan who exercised a powerful influence over Oliphant and relieved him of most of his fortune. Oliphant then sued Harris and recovered several thousand pounds. Further details will be found in *Heavens on Earth*, by Mark Holloway (*Turnstile Press*, 1951).

with Wilkie which took place in the large double drawing-room at 90, Gloucester Place. Near the window stood a massive writing-table fitted with a small desk of the same design as Dickens'; beside it was a japanned tin box containing what he called his 'stock-in-trade'—outlines of plots, notes for stories and two books of newspaper-cuttings from *The Times*, *Echo*, and *Pall Mall Gazette*. One of these volumes was classified under three headings, 'Our civilisation,' 'Hints for scenes and incidents' and 'Hints for character.' He told Yates that he was never at a loss for a plot, his difficulty always being to work it out to his satisfaction. He was, he said, a rapid inventor and a slow producer. Yates led him to speak of his literary models and invited his opinion of various writers. 'I don't attempt the style of Addison, because I hardly think it worth while. Addison was a neat but trivial writer, not in the least vigorous or dramatic; but the very reverse—analytical and painfully minute. His style bears about as much resemblance to good strong nervous English as a silver filigree does to a bronze statue. Lord Byron's letters are the best English I know—perfectly simple and clear, bright and strong.' Of Fielding and Smollett he said that they were now only read by scholars, 'admirable painters of manners' though they had been. Goldsmith, on the other hand, who possessed the poetic insight which they lacked, 'had left an imperishable work in *The Vicar of Wakefield*.' They talked of a current biography of Napoleon which sought to show that its subject was 'a mean scoundrel and a shameless liar,' and was so regarded by his contemporaries. 'It is good to tell the truth about Napoleon, of course,' was Wilkie's comment. 'But you cannot break the idol, for his deeds strike the imagination. He was a dramatic man.'†

During the year 1879 more links with the past were severed. In January his old friend E. M. Ward died, and to his son, Leslie ('Spy', the cartoonist) Wilkie wrote: 'No ordinary engagement would prevent me from paying the last tribute of affection to my dear lost friend. Illness alone makes it impossible for me to join those who will follow him to the grave tomorrow . . . I first knew your father when I was a boy—forty years since—and it is no figure of speech, it is only the sad truth, to say that I do indeed

† The account of the interview was subsequently reprinted in *Celebrities at Home* (Third Edition). Edmund Yates. (*World Office*, 1879).

share in your grief, and feel the irreparable loss that you have suffered as, in some degree at least, my loss too.' August of the same year brought news from across the Atlantic of the death of Charles Fechter. In November Dickens' widow died after an illness of some months. Kate Perugini recalls that Wilkie, 'ever a dear friend of the family,' called frequently at her mother's house in Gloucester Crescent to enquire after her progress.

Other friends of his younger days had gone too. When he published *The Frozen Deep* in 1874 the playbill of the famous performance at the Free Trade Hall, Manchester, had been reproduced as a frontispiece. In the preface Wilkie pointed out the melancholy fact that of the nine male actors on that occasion, all friends of his, only three were still alive. His brother Charley, Dickens and his son Alfred, Shirley Brooks, Egg and Mark Lemon were all dead. Besides himself only Pigott and Charles Dickens Junior were left. The ranks were being thinned indeed.

16

Last Years

DURING the last ten years of his life Wilkie withdrew from
society more and more. Whilst it is an exaggeration to
state, as does the *Dictionary of National Biography*, that
he became a hermit, he certainly avoided public functions almost
entirely, dined out infrequently and then only at the homes of his
more intimate friends such as the Lehmanns, and entertained hardly
at all. This way of living was not so much of his own choosing as
dictated by health considerations. By the year 1880 he was a semi-
invalid, immured in his house for long periods. Though still in his
middle fifties, he was already an old man. 'Your Wilkie is getting
old,' he had written a year earlier, 'there is no mistake about that!'
He was often unable to eat a normal diet. Sometimes at dinner he
would take only bread soaked in meat gravy, and would then get
up in the middle of the night and have cold soup and champagne
—dry champagne, of course. His doctor warned him against meat,
but his adherence to doctor's orders was not always strict. Writing
to thank the Padrona for a parcel of butter which arrived 'on the
very day when I was thinking of keeping a private cow in the
backyard and presiding myself over the pastoral churn,' he added
a postscript: 'Oh! I was foolish enough to eat slices of plain
joints two days following. The bilious miseries that followed
proved obstinate until I most fortunately ate some *pâté de foie
gras*. The cure was instantaneous—and lasting.' A year or so later
he is requesting 'weak brandy-and-water and NO wholesome joints'
in his acceptance of an invitation to lunch; on another occasion
he asked the Padrona to order a handy stick with which to rap
him over the knuckles 'if you find me raising to my guilty and
gouty lips any other liquor than weak brandy-and-water.'

An affecting letter to Frederick Lehmann describes what had

become virtually his normal state of health: 'The inflammatory and painful part of this last gouty visitation is at an end. Weakness is now the obstacle to be got over—my knees tremble on the stairs and my back aches after half an hour's walking—no, *tottering*—on the sunny side of the street. I am told to drive out—but I won't. An airing in a carriage is (to me) such a depressing proceeding that I am ready to burst out crying when I only think of it. I will get stronger on my wretched old legs, and report myself in Berkeley Square as soon as I have ceased to be a human wet blanket.' Wybert Reeve records that for exercise he used often to walk up and down stairs with the aid of the balusters, many times on end. Few of his friends expected that he would last another ten years.

Early in 1880, at Frederick's request, he sat to Rudolf Lehmann for a portrait which was to be a present to the Padrona, and the artist has left his impressions of the sitter, in print as well as on canvas. Wilkie would arrive at the studio muffled up in the heavy fur coat which he had acquired during his American tour. He was a good sitter, as befitted 'the true son of a Royal Academician.' His face was pallid and smooth, with hardly a wrinkle. Rudolf Lehmann remarks, as others have done, upon the curious congenital swelling on the right side of his forehead, and tells us that he chose for the portrait an aspect which partly concealed this malformation. Wilkie himself used to refer to it, complaining that Nature had got him 'all out of drawing,' in addition to giving him a short body quite out of proportion to his unusually large head. His eyes, according to the painter, had a weird, far-off look about them, giving the impression that they 'invested almost everything with an air of mystery and romance.' He would ply Lehmann with questions about this or that object which caught his attention. Once it was a door which formed part of an improvised partition. Having stared at it for some time he asked in a whisper, 'Where does that lead to? It looks as if it opened into a subterranean vault or passage, and might easily be an escapada in case of sudden surprise,' and fell into a deep reverie. He never lost this desire—it was indeed almost a compulsion—to weave a story around the most trivial incident. In one of the later books he wrote: 'Not one man in ten thousand, living in the midst of reality, has discovered that he is also living in the midst of romance.' He himself made this discovery very early in his life, and saw in that special awareness the quality which, basically, distinguishes the novelist from his fellow-men.

Broken down in health though he was, he carried on writing as hard as ever to meet the steady demand for his books, resting only when blinded with gout and tortured by rheumatic pains. Work was for him an anodyne hardly less effective than his opium. In eight out of the ten years that were left to him a new book by Wilkie Collins appeared in Chatto and Windus' list. In 1880, they published *Jezebel's Daughter*, adapted from his play *The Red Vial* which had so miserably failed twenty years before. For some time he had been pondering this notion of turning it into a book. Twelve years before he had even lighted upon 'a splendid idea for boiling down *The Lighthouse*, *The Frozen Deep* and *The Red Vial* into *one* novel,' and offering it to 'the penny journals.' The operation may have involved more boiling than he anticipated, for he proceeded no further.

It is not difficult to detect the germ from which this somewhat crude melodrama sprang. As a young man he had visited Frankfurt and had been shown round the mortuary, or Deadhouse, as he preferred to call it. In the course of his inspection he learned that at one time a superstitious fear of being buried alive had been common throughout Germany, and that it still prevailed to some extent in Frankfurt. As a precaution against such a calamity the Deadhouse authorities had long since established, and still carried on, a particularly grisly practice. To the fingers of each corpse a series of strings was attached, leading to a bell. Any movement on the part of the 'corpse' would thereby automatically ring the bell and rouse the attendants. It hardly needed the macabre imagination of a Wilkie Collins to reflect upon the situation of a cadaver thus dramatically announcing its own resurrection. Such indeed is the climax of *Jezebel's Daughter*, a kind of Walpurgis-nacht performed by a madman, a murderess and a drunken nightwatchman. Of the authenticity of the setting we are left in no doubt, being told in the Preface 'that the accessories of the scenes in the Deadhouse of Frankfurt have been studied on the spot. The published rules and ground-plans of that famous mortuary establishment have also been laid on my desk, as aids to memory while I was writing the closing passages of the story.'

The story, as a whole, though readable enough, is merely a structure to support the sensational climax and displays little of the ingenuity that might have marked its development had he written it twenty years earlier. None of the characters come fully to life, and if Madame Fontaine, the Jezebel of the title, occasionally recalls Lydia Gwilt she also serves as a melancholy reminder of how far below that standard his writing had fallen; nor can we share the author's interest in Jack Straw, yet another of his mentally deranged characters. For the rest, there is more than enough of obscure poisons and their antidotes—a subject which never ceased to fascinate him—and too little of that careful creation of atmosphere in which the most sensational event carries conviction.

The Black Robe, published a year later and serialised in *The Canadian Monthly*, is probably the best of the later books. Begun as an attack on the Jesuits, whom he depicts as engaged in a world-wide conspiracy to further their power and influence, it develops into a fairly straightforward sensation-novel. The propaganda element is kept well in check. The pace seldom drags and there is far less padding than is usually found in these later novels. Two characters stand out. In Mrs. Eyrecourt, the heroine's mother, Wilkie succeeds for once in drawing a satirical portrait which stops short of caricature. We are introduced to a vain, sophisticated, frivolous woman of Society, pursuing with tireless energy the seasonal round of social engagements. Only when her daughter's interests are threatened does Mrs. Eyrecourt reveal beneath this brittle exterior not only the normal instincts of a mother but unsuspected strength of character. In acumen and resourcefulness she becomes a match for Father Benwell, the Jesuit priest who dominates the story. Father Benwell, an important figure in a network of religious intrigue with headquarters in Rome, makes a most satisfying villain. In plotting the restitution to the Catholic Church of a valuable estate, he displays something of Count Fosco's ingenuity and suave arrogance.

Sending a copy of *The Black Robe* to his friend Winter in New York, Wilkie wrote: 'It is thought, on the European side of the Atlantic, in Roman Catholic countries as well as in Protestant England, to be the best thing I have written for some time. And it is memorable to *me* as having produced a freely offered gift of forty pounds from one of the pirates who have seized it on the American side!'

During the year 1881, he sought the services of A. P. Watt, founder of the earliest firm of literary agents, in disposing of the rights of his next book. This was a remarkable move for one who had in the past revelled in the commercial side of his calling, who so obviously delighted in bargaining with publishers and making the most of his market. But with advancing years he had lost some of his zest for these things, and may have found that competition was becoming stiffer. The initial transaction with Watt, successfully concluded, was followed by others, and within a few months he established himself as Wilkie's literary agent, handling nearly all negotiations on his behalf. His letters to Watt have been preserved and reveal the steady development of a professional association into a warm personal friendship. They also show, incidentally, the elaborate care with which Wilkie tackled the intricacies of serial publication, his strict routine for the correcting of proofs and for the despatch of advance sheets to foreign periodicals. By appointing Watt his sole literary executor Wilkie demonstrated his confidence in him both as adviser and friend.

In the autumn of 1881, Wilkie had a particularly bad attack of gout which compelled him to rest for some months. He spent this period of enforced idleness at Ramsgate, which had long been his favourite watering-place and became almost a second home. During the remaining years of his life he would never leave his home in London except to go to Ramsgate. He seems invariably to have stayed at 14, Nelson Crescent, where he probably rented an apartment. The town figures in a number of his later books, including *Poor Miss Finch*, *The Two Destinies*, and *The Fallen Leaves* and he paid many a tribute to its climate, which suited him admirably. To a friend convalescing at nearby Broadstairs he wrote:

We are the Corsican Brothers of human infirmity. For three months the gout has again tortured my eyes—and here I am recovering within two miles of you! Are you well enough to get here by railway (if walking is still bad for you) and take your luncheon, on any day you like, from 2 to 2.30? I could then answer your questions in the pleasanter way—besides sparing my eyes letter-writing at length, in the interests of some light work which I am just able to do after four months of utter literary eclipse. Why don't I go to you at Broadstairs? It is the most dreadful place in the world to me now. The ghosts of my brother, Dickens, Augustus Egg, and of two other dearly-loved friends—who all lived with me at Broadstairs—now haunt the place. Two years ago I *tried* to go to Broadstairs. At the first view of 'The Fort House' the old and dear associations completely overwhelmed me and I turned back to Ramsgate.

From Ramsgate he would often go yachting in the Channel, or perhaps further afield. As late as the summer of 1886 we find him writing to Archer from Nelson Crescent: 'I have been sailing and I have just found your letter waiting for me here. Send the story to this address (headquarters for work after idling at sea) and I will read it with the greatest pleasure.' His enthusiasm for sailing and the sea did not diminish with the years. He could of course no longer command the physical agility and alertness which such expeditions as the 'Tomtit' cruise of his younger days demanded. Of necessity his yachting became a staider pastime. Winter recalls his dictum that the perfection of enjoyment could only be obtained 'when you are at sea in a luxurious well-appointed steam-yacht in lovely summer weather.'

As soon as he felt well enough for sustained work he began a new novel, not very happily entitled *Heart and Science*, which was to expose the horrors of vivisection. It may well have been a case heard some six months before at Bow Street which enlisted his support for the cause of dumb animals. The facts of the case have been recalled by S. M. Ellis.† David Ferrier, Professor of Forensic Medicine at King's College, was charged under the Vivisection Act with performing experiments calculated to cause suffering to two monkeys. The proceedings were brought by the Victoria Street Society for the Protection of Animals who showed that experiments had resulted in the total deafness of one monkey and paralysis of the other. The magistrate, however, dismissed the summons. Professor Ferrier is mentioned by Wilkie in the Preface.

In August, 1882, he describes himself as 'just now immersed in physiology, in my spare hours, in preparation for coming numbers of *Heart and Science*.' For six months he wrote furiously—'one part sane and three parts mad,' he told the Padrona—during the

† *Wilkie Collins, le Fanu and others.* S. M. Ellis. (*Constable*, 1931).

S

whole of which time he was miraculously free of his ailments. As soon as the book was finished he realised that he was 'half dead with fatigue,' and the very next day the gout had attacked his right eye. Henceforth he was compelled for long periods to shade the eye with a black patch. At the end of February he wrote to the Padrona: 'I am nearly well, and I pull off my black patch indoors. But I am forbidden the night air, and I am so weak that I slip down in my chair towards night, like old Rogers. But *he* was only eighty—I am a hundred.'

Heart and Science, published in April, 1883, is yet another failure. This time even the plain narrative is handled clumsily and fails to grip. The persons of the story, Ovid Vere, the vacuous hero, Mrs. Gallilee, Dr. Null and Mr. Mool, are as unreal as their names; apart from Dr. Benjulia in the last volume, only the little girl Zo, who enchanted Swinburne, has any semblance of life. The anti-vivisection propaganda is hardly more than incidental to the plot, and argument is limited to the bare assertion that medical research has no need of such practices. Concern for his readers' feelings precludes him from taking them inside the laboratory. We are allowed to listen, but may not see. The book's purpose is further weakened by his belated sympathy for the vivisector himself. The character of Dr. Benjulia develops almost in spite of his creator, who shows us not an inhuman sadist, as he seems to have intended at the outset, but a man suffering deeply because of the pain he is compelled to inflict in the course of his researches.

Wilkie's immersion in the scientific literature of his day, claimed in the Preface as evidence of technical authenticity, merely enable him to sprinkle his pages with the current jargon of science. There is no awareness of the rapidly widening horizons of scientific discovery, only a spurious air of topicality which no doubt impressed the casual reader. The conflict suggested by the title is a conflict within the author himself. He found himself in a fast-changing society, a world, to use his own words, 'in the most rampant stage of development.' The old, familiar world was dying and he was inclined to be suspicious of, because he no longer fully understood, the new. The march of Science he regarded in some vague way as a threat even to those basic human emotions which endure from age to age, and for this reason he felt impelled to restate their validity. In short, he was growing old and a little out of temper with his time.

Very different, but no less disappointing, is *I Say No*, the oddly-named novel which appeared a year later. The plot follows the pattern of his early books in that there is a 'secret' hidden, or half-hidden, from the reader until the final chapters, but there the resemblance ends. In the later novels there is a growing tendency to rely upon pure coincidence as the very mainspring of plot-construction. In *I Say No* everything hangs upon coincidence. At every turn some chance meeting, some unsuspected relationship, or some other fortunate accident is required to carry the story along. Every law of probability is heedlessly jettisoned. The result is a story which will beguile only those whose credulity can stand the strain.

I Say No marked a further round in the continuous war waged by Wilkie Collins and Harpers against the American pirates. As the story appeared in *Harper's Weekly* a Philadelphia paper was copying the instalments week by week. Since there was every chance that Harpers would be forestalled in publishing the book, Wilkie co-operated by sending them the concluding chapters in manuscript as he wrote them instead of waiting for corrected proofs of the English serial version. The result was that the book was published in New York in July, 1884, a good four months prior to its London publication.

It had been hinted more than once that Wilkie Collins during his last years had recourse to the practice known as 'ghosting.' Not a shred of evidence has been produced in support of the theory, which seems to have appeared first in an article by Arthur Waugh entitled 'Wilkie Collins: and his Mantle.'† Waugh speaks of 'that period in which, so I have been told, the pens of kindly companions helped his failing vigour to keep pace with the demands of the market.' The charge is repeated by Lewis Melville in his book, *Victorian Novelists*. All the facts seem, however, to contradict such a theory. First of all, Wilkie's style, undistinguished though it was—particularly in the later books, is consistently recognisable. There is a flat sameness about the last half-dozen novels, whatever may be the differences of plot and background. The falling-off in quality is fairly steady, and shows none of the

† *Academy Magazine*, 5th April, 1902.

sharp variations one would expect to follow the interventions of
'kindly companions.' The virtues of the later books, such as they
are, are essentially Wilkie's own; clarity of expression, a certain
narrative fluency and some measure of ingenuity can still be seen.
Similarly, their shortcomings are his too, the overworked repertory of melodramatic tricks, the stilted dialogue, the passion for
the fortuitous and the rather arch attitude towards the reader.
Then there is the undoubted fact that throughout the 1880's his
literary output bore a direct relationship to the state of his health;
we can easily trace the periods of serious illness as being also
periods of literary inactivity. In handing over his last novel to
Walter Besant to complete, Wilkie provided him with a minutely-
detailed scenario of the unwritten chapters. Why go to Besant at
all, during his last illness, if anonymous pens were already in his
service? But the most compelling argument of all is that the
practice of employing ghosts would have been utterly alien to
Wilkie's character and to his integrity as a writer. Throughout
his career he took his work, and his duty to his readers, with the
utmost seriousness. In correspondence and in the Prefaces there
is the fullest evidence of this. It would be wholly inconsistent with
this attitude for him to have palmed off upon a faithful public
work under his name which was not entirely his own.

In April, 1883, he wrote to Frank Archer: 'Miss Lingard is to
play the chief part in that new piece of mine which has been
waiting for a true artist with such special capacities as the part
needs.' The 'new piece' was an original melodrama in four acts
entitled *Rank and Riches*, and accepted for production at the
Adelphi Theatre, rival of the Olympic, as a home of melodrama.
A strong cast had been assembled including George Alexander,
G. W. Anson, Miss Lingard, and, in a small part, Charles Hawtrey.
Everything was set for a great success. The producer, Edgar Bruce,
was very confident, telling everyone, not quite accurately, that
Wilkie Collins had never had a failure with any of his plays. On
the first night, June 9th, 1883, A. W. Pinero recalls standing beside
the author at the back of the dress-circle, just before the rise of
the curtain. He noticed that Wilkie was sporting a large camelia
in his buttonhole, expecting no doubt to take his bow in due time.
Nothing went right from the start. Finding the dialogue some-

what stilted and seizing upon a phrase here and there capable of more than one interpretation, the audience began to titter. Then G. W. Anson made his entrance as Mr. Dominic, a 'bird-doctor,' scattering birdseed around the stage. This was too much for the audience; the laughter became an uproar, the actors could carry on only with great difficulty and poor Miss Lingard was reduced to tears. The first act curtain came down to a chorus of 'howling, hooting and hissing,' mingled with raucous counter-cheering from the partisans of author and producer. At the end of the third act Anson, courageous if ill-advised, came before the curtain and made a short speech in which he upbraided the audience for their hostility towards the work of 'a great master' and begged them at least to show courtesy to Miss Lingard. They were, however, in no mood to be lectured and showed their resentment by a renewed clamour. There were shouts, according to *The Times*, of 'Bosh,' 'Nonsense,' and 'Get on with the play.' Whereupon Anson finally lost his temper, shook his fist and called them 'a lot of damned cads.'† The company got through the last act somehow, and the effect of the evening on Wilkie Collins, who was acutely nervous even at a successful first-night, can be imagined. The play was quickly withdrawn.

Rank and Riches marked the end of his theatrical ventures, if one excepts the dramatisation of *The Evil Genius*, which received a single performance for copyright purposes in October, 1885. The fiasco suggests that his particular style of melodrama had outlived its vogue and that he could no longer satisfy the changing demands of the theatre-going public. It is true that *Man and Wife* and *The New Magdalen* were still considered worth reviving, and that *The Woman in White* continued to turn up in the provinces, but these plays survived as adaptations of novels still widely read, and as theatrical successes in their own right. He was still a popular dramatist in America, where, strangely enough, *Rank and Riches* enjoyed a considerable success.

In April, 1884, he suffered a great personal loss in the death

---

† Sir Charles Hawtrey tells us in *The Truth at Last* (Thornton Butterworth, 1924) that the regular first-nighters never forgave Anson, greeting him with yells and boos at every subsequent first-night. This treatment forced the wretched actor to leave the country for Australia, where he ended his stage career.

of Charles Reade. To an American correspondent he wrote: 'In this country we have lately lost one of the "last of the Romans" —my dear old friend, Charles Reade. I look out for the new writer among us who is to fill that vacant place—and I fail to see him.' George Eliot had died in 1880, Trollope two years later. Of the great names of mid-Victorian fiction, Wilkie Collins survived almost alone. Who would have forecast, at the time of *The Moonstone's* appearance, that this sick man, addicted to laudanum as he was, would not only outlive his literary contemporaries, but would still retain twenty years later his hold upon the great mass of the reading public? His later work may have been inferior stuff which the critics no longer took seriously, but in a ballot organised about this time by the *Pall Mall Gazette* to decide the most popular author, Wilkie Collins outdistanced all his competitors.

In America, too, he was still a best-seller. Within a year or so he achieved eponymous fame of a somewhat unexpected kind. A well-known trotting stallion in the United States was named after him and he was delighted to receive a pamphlet outlining the horse's virtues and stating that 'Wilkie Collins covers mares at $75 each.'

If many of his old friends were dead, he had not lost his gift for making new ones. Early in 1885 he met, through an introduction of William Winter, the young American actress, Mary Anderson, who had just made her London *début*. Despite the thirty-five years that separated them, they became the greatest of friends. Though generally disinclined to pay social calls any more —he used to describe himself as 'completely out of the world'—he would often visit Mary at the house in Cromwell Road where she lived with her mother and brother.

In later years Wilkie seems to have felt more at home among theatrical folk than in any other society, apart from one or two intimate friends like the Beards or the Lehmanns. Mary Anderson tells in her Memoirs† of many entertaining evenings they spent in his company, when he would tell stories of Dickens, Reade and Thackeray. She remembers his describing the feeling of desolation when he, the last of the four, stood at the edge of Reade's grave. He talked frankly to her of his drug-taking, telling how the

† *A Few Memories.* Mary Anderson (Mme. de Navarro), (*Osgood, McIlvaine & Co.,* 1896).

laudanum, though it numbed the pain, used to excite his mind so that when going up to his room at night, the staircase seemed crowded with ghosts trying to push him down. She considered him excessively modest; on an occasion when she praised one of his books he brushed the tribute aside with the words: 'Ah, I am only an old fellow who has a liking for story-telling, nothing more.'

His letters to Mary Anderson are full of references, in the usual light-hearted vein, to his ailments. In March, 1885, a new complication had been added.

Illness, nothing but illness, has kept me away. My heart has been running down like a clock that is out of repair. For the last fortnight the doctor has been winding me up again. He is getting on well enough with his repairs, but I have been (medically) intoxicated with sal volatile and spirits of chloroform; and the result has been a new idea of a ghost story.

And a month later:

If I can get to the theatre, it is useless to say that I will seize the opportunity. But the weather is terribly against me. I may tell you (between ourselves) that the mischief this time is a deranged condition of the nerves near the heart, and a very slight cause sets in action a terrific pain in the chest and in the arms. But I am getting stronger ...

For a time he toyed with the idea of writing a play for her, once going so far as to submit a first-act scenario. Mary considered her part unsuitable, and described in a letter the kind of role she had in mind. Wilkie replied: 'I already understand what is wanted —and I am eager to consult with you as to the details—to ask hundreds of questions and to try if we can together meet the one serious difficulty that I see—finding a good subject. If something could be found in *American* history—not connected with wars—I should like it best, because the dramatic writers of the United States have left that field free.' But not even a perusal of Bancroft's long *History of the United States* could produce a suitable theme, and the idea was ultimately dropped.

Wilkie's friendship with Mary Anderson lasted until his death. It was a happy association, as can be seen from the last letter she quotes, dated January 20th, 1888:

Mr. Terriss, dear Mary Anderson, is not Romeo. I am Romeo—
because I am in sympathy with you. At the time when by my
calculation, you must have been writing your nice little note, I
was asking myself at what time in the afternoon I should be
most likely to find you at home and disengaged, if I put my
patch on my weak eye and called at Cromwell Houses. When
may I climb the area railings, with my umbrella in one hand and
my guitar in the other, and hope to see Juliet in the balcony
(well wrapped up)? . . . Over and over again I have thought of
writing, and have put it off in the hope of being well enough to
speak for myself. At last there is nothing the matter but weakness and certain vagaries of the optic nerves, which persist in
seeing a pattern of their own making, as black as black lace,
in this form: [a sketch follows]. It might be prettier, might it
not? I think it is a reptile of the pre-Adamite period.

Always yours affectionately,

Wilkie Collins.

His next book, *The Evil Genius*, published in 1886, marked a
departure from the type of novel with which his name had become
associated. Sub-titled *A Domestic Story*, it is concerned not with
crime but with forbidden passions and divorce, a field he would
have been better advised to leave to those who were already
exploiting it successfully. It is an uninspired performance, containing many echoes both of character and incident from his
earlier works. Technically, it suffers from the same defect as *Man
and Wife* and *The New Magdalen* in being written in such a way
as to permit easy stage adaptation, and is full of obviously contrived exits and entrances. The story embraces no special 'purpose'
but Wilkie could not resist a passing dig at the American law of
copyright. The subject is dragged by the ears into a conversation
between a lawyer and his friend:

'What made you go to America? You haven't been delivering
lectures, have you?'
'I have been enjoying myself among the most hospitable people
in the world.'
Mr. Sarrazin shook his head; he had a case of copyright in hand
just then. 'A people to be pitied,' he said.
'Why?'
'Because their Government forgets what is due to the honour
of the nation.'

'How?'

'In this way. The honour of a nation which confers the right of property in works of art produced by its own citizens, is surely concerned in protecting from theft works of art produced by other citizens.'

'That's not the fault of the people.'

'Certainly not. I have already said it's the fault of the Government.'

In the *dénouement* of the story a couple who were divorced in the first volume are brought together again in marriage. Such an event was almost unheard of at the time, and the author was regarded as having overstepped the bounds of probability. He might have claimed that he was merely anticipating the social habits of a generation still to come. This was not the first occasion on which Wilkie was ahead of his time.

Whatever the merits or demerits of *The Evil Genius*, it was at least a commercial success for its author. Writing to Wybert Reeve in Australia, he said:

My new novel, now shortly to be published in book form, has appeared previously in various newspapers, and the speculator purchasing all serial rights in England and the Colonies has given me the largest sum I have ever received for any of my books before.

As for my health, considering I was sixty-two years old last birthday, that I have worked hard as a writer (perhaps few literary men harder) and that gout has tried to blind me first and kill be afterwards on more than one occasion, I must not complain. Neuralgia and nervous exhaustion generally have sent me to the sea to be patched up, and the sea is justifying my confidence in it. I must try, old friend, and live long enough to welcome you back when you return to be with us once more.

The serial rights of *The Evil Genius* were purchased by Tillotson's of Bolton, a progressive firm who were pioneers of the practice known as syndicating. They controlled several Lancashire newspapers and used to provide for their own and other papers a weekly service of serial fiction. For many years this was carried on by the stereo method, stereos of each instalment being produced in Tillotson's works and furnished weekly to the newspapers subscribing to the service. The aggregate fees received by the firm enabled it to enter the market for serial fiction with some success, and Wilkie Collins was perhaps the first front-rank novelist to have dealings with Tillotson's. His association with them began in 1879 when *Jezebel's Daughter* appeared as a serial in the *Bolton Weekly Journal* and twelve other Northern newspapers. For the serial copyright and German translation rights he received £500. Then followed one or two shorter stories, each spread over about three instalments, for which he was paid sums varying from £35 each for 'Who Killed Zebedee' and 'The Devil's Spectacles,' to £150 for 'The Ghost's Touch.'† As the syndicating business prospered and the name of Wilkie Collins proved an attraction, so the price rose and for *The Evil Genius* Tillotson paid £1,300, to cover 'the sole rights of consecutive serial publication in English newspapers.' This was almost certainly the largest figure he ever received for serial rights in the United Kingdom. His last book to be syndicated by Tillotson was *The Legacy of Cain* for which he was paid £1,080. If one adds the payments from Chatto and Windus for book publication, from Harpers for serial and book publication in America, as well as sundry amounts for translation rights,‡ it is clear that he was still able to earn large sums with every book he wrote.

Another lively publisher with whom he made contact was J. W. Arrowsmith, of Bristol, for whose 1886 *Christmas Annual* he wrote a short novel entitled *The Guilty River*. It was a rushed job from the start. He did not begin writing until September and on October 12th he told Archer: 'I am still hard at work on my Christmas book—and, woe is me, working against time. But the shade is off my eye and, though I am feeling weary, I hope to get through my work in (say) three weeks more.' Less than a month later it was finished, and its author exhausted. 'I am like the old posting horses in the old posting days. While I was whipped my pace was wonderful. Now we have got to our destination my head hangs down and my forelegs tremble. But, considering that I was twelve hours a day at work for the last week of my labours, I

---

† 'The Devil's Spectacles' never appeared in book-form in this country, although it was published in the American *Seaside Library* as 'The Magic Spectacles.' The other two stories were included in *Little Novels* under different titles.

‡ He had recently learned that his books, beginning with *The Woman in White*, were in process of being translated into Bengali.

have no reason to complain of my constitution.' By the middle of November the book was in the shops, and the publisher engaged upon a big campaign of sales promotion. 'The good man himself (Arrowsmith) was here on Tuesday last to report what he had done in the way of launching *The Guilty River*. He likes the story and believes in it—and he has advertised by posters, shopcards, news-papers—*and* by a hundred "sandwich men" promenading London with *Guilty River* all over them—and this for a shilling book! . . . We had sold 20,000 copies between Monday and Friday last.'

He looked forward to a period when 'pen and brain shall rest together.' When an idea knocked at his head, he told a friend, the answer was 'Not at home.' But his body exacted the penalties of overwork. Neuralgia set in, and he was permitted only short walks 'followed by bathings and rubbings and restings.' Beard managed to beat back a threatened attack of gout, but the remedies employed so weakened the patient that he had to recuperate by the sea. The Padrona, wintering in Cannes, was always a sympathetic audience and he wrote to her on February 2nd, 1887:

> If you were only at the North of Scotland—say Thurso—I would rush to you by steamer and become young again in the fine cold air. But when I think of that fearful French railway journey, and of the Southern climate of Cannes, I see madness on my way to the Mediterranean and death in lingering torments on the shores of that celebrated sea. We have had here—after a brief paradise of frost—the British sirocco. Fidgets, aching legs, gloom, vile tempers, neuralgic troubles in the chest—such are the conditions under which I am living and such the obstacles which have prevented my writing to you long since.

Although he boasted that he was not even thinking of another book, Wilkie could not be completely idle for long. He occupied himself with arranging the collection in book-form of various stories he had contributed over the past ten years to periodicals on both sides of the Atlantic. *Little Novels*, in three volumes, was published by Chatto and Windus in the spring of 1887. The quality of the stories is far below that of *After Dark* and *The Queen of Hearts*, as he himself recognised.

About this time there appeared in the *Contemporary Review* a eulogistic article on Wilkie Collins and his work written by a

dilettante of the arts named Harry Quilter. His avowed purpose
was to secure 'some public recognition of Wilkie Collins' long
service to literature.' This was something of a change from the
apathy, or at best the tepid respect, which the name of Collins
now seemed to evoke in critical circles, and it is not surprising
that the novelist invited Quilter to call at 90, Gloucester Place.
Quilter was charmed by the old man, as he had been entranced by
his books, and became an even more ardent propagandist. If his
attempt to redress the critical balance erred on the side of idolatry,
it must have warmed Wilkie's heart to find himself refered to as
having 'told stories better than they have ever been told in the
world before, and probably better than they will ever be told again.'

Quilter was one of many who testify to the unstinting help and
advice that Wilkie was always ready to offer a younger writer.
'I know how,' he wrote, 'with no slightest call upon him, towards
the end of his life, jaded, suffering, and with insufficient strength
for his daily work, he helped me freely, unaffectedly and continually.' After Wilkie's death he heard from several others 'the
same story of how unselfishly this man helped them when they
were young and struggling.'

These were no isolated instances. Frank Archer—who ultimately
deserted the stage for literature—submitted his first short story
to Wilkie for his criticism, and received in reply a long letter in
which he analysed the story in great detail, made a number of
constructive suggestions, and promised an introduction to a
periodical. Another friend wrote that 'he was always most kind,
attentive and encouraging to all young literary aspirants who
applied to him for advice, and took the greatest pains to read
their MSS. and pass judgments on them.' He would always do this
with diffidence, pointing out that it was only his opinion. Many
a letter still exists in which he sought to place with a publisher
or editor the work of authors often quite unknown to him. These
were the actions of a man of whom it has been unjustly said that
he was embittered and jealous of the younger generation of writers.

He was faced, towards the end of 1887, with the prospect of
tearing up the roots of more than twenty years' residence at 90,
Gloucester Place. For a man of his age and settled habits, and in
his state of health, it was a bitter blow. To Mary Anderson he
wrote: 'My lease at Gloucester Place has expired, and my landlord,

the enormously rich Lord —, asked me such exorbitant terms for allowing me to continue to be his tenant that I confronted the horror of moving in my old age.' So Caroline went house-hunting and eventually found a suitable 'upper part' at 82, Wimpole Street, still within the boundaries of St. Marylebone. On February 3rd, 1888, he wrote to Fred Lehmann:

> After a month's confinement in the house (nervous seizure) I am soon to be turned out of the house. Half my furniture has gone already—I live in a dressing-room. The new house is at 82, Wimpole Street. On or before the 25th (when my lease expires) I must be moved—perhaps in the van, unless the weather improves.

A few days later he sent Hall Caine an invitation to call and see him: 'If you don't object to a room without a carpet or a curtain, I can declare myself still possessed of a table and two chairs, pen and ink, cigars and brandy-and-water, and I should be delighted to see you.' In the circumstances it is not surprising that Hall Caine found the large house rather dingy and cheerless. The door was opened by a manservant—his valet George—whose nervous questioning betrayed the fact that to unexpected visitors the master was nearly always 'not at home.' This is confirmed by a letter Wilkie wrote two years before to Ada Cavendish's husband:

> If I go down on both knees to Ada—with the tears rolling over my cheeks—will she send me a postcard the next time she thinks of kindly coming to see me? How am I—working at the back of the house—to know who it is who honours me with a visit? And if I say 'at home to everybody who calls' reckon up (if you understand Algebra) the number of ladies and gentlemen with manuscripts, the number who want introductions to publishers, the number who want advice on their affairs in general and the number who are anxious to borrow a little money —whom I should have the pleasure of receiving.

Although Wilkie had been pointed out to Hall Caine by his friend Rossetti some years earlier, this was their first meeting. Hall Caine noticed that he looked more feeble and had grown paler and more flabby in the interval. 'His eyes were large and protuberant, and had the vague and dreamy look sometimes seen in the eyes of the blind, or those of a man to whom chloroform has just been administered.' Noticing his guest staring at them, Wilkie said, 'I see that you can't keep your eyes off my eyes, and I ought to say that I've got gout in them, and that it is doing its best to blind me.'

At this first meeting they talked of many things, among them the law of copyright, a topic ever near Wilkie's heart; he was 'very full, very precise and very emphatic on the subject.' Among fellow-novelists he expressed admiration of Victor Hugo and of Dumas *père*, whom he had several times been on the verge of meeting in his younger days. Scott, of course, was spoken of in terms of reverence.

In these last two years Hall Caine saw him fairly often, and has left a sympathetic picture of the novelist in old age.

Wilkie Collins was a good and animated talker, never spontaneous, but always vigorous and right. His voice was full and of even quality; a good voice, not at all a great one. In manner he was quiet, a little nervous, and not prone to much gesture. He sat while he talked with his head half down, and his eyes usually on the table; but he looked into one's face from time to time and his gaze was steady and encouraging. He had many good stories and told them well. His style was quiet but emphatic, precise and perhaps slow, the points cumulative in their effect, most carefully led up to, and ending always in complete success. The pistol never missed when Wilkie pulled the trigger.

Without being the most magnetic of men, Collins was a man to set one at ease, to get the best out of one, to send one away with a comfortable feeling towards oneself; and yet a man with a proper sense of personal dignity. You never knew it for dignity and that was exactly where its strength lay. The same large grasp of fact and command of detail which one found in the novels, one found in the novelist. If his conversation was not luminous and large, if his outlook on life was not wide, if his horizon was not far away, neither were they little and narrow and near. His insight was sure, his memory unfailing, and his invention strong.†

He was a methodical worker and even when writing against time permitted himself an hour's relaxation between four and five

† *My Story*. Hall Caine. (*Heinemann*, 1908).

p.m., 'when a friend is always welcome.' Frank Archer recalls an afternoon spent with him about this time, in response to an invitation to keep him company with a cigar. There had been a time when Wilkie smoked almost continuously but finding that it interfered with his sleep, he had now to limit himself to a very occasional cigar. At this meeting—the last time Archer saw his friend—the conversation turned to the subject of actors. Wilkie talked of his experiences of the French stage, of actors such as Coquelin, Got, Regnier, Lafont, and the greatest of all in his opinion, Frédéric Lemaitre. So many of his friends in Paris were dead that it was for him a sad place which he no longer cared to visit. Among English actors, it was his great regret that he had never seen Kean; and as for the elder Farren, whom he at one time idolised, he had experienced the disappointment of meeting him and finding him 'quite stupid.'

Although Archer thought he looked well, if rather more bent than usual, others were remarking how decrepit he had become. One evening after he had dined with the Beards, they stood on the doorstep watching him walk slowly up the street. Bent almost double and leaning on his heavy stick, he looked like an old man of eighty. 'Who could suppose,' asked Frank Beard, 'that he was ten years younger than I?' It was said that he had a morbid terror of being written about as a dying man.

On moving into 82, Wimpole Street, his immediate task was to keep up the instalments of his new book. *The Legacy of Cain*, which had just begun serial publication in Tillotson's newspapers. He managed to finish the work by early summer and in July, 1888, a copy was filed in New York for copyright purposes, six months before its appearance in book-form in England. By enabling Harpers to publish not only well in advance of London publication, but also before the serial came to an end, he fired his last and perhaps most effective shot in his campaign against the American pirates. To his English publisher, Andrew Chatto, he wrote on December 7th: 'Five and twenty years ago I should have felt tolerably sure of the reception of *The Legacy of Cain*. Today, I don't know that I may not have aimed over the heads of the present generation of novel-readers. For your sake, and mine, I will hope.' Could he really delude himself into thinking that *The Legacy of Cain* stood comparison with the books he was writing twenty-five years earlier? For it is one of his very worst novels. Crime and madness, poison and mistaken identity, all the familiar ingredients are there, but it is no longer the old expert hand that mixes them. In fact *The Legacy of Cain* might almost be mistaken for a parody of the Collins sensation-novel.

For *The Universal Review* of June, 1888, he wrote an article entitled 'Reminiscences of a Story-Teller.' It is disappointing to find this merely a collection of anecdotes dealing mainly with the reactions of his books upon various types of reader. There was the woman who, having failed to catch his name on being introduced, talked to him at dinner of novels. 'To a man who has been hard at work all day writing a novel,' he comments, 'this interesting subject fails to produce the effervescent freshness which stimulates the mind.' He listened languidly until his companion suddenly said, 'I hope you don't like Wilkie Collins' novels.' Searching frantically for a way of saving her embarrassment he quickly replied: 'I haven't read them.' But the lady discovered her mistake later in the evening and never forgave him. Then there were the people who had recognised themselves or their friends in his books and wrote indignant letters; and the prudes, who throughout his life bombarded him with protests against this scene or that incident. Finally there was the host of readers who would rush to correct any mistake of fact, as when he allowed a character in a story of 1817 to travel by train. Among his correspondents on this occasion was a young man who described himself as a mine of information, and 'suggested living with me (on a sufficient salary), so as to be always on hand, and able to enlighten me on a subject at any hour of the day or night.' Quite unable to face the idea 'of this living encyclopædia getting into the house, and dropping useful information all the way along the hall and up the stairs,' Wilkie declined the offer. For a time he toyed with the idea of writing a book of reminiscences, and talked eagerly of the project on the last occasion he met Hall Caine. The work did not however progress very far, if indeed it was ever begun.

For his last book, *Blind Love*—originally entitled *The Lord Harry* —he had the advantage of a ready-made plot from real life. Towards the end of 1887, when lunching with the Lehmanns, a fellow-guest told him the story of the notorious von Scheurer insurance fraud, perpetrated some four years earlier but only just discovered. Briefly the facts were these. The young and handsome Baron von Scheurer had insured his life with five London offices for a total of £15,000, the policies being in favour of his mistress, Juliana Metz. They then took up residence in France, leasing a cottage in the village of Meudon where they employed a German maid. Having taken into their limited confidence a rascally doctor named Castelnau, they embarked on a series of philanthropic visits to the pauper wards of the Paris hospitals, until one day, seeing a man in an advanced stage of consumption, they offered very kindly to take him to the cottage, where he would have the benefits of fresh air and personal attention. Since the man had been chosen for his strong resemblance to the Baron, it was inconvenient when he began to recover, and Dr. Castelnau was compelled to administer a lethal dose of poison. The corpse was then photographed but its resemblance to the Baron was less marked than in life, and the Baron had himself to pose on the deathbed. The false 'Baron' was interred at Père Lachaise cemetery with great ceremony and a monument erected. Juliana submitted the claim to the insurance companies, supported by all necessary 'proofs.' The insurers were suspicious from the first, finding it incredible that a man passed as a first-class life in June should die of consumption the following December, and held up payment as long as possible; they were unable, however, to prove fraud and the monies were eventually paid. By this time the Baron was living in a Paris hotel as the Comte de Ségur. Then coincidence stepped in. Dr. Castelnau ran across the German maid from the cottage, and made advances to her which she strongly resented. Unsuspected by the conspirators she had been able to understand French and was well aware of what had been going on. She promptly told the whole story to her journalist fiancé who passed on the information to the insurance companies. Dr. Castelnau, who had been tricked into accepting £1,000 as his 'half' share of the proceeds, made a full confession. The Baron and his mistress were traced to Vienna where Juliana was arrested, but the Baron managed to escape. He wrote to the police in a chivalrous attempt to exculpate his mistress, and then committed suicide by blowing his brains out. Eventually £11,000 was recovered, and the two other conspirators received long prison sentences.

Wilkie recognised the story at once as a plot for a sensation-

T

novel, and wanted to jot down the details there and then. His informant, a director of one of the insurance companies concerned, promised, however, to send him a full account by post, which he did the next day. Wilkie wrote in acknowledgement:

> My one regret is that I am not able to begin making use of my materials at once. But a new serial story, which is to begin in February next, claims all my working hours . . . How the law disposes of the two surviving conspirators—and especially what became of the interesting Juliana—will probably appear in the newspapers. In any case, I shall keep a wary eye on the foreign news in *The Times* . . .

The letter concludes:

> As I get older I find it more and more difficult (in the matter of literary workmanship) to please myself. By comparison with my late colleague Anthony Trollope, with his watch on the table, and his capacity for writing a page in every quarter of an hour, I am the slowest coach now on the literary road.

The last year of his life started badly. In January he was travelling in a four-wheeled cab when it collided with another vehicle. The cab overturned, smashed glass flew all about him, and the unfortunate Wilkie was thrown out on the pavement. Miraculously he escaped both cuts and bruises but was badly shaken. A few weeks later he developed bronchitis, followed almost immediately by an attack of angina. By April, however, he had recovered sufficiently to be able to dine out on oysters.

With *The Legacy of Cain* off his hands he turned eagerly to the story he was destined never to finish. There is good reason to believe that in his younger days he might have fashioned this admirable material into another *Woman in White*; as it was, without realising the full dramatic possibilities of the story, he did at least produce in *Blind Love* one of the best of the later books. A needlessly elaborate preamble to the conspiracy occupies the entire first volume; thenceforward Wilkie sticks fairly closely to the original case. The Baron becomes a dissolute Irish lord, involved in the plottings of a secret political society—an echo of *The Woman in White*. Iris Henley is a less guilty accomplice than Juliana Metz; it is 'blind love' which drives her to condone the misdeeds of the raffish Lord Harry, to whom, no doubt to appease the strait-laced,

Wilkie marries her. Doctor Vimpany is a satisfactorily odious villain. There is no attempt at mystery, and it is hard to understand Wilkie's description of this straightforward narrative as 'Another *Moonstone.*'

On June 30th, 1889, a day or two before the first instalment appeared in the *Illustrated London News,* he had a paralytic stroke. His general physical condition was not such as to encourage hopes of recovery, and for some weeks he lingered near to death. Frank Beard, in consultation with a specialist, did what little could be done. Harriet Bartley, his adopted daughter, wrote to Archer on July 11th: 'We are terribly anxious . . . his brain is what we now fear for. He knows all of us, but he cannot command his wonderful imagination . . . He had a restless night and is weaker. Mr. Beard says the paralysis left his heart more affected by it than we thought.' Caroline and a nurse took it in turns to watch over the patient; the doctors allowed no one else in the sick room. Harriet, besides keeping his many friends posted with news, did much of the fetching and carrying. Two days later she wrote: 'The dear patient is weaker, because he gets no sleep. But he has taken a *little* nourishment—and so we keep on hoping.' Soon afterwards, amazingly, he rallied and began to make steady progress. Within a week or two he was allowed to get up and by August he was able to leave his sickroom on the third floor and move about the house.

Work was, however, out of the question. Eighteen weekly instalments, or about two-thirds, of *Blind Love* were written, but he realised that he would never be able to finish it. About the middle of August he said to A. P. Watt, 'Ask Walter Besant if he will finish it for me. Tell him I would do as much for him if he were in my place and I in his. If he has the time I think he will do this for me. We are both old hands at the work and we understand it.' Besant, who was on holiday in Yorkshire, readily agreed and asked for Wilkie's notes to be sent on to him. In the Preface to *Blind Love* he writes:

I found that these were not merely notes such as I had expected —simple indications of the plot and the development of events— but an actual detailed scenario, in which every incident, however trivial, was carefully laid down: there were also fragments of dialogue inserted at those places where dialogue was wanted to emphasise the situation and make it real . . . The plot of the novel, every scene, every situation, from beginning to end, is the work of Wilkie Collins.

On September 3rd Frederick Lehmann received this note from him, the close of a correspondence extending over thirty years:

A word to report myself to you with my own hand. I am unable to receive Martin today, for the reason that I have fallen asleep and the doctor forbids the waking of me. Sleep is my cure, he says, and he is really hopeful of me. Don't notice the blots, my dressing-gown sleeve is too large, but my hand is still steady. Goodbye for the present, dear old friend, we may really hope for healthier days.

My grateful love to the best and dearest of Padronas.

The improvement in his condition continued until mid-September when he developed bronchitis and suffered an immediate relapse. Early in the morning of September 23rd a messenger hurried round to Beard's house with a note, the last thing Wilkie wrote. It was a small piece of notepaper with the words: 'I am dying—come if you can,' faintly and almost illegibly pencilled upon it.

Frank Beard went across to Wimpole Street at once. The curtains of Wilkie's room were drawn, the lights dim, a fire blazed in the grate. Beside it, leaning back in his big armchair, his head sunk in a pillow, surrounded with blankets, lay his old friend, pale and emaciated. For many days he had been able to eat nothing. Beard sat down beside him and from time to time felt his pulse, which was growing steadily weaker and more irregular. Though his eyes opened now and then, Wilkie was past consciousness. His life was ebbing away in perfect calm. Just after half-past ten in the morning there was a slight convulsive movement, the head sank to one side, and the heart ceased to beat.

17

Post Mortem

THE funeral took place on September 27th at Kensal Green Cemetery. During the service the sky was overcast, threatening rain, but just as the procession came down the steps of the church, the sun burst through the clouds. From these north-western heights one can see far over London, and the city, bathed in the autumn sunshine, was looking its best for the final journey of one who was, in the truest sense, a Londoner. Nearly all his more intimate friends attended the ceremony: Caroline Graves and her daughter, Frank Beard, Holman Hunt, Pigott, Ada Cavendish, Hall Caine, Chatto, Edmund Yates, Bancroft and Pinero, E. M. Ward's widow, and Charles Dickens Junior. Among those who came to pay tribute to a literary colleague were Edmund Gosse, representing the Society of Authors, and Oscar Wilde. Mamie Dickens and her sister Kate Perugini sent wreaths, as did Martha Rudd, Miss Braddon, the Comte de Paris and many of Wilkie's theatrical friends.

In addition there was a large crowd of spectators, and a contemporary report describes a scene which might almost have figured in one of Wilkie's novels. 'There must have been at least a hundred of those unwholesome creatures who call themselves women, who seem to live in graveyards. When the coffin had been lowered into the bricked grave there was a general rush of these people who craned over into space, and clawed the wreaths of flowers, and pulled about the cards which were attached to the wreaths, and laughed and cried and chattered until they were moved on by the graveyard police.' A memorial service was held two days later at St. George's Chapel, Albemarle Street.

His Will was drawn up with the precision and attention to detail that one would have expected. It is dated March 22nd, 1882, and a codicil, added a couple of months before his death, appointed two further executors. First there are instructions with regard to his funeral, the expenses of which, apart from the purchase of the grave and the erection of 'a plain stone cross,' shall not exceed £25; 'no scarves, hatbands or feathers shall be worn or used.' There are detailed instructions as to the sale of his books and pictures; small annuities are to be given to two aunts and there are the usual bequests to servants. Holman Hunt's chalk drawing of Charles Collins was to be returned to the artist. To Caroline he left his gold studs and links and the furniture of two rooms. The rest of his property was to be disposed of and the proceeds invested in trust, half the interest going to Caroline for her lifetime and then to her daughter for her lifetime, the other half to Martha Rudd (Mrs. Dawson). Remainder in each case was left to his three illegitimate children, whose parentage he frankly acknowledged in the Will.

The sale of his effects produced less than was expected, especially the pictures and books. His manuscripts realised over £1,300, however, £320 being paid for that of *The Woman in White*. From a newspaper report we learn that the collecting of antique furniture had been a pastime of his, and that several items in the sale were bought on behalf of an American museum. The estate was finally sworn at £11,414, not a large figure having regard to his earning capacity over thirty years.

Within a few days of Wilkie's death Harry Quilter had formed a committee for the purpose of providing him with a suitable memorial, and an appeal over Quilter's signature was published in various newspapers. Meredith and Thomas Hardy were on the committee, in addition to personal friends such as Frank Beard, Pigott, Besant and Hall Caine. Quilter somewhat overstated his case in claiming that 'it would be a little short of a national disgrace were such an author, whose books have long been famous throughout the world, to pass away without some permanent mark of honour from the English public whose pleasure he has so long enhanced, and from the brotherhood of literature of which he was so distinguished a member.' No sooner was it put around that their idea was to erect a memorial in either Westminster Abbey or St. Paul's, than the *Daily Telegraph* came out in loud condemnation, in its leader of October 5th:

There is no duty so invidious and so distasteful as that of subjecting the work of any highly gifted and deservedly popular writer, recently deceased, to severely critical scrutiny and strict appraisement on its merits. In the case of the late Mr. Wilkie Collins the task is a particularly unwelcome one . . . When the pleasure which he has given to thousands has been so lavishly and liberally bestowed it seems almost ungracious to enquire curiously into the status of the literary powers which enabled him to confer it . . . The mere fact that it is found necessary to 'agitate' for the memorial to a deceased English worthy to be erected in Westminster Abbey or St. Paul's Cathedral affords the strongest possible presumption that the proper place for such a memorial is elsewhere. To form committees, to distribute circulars, to 'tout' for subscriptions, and to take steps for bringing 'influential' pressure to bear upon Deans are steps which ought not to have, and would not have, to be resorted to in the case of any man of distinction in art or letters, war or politics, whose title to admission was of that clear and indisputable kind which ought alone to be recognised. The national Valhalla will not require to be filled by the same sort of methods as is employed to obtain the election of a candidate to a charitable institution. The great dead who alone deserve to occupy it do not need the canvassings of a clique to procure their admittance. They are summoned to that glorious resting-place by the spontaneous voice of the nation.

Without accepting the infallibility, so apparent to the *Telegraph*, of contemporary judgment in these matters, we may agree that Wilkie Collins was hardly a suitable subject for such a memorial. There is something pathetic about this public wrangle over the claims of a man who in his lifetime avoided personal publicity, to an honour which he almost certainly never desired. The *Telegraph* leader virtually killed the Fund at its inception, and, if this were not enough the Dean and Chapter of St. Paul's reported adversely on the proposal, having taken, according to an American paper, 'other considerations than Mr. Collins' literary excellence into account.' Although the general public failed to subscribe, Quilter contrived to scrape together over several months some £300, mainly from Wilkie's friends and literary colleagues. The money was devoted towards establishing at the People's Palace, in the East End of London, the 'Wilkie Collins Memorial Library' of fiction.

Six years later, in June, 1895, Caroline Graves died at 24, Newman Street, at the age of 61. She was buried in Wilkie's grave at Kensal Green, possibly in accordance with instructions contained in an envelope which we know to have been enclosed with his Will. Her name does not appear on the tombstone. For some years after Caroline's death, the grave was tended by Martha Rudd until she too vanishes from the story. The 'morganatic family' soon lost themselves among London's nameless millions.

It is not easy to assess Wilkie Collins as a writer and his place in English fiction will probably remain a matter of some controversy. The issue is to some extent confused by the quantity of inferior work which he produced during the last twenty-five years of his life, work which, taken by itself, might entitle him to a place among such conscientious purveyors of popular fiction as Miss Braddon, William Black or Charles Lever. But who would place in such a mediocre gallery the author of *The Moonstone* or *The Woman in White*? And it is upon his best work—not the worst, nor even the average—that a writer may claim to be judged. Wilkie Collins' reputation must stand or fall by these two books, together with *Armadale*, *No Name* and perhaps *Man and Wife*. On the strength of these he can surely claim at least to be measured against the great literary figures of his time, to stand alongside Dickens, Thackeray, George Eliot, Trollope and Reade. His work fell short in many ways, of course, where they excelled. He could not approach Dickens' sheer overflowing genius; he had not Thackeray's style or versatility, nor George Eliot's intellect; he could not, as Trollope could, move about a little world of his own creation; his writing was less vigorous than Reade's. In one respect, however, Wilkie outdistanced them all. His ability to tell an absorbing story in such a way as to extract from it the last ounce of mystery and suspense and excitement, remains in these few books unsurpassed. In them he did something better than it had been done before. As Trollope wrote in his Autobiography: 'Of Wilkie Collins it is impossible for a true critic not to speak with admiration, because he has excelled all his contemporaries in a certain most difficult branch of his art.' Trollope could not, it is true, 'lose the taste of the construction,' but he readily admitted that the construction was superb.

To Wilkie Collins belongs the slightly paradoxical achievement of elevating the sensation novel to the level of serious fiction, and at the same time of reaching a wider circle of readers than any of his contemporaries save Dickens. In stripping the old-fashioned sensation novel of its Gothic trappings and relating it to the everyday Victorian world, the world his readers knew, he transformed it into something at once more credible and more fearful. For the supernatural forces of the earlier romances he substituted the criminal plottings of real people, actuated by simple, plausible motives of greed or revenge. He was wise enough to see that by this means, and by setting his tales among familiar surroundings, the effect he achieved would be more, and not less, sensational. With his characters, for the most part, it is the same. They are essentially ordinary people. Though they move in a world charged with mystery and suspense, among fleeting shadows and strange sounds, often caught in a web of diabolical intrigue, they still behave as ordinary people, with simple, sometimes almost primitive emotions. However unusual the situation in which they find themselves they behave sensibly and rationally. If this is sometimes less true of his villains even the most bizarre of these is firmly rooted in reality.

The charge that Wilkie Collins was incapable of creating character has been so often repeated as to become almost a truism. Always nettled by it, he himself was apt to reply: 'What about Fosco?' inviting the retort that one swallow hardly makes a summer. But if we apply the test of whether or not a character lives on after the final page has been turned, there are surely other swallows. He might equally have cited Rosanna Spearman, or Marian Halcombe, or Captain Wragge, or Magdalen Vanstone, or half-a-dozen others. These are no mere puppets, jerked hither and thither by an elaborately contrived mechanism, but living creatures who linger in the memory long after their part in the drama is over. This is not to say that he could breathe life into a character at will. His touch was unsure, and even the most convincing of them lack a certain subtlety of drawing. There are, too, occasions when it seems that Wilkie is playing all the parts himself, dashing frequently into the wings like a Protean actor, to return in a different costume and with a voice imperfectly disguised.

He was no stylist. He wrote simply, and with perfect clarity and directness. If his style lacks distinction, it is at least an instrument well-suited to its purpose, which, after all, is to tell a story. 'Everyone writes novels nowadays,' he told a friend, 'but nobody tells stories.' This absorption in the purely narrative side of his art continued to the end. Not only did it colour all his literary opinions, but it rendered him incapable of appreciating the way in which the whole scope of the novel was being expanded. If the younger writers were experimenting with new forms, it was only because in his view they were no longer able to tell a good story in the old way. As we have seen, he regarded Scott as the model for all fiction-writers, and never missed a chance of extolling 'the Prince, the King, the Emperor, the God Almighty of Novelists.' To one aspirant he wrote: 'Study Walter Scott. He is beyond all comparison the greatest novelist who has ever written. Get *The Antiquary*, and read that masterpiece over and over and over again.' Some way after Scott in his regard came Balzac, Victor Hugo, Dumas *père*, and Fenimore Cooper—all masters of narrative in their way.

The apparent fluency of Wilkie's writing is deceptive. The act of writing was for him always a labour, and often an agony. His manuscripts are black with deletions and alterations. The early *Basil* manuscript in the British Museum is in parts almost undecipherable, and must have presented a formidable problem to even the most experienced copy-reader. It was the same, we are told, with his proofs. 'The mere writing of a story is nothing,' he said on one occasion, 'it is in the revise—the amendments, the reconstruction, that the hard work really begins.' He took his job with utter seriousness and held in the greatest contempt those whom he termed 'the holiday authors,' who 'sit down to write a book as they would sit down to a game of cards, leisurely-living people who coolly select as an amusement to kill time, an occupation which can only be pursued, even creditably, by the patient, uncompromising, reverent devotion of every intelligent faculty which a human being has to give.'

The extraordinary disparity between the best and the worst of Wilkie Collins has given rise to a good deal of speculation. What was the reason for that steady decline in the quality of his later books? Why was such an apparently rich vein of ore so soon worked out? Why, in his last twenty years, did the mechanism become progressively more obtrusive, the characters more common-place, the situations more repetitive, the coincidences more frequent and far-fetched? Three main explanations have been advanced; over-production, ill-health and opium. The first we can dismiss, since during the relevant period his output declined, if anything. In the twenty years up to 1870 he produced nine long novels, and in the following twenty years thirteen, of little more than half the length; he wrote roughly the same number of shorter stories in each period. Ill-health may have contributed to the decline, though one recalls that much of *The Moonstone*, for example, was written at a time of acute physical and mental distress. The chief cause must almost certainly have been opium. The type of book at which Wilkie excelled, and which he was always trying to repeat, required above all a continuously clear intellect. One cannot expect a complex, elaborately constructed plot to emerge from a brain alternately clouded and stimulated by narcotics; and without the inspiration of such a plot Wilkie Collins seldom rose above the second-rate. Latterly his capacity for self-criticism dwindled. He seemed genuinely unaware of the extent to which his talent had decayed. Of one thing, however, we may be certain; there was no falling-off of effort. Large and uncritical though his public remained, he never offered them less than the best he could do.

It is hardly surprising that so uneven a writer should evoke such widely differing views. At the time of his death his reputation with the critics, if not with readers in general, had sunk very low. He had lingered too long upon the literary stage. The appreciations of his work which appeared in various periodicals harked back to the earlier romances and, for the most part, passed over his more recent writing in kindly silence. Among the sincerest tributes was that of Edmund Yates, who wrote in *Temple Bar*: 'The world is the poorer for want of one of the most fearless and honest fictionists who ever fed the public's sensation hunger, while seek-ing to influence the public's serious sentiments.' Swinburne, in a balanced critical study of Wilkie Collins' work,† summed him up as 'a genuine artist' despite occasional lapses. It was, he con-sidered, to the credit of France that Collins should be more highly regarded there than in his own country, and he looked to a later

† *Studies in Prose & Poetry*. A. C. Swinburne. (*Chatto & Windus*, 1894).

generation to accord him the full recognition he deserved. Twenty years later Thomas Hardy wrote: 'He probably stands first in England as a constructor of novels of complicated action,' and remarked that those who ridiculed him in his lifetime were soon praising second-rate imitations of his methods. By this time *The Moonstone* and *The Woman in White* had found their way into the category of lesser Victorian classics, but about their author or his other books the reading public was incurious. The centenary of his birth passed unnoticed, and not until some twenty years ago was interest re-awakened in Wilkie Collins. His re-discovery by three contemporary writers, T. S. Eliot, Walter de la Mare and Dorothy L. Sayers, coincided to some extent with the resurgence of interest in and re-valuation of the Victorians in general. Following her researches into the history of the detective-novel and the thriller, Dorothy L. Sayers paid an authoritative tribute to Collins' pioneer work in both fields, and to his competence as a writer. T. S. Eliot saw him as the master of melodrama. 'There is no contemporary novelist,' he wrote in *The Times Literary Supplement*,† 'who could not learn something from Collins in the art of interesting and exciting the reader. So long as novels are written, the possibilities of melodrama must from time to time be re-explored. The contemporary "thriller" is in danger of becoming stereotyped . . . The resources of Wilkie Collins are, in comparison, inexhaustible.' A year or two later Walter de la Mare delivered a paper to the Royal Society of Literature on 'The Early Novels of Wilkie Collins'‡ in which he discovered the rich quality and brilliant craftsmanship of Collins' best work, and redefined its limitations. In one vivid paragraph he illustrates that strange chiaroscuro effect which is the very essence of Wilkie Collins; his work resembles 'a cheerful sunlit morning—the flutter of birds, the sound of distant voices—when, slowly and furtively, there seeps in upon every object within it the gloom and the hush, the sullen ominousness, the leaden lull of an advancing eclipse; it is the actuality of a summer evening lit suddenly by the wide refulgent flicker of distant lightning. Quiet and blue his sea may lie, but lo!—high in the heavens—a remote, serene drift of warning clouds.'

† Reprinted in *Selected Essays, 1917–1932*. T. S. Eliot (*Faber*).
‡ Reprinted in *The Eighteen Sixties*. (*Royal Society of Literature*, 1932).

These three diverse writers treated his work with a serious critical attention it had not received since his death. Together they are largely responsible for establishing his position as a novelist of some importance and as a pioneer in one of the most productive fields of English fiction.

The simple art of telling a story is one which it is from time to time fashionable to disparage. Yet it is as old as the power of speech, and as new as today's film or tomorrow's radio play. To this art Wilkie Collins dedicated himself from first to last. No man has pursued it with a more whole-hearted devotion, and few have told stories better than he.

As with most writers, it is in his books no less than in his letters and in the recollections of those who knew him that we must seek the real Wilkie Collins. From his friends we have learned that he was modest, kind, courteous and, above all, sincere; that he possessed a fairly strong, though not a dominating personality. They found him a delightful and stimulating companion, an excellent host, an amusing, if not a witty talker. Some refer to his erratic temperament, alternating between lively good humour and deepest gloom or irascibility, without mentioning that this may have been no more than the normal temperament of the drug-addict. All testify to his genius for friendship. Their collective opinion can be summed up in the words of his friend William Winter, 'I have not known any person, distinguished or otherwise, whose society—because of mental breadth, generous feeling, quick appreciation, intrinsic goodness and sweet courtesy—was so entirely satisfying.'

None of this goes very deep. Wilkie Collins was a more complex character than most of his friends would have us believe. As to his less superficial qualities they are more reticent, but we can learn a good deal from his life and his writings. Gentle by nature, he was tolerant of most things, save cruelty, humbug and intolerance. If he was impatient of fools, it was because he had seldom met a fool who was not also cruel. Towards the narrow-minded, the prudes, the hypocrites, he was implacably hostile. Indifferent to convention he lived the life he chose and wrote what he wished to write. If the world was shocked—as often happened—he might be sad, or angry, but he did not compromise. His will was strong, often to the point of stubbornness. Courage and will-power enabled him to resist, with the help of opiates, twenty-five years of intermittent sickness and physical pain which would have broken most men. Nothing less than utter prostration could keep him away from his work. In the labour of writing he could escape, in the words of Walter de la Mare, 'lapped in the condition of the worm in the cocoon spun out of its own entrails; ink his nectar, solitude his paradise, the most exhausting earthly work at once his joy, his despair, his anodyne and his incentive.'

Though he took little interest in politics as such, he was a true Radical, with all the Radical's determination to fight oppression and to set right injustice. His pen was ever at the service of the weak, the sick and the disinherited. He had a deep sense of pity; but this alone cannot explain his intense, compelling interest in disease, deformity and death. Here was the morbid expression of some deep psychological maladjustment, the causes and precise nature of which are obscure.

There remains a sense of incompleteness about this picture of one who was in many respects an extraordinary man. If here and there the outline is blurred, perhaps the fault is largely his own. From all but his closest friends he seems to have kept something in reserve, to have withheld something of himself. Of those who might have told us more of the real Wilkie Collins—Caroline Graves, his mother and brother, Dickens, Martha Rudd—none but Dickens has left so much as a line about him; and even Dickens tells us little. Wilkie's letters, though far from being impersonal, reveal few of his inner thoughts. Like his books they are for the most part narrative. He kept no diaries. All correspondence with Caroline, which might have made clear much that is now obscure, has vanished. He himself destroyed a quantity of letters which contained matter he wished to conceal. Eighty-five years have obliterated many clues.

Wilkie Collins was a master of the story which hangs upon the well-kept secret. The steps he took suggest that he wished the story of his own life to remain something of a mystery to all but his closest friends. Perhaps more has emerged than he intended, but if some dark places remain it was he himself who withheld the light.

Bibliography 1

WORKS

Memoirs of the Life of William Collins, R.A. (2 vols.)

LONGMANS, 1848.

Antonina, or the Fall of Rome. (3 vols.)　　BENTLEY, 1850.

Rambles beyond Railways: or Notes in Cornwall Taken A-foot. (1 vol.)　　BENTLEY, 1851.

Mr. Wray's Cash Box: or the Mask and the Mystery: a Christmas Sketch. (1 vol.)　　BENTLEY, 1852.

Basil: a Story of Modern Life. (3 vols.)　　BENTLEY, 1852.

Hide and Seek: or the Mystery of Mary Grice. (3 vols.)

BENTLEY, 1854.

After Dark (six stories with connecting narrative). (2 vols.)

SMITH & ELDER, 1856.
containing A Terribly Strange Bed, The Stolen Letter, Sister Ross, Gabriel's Marriage, The Yellow Mask (all reprinted from *Household Words*) and The Lady of Glenwith Grange.

The Dead Secret. (2 vols.)　　BRADBURY & EVANS, 1857.

The Queen of Hearts (ten stories with connecting narrative). (3 vols.)　　HURST & BLACKETT, 1859.
containing The Dream Woman, The Dead Hand, The Parson's Scruple, Fauntleroy, and Anne Rodway (all reprinted from *Household Words*), The Black Cottage and A Plot in Private Life (*Harper's Monthly Magazine*), The Family Secret (*National Magazine*), Mad Monkton (*Fraser's Magazine*) and The Biter Bit.

The Woman in White. (3 vols.)　　SAMPSON LOW, 1860.

No Name. (3 vols.)　　SAMPSON LOW, 1862.

My Miscellanies (articles reprinted from *Household Words* and *All the Year Round*). (2 vols.)　　SAMPSON LOW, 1863.

Armadale. (2 vols.)　　SMITH, ELDER, 1866.

The Moonstone: a Romance. (3 vols.)   TINSLEY, 1868.

Man and Wife: a Novel. (3 vols.)   F. S. ELLIS, 1870.

Poor Miss Finch: a Domestic Story. (3 vols.)   BENTLEY, 1872.

The New Magdalen: a Novel. (2 vols.)   BENTLEY, 1873.

Miss or Mrs.: and other stories in outline. (1 vol.)   BENTLEY, 1873
    containing Miss or Mrs. (*Graphic*) and Blow up with the Brig
    and The Fatal Cradle (*All the Year Round*).

The Frozen Deep: and other tales. (2 vols.)   BENTLEY, 1874
    containing The Frozen Deep, The Dream Woman (revised), and
    John Jago's Ghost.

The Law and the Lady: a Novel. (3 vols.)   CHATTO & WINDUS, 1875.

The Two Destinies: a Romance. (2 vols.)   CHATTO & WINDUS, 1876.

The Haunted Hotel: a Mystery of Modern Venice; to which is added
    My Lady's Money (*Belgravia*). (2 vols.)   CHATTO & WINDUS, 1879.
                                            (published Nov. 1878).

A Rogue's Life: from his Birth to his Marriage (*Household Words*).
    (1 vol.)   BENTLEY, 1879.

The Fallen Leaves: First Series. (3 vols.)   CHATTO & WINDUS, 1879.

Jezebel's Daughter. (3 vols.)   CHATTO & WINDUS, 1880.

The Black Robe. (3 vols.)   CHATTO & WINDUS, 1881.

Heart and Science. (3 vols.)   CHATTO & WINDUS, 1883.

I Say No (3 vols.)   CHATTO & WINDUS, 1884.

The Evil Genius: a Domestic Story. (3 vols.)
                                    CHATTO & WINDUS, 1886.

The Guilty River. (1 vol.)   ARROWSMITH, 1886.

Little Novels (Fourteen stories). (3 vols.)   CHATTO & WINDUS, 1887
    containing Mrs. Zant and the Ghost, Miss Morris and the
    Stranger, Mr. Cosway and the Landlady, Mr. Medhurst and
    the Princess, Mr. Lismore and the Widow, Miss Jeromette and the
    Clergyman, Miss Mina and the Groom, Mr. Lepel and the House-
    keeper, Mr. Captain and the Nymph, Mr. Marmaduke and the
    Minister, Mr. Percy and the Prophet, Miss Bertha and the Yankee,
    Miss Dulane and My Lord, Mr. Policeman and the Cook. (All
    reprinted from various periodicals.)

The Legacy of Cain. (3 vols.)   CHATTO & WINDUS, 1889.
                                              (published Dec., 1888.)

Blind Love (completed by Walter Besant). (3 vols.)
                                              CHATTO & WINDUS, 1890.

The Lazy Tour of Two Idle Apprentices and other stories. (By
    Charles Dickens and Wilkie Collins.) (1 vol.)
                                              CHAPMAN & HALL, 1890
    containing The Lazy Tour, No Thoroughfare and The Perils of
    Certain English Prisoners (*Household Words* and *All the Year
    Round*).

Bibliography 11

*The following are among the more important sources
of information concerning Collins' life and work*

Wilkie Collins, le Fanu and others. S. M. Ellis. CONSTABLE, 1931.

Victorian Wallflowers. Malcolm Elwin.   CAPE, 1934.

Memories of Half a Century. R. C. Lehmann. SMITH, ELDER, 1908.

The Eighteen Sixties. (The Early Novels of Wilkie Collins, by Walter
de la Mare.)   ROYAL SOCIETY OF LITERATURE, 1932.

Wilkie Collins and the Woman in White. Clyde K. Hyder.
P.M.L.A., 1939.

Wilkie Collins in America. Clyde K. Hyder.
KANSAS UNIVERSITY, 1940.

An Actor's Notebooks. Frank Archer.   STANLEY PAUL.

My Story. Hall Caine.   HEINEMANN, 1908.

On and Off the Stage. Mr. and Mrs. Bancroft.   BENTLEY, 1885.

Selected Essays, 1917–1932. (Wilkie Collins and Dickens.) T. S. Eliot.
FABER.

Studies in Prose and Poetry. (Wilkie Collins.) A. C. Swinburne.
CHATTO & WINDUS, 1894.

Old Friends. William Winter.   NEW YORK, 1909.

Wilkie Collins and Charles Reade. (Dormy House Catalogue.)
CONSTABLE, 1940.

Some Recollections of Yesterday. Nathaniel Beard.
TEMPLE BAR, VOL. CII, July, 1894

Recollections of Wilkie Collins. Wybert Reeve.
CHAMBERS'S JOURNAL, VOL. IX, June, 1906.

Wilkie Collins. Arthur Compton-Rickett. THE BOOKMAN, June, 1912.

The Letters of Charles Dickens.   NONESUCH PRESS, 1938.

The Dickens Circle. J. W. T. Ley.   CHAPMAN & HALL, 1918.

Dickens. Hesketh Pearson.   METHUEN, 1949.

Index